CW00434678

Integrated Learning Systems: Potential into Practice

Edited by:

Jean D.M. Underwood, University of Leicester and ESRC Centre for Research in Development, Instruction and Training

Jenny Brown, National Council for Educational Technology (NCET)

Heinemann

Heinemann Educational Publishers
Halley Court, Jordan Hill, Oxford OX2 8EJ
a division of Reed Educational & Professional Publishing Ltd

Editors:
Jean D. M. Underwood, University of Leicester and the ERSC Centre for Research in Development, Instruction and Training
Jenny Brown, National Council for Educational Technology (NCET)

Contributors:

John Barret	Prof. John Gardner	Maeve Stone
Dr Susan Cavendish	Prof. Colin Harrison	Prof. Carol Taylor Fitz–Gibbon
Neil Defty	Jim Houghton	Prof. Geoffrey Underwood
Sheila Dowling	Malcolm Hunt	Prof. David Wood
Tony Lawson	Dr Ann Lewis	
Dr Angela McFarlane	Don Passey	
Dr Susan Rodrigues	Jane Spilsbury	

OXFORD BLANTYRE MELBOURNE
AUCKLAND IBADAN JOHANNESBURG
GABORONE PORTSMOUTH NH (USA) CHICAGO

First published 1997
Reprinted 1999
Reprinted 2000

10 9 8 7 6 5 4 3
00 01 02

ISBN : 0 435 09690 7
Typeset and illustrated by TechType, Abingdon, Oxon
Printed and bound in Great Britain by
Biddles Ltd, www.biddles.co.uk

Acknowledgments

- To all the staff and pupils of the participating schools for their time, effort, and co-operation.
- To all the researchers and the legions of support staff.
- This is an NCET/DfEE funded project.

About this book

This book traces the impact of ILS technology on children's learning, teachers' development, and the organization and management of schools throughout a two year project in the UK.

Section One: A framework for the evaluation describes the background to the project and its relationship to previous studies of ILS usage. The general concept of an ILS is explored, and the software packages used in the trial are described in detail.

Section Two: Focus on learning looks at learners' response to ILS, and includes details of the key learning outcomes identified over the trial period. The evaluation looked at whether basic skills in numeracy and literacy can be enhanced, and at the value of ILS in developing a wider skills base.

Section Three: Focus on teachers explores the relationship between teachers and ILS, looking at attitudes to the systems, at the use of diagnostic information they provide, and at opportunities for professional development.

Section Four: Putting ILS into school considers key management issues related to the introduction of ILS. Case studies of implementing ILS in a variety of learning environments provide evidence of the widespread applicability of the concept.

Detailed references for those wishing to read further are included at the end of the book, together with a glossary of key terms.

What is an integrated learning system?

Integrated Learning System is an ill-defined and often misused term. It derives from the USA and is held to mean a system that includes extensive courseware plus management software, usually running on a networked system.

Integrated Learning Systems (ILS) traditionally operate on the behaviourist model of learning which uses drill and practice to deliver core curriculum content and skills, through individualized tutoring and practice. More problem oriented systems are now under development.

There are three essential components to any such system:

- the curriculum content
- the record-keeping system
- the management system

Much of the subject specific software in the UK and elsewhere incorporates the first two components: that is, a range of tutorial materials and assessment modules, linked to a student record system. One distinction between ILS and many of these tutoring packages is that of scale. An ILS will have substantial course content and aggregated learner records.

Contents

Why read this book?

The use of Integrated Learning Systems (ILS) in schools is relatively new. The ideological and theoretical positions which divide opinion about their educational value are decidedly old. How open-ended and exploratory should be the approach to learning that they promote? To what extent should they control the learning experience? Should they minimise the possibilities for learner 'error'? How are the lessons offered by such systems to be integrated within the general curriculum? The significance afforded to such questions and the evaluation of any answers offered to them are symptomatic not only of specific attitudes towards new technology but of a general stance on old issues concerning the nature of human learning and of the nature and role of instruction.

One of the systems (SuccessMaker) which comes out well in the formal evaluations offered in this book has a distinct behaviourist feel to it. The system focuses on details of a learner's procedural activity, seeking to identify and repair any errors, providing frequent feedback and forcing the learner along specific solution paths based on predetermined algorithms. Many educational researchers and theorists will abhor it! But pupils appear not to; nor do many of their teachers who have many good things to say about the ILS. To whom should we listen?

The findings presented in this volume are not the first to show evidence of enhanced learning outcomes fostered by ILS use in the classroom. However, the evidence displays a number of original and important features. First, more than one ILS has been evaluated, helping to forestall criticism that any benefits found stem simply from novelty and enhanced learner motivation. Not all systems conferred measurable benefits and no one system evidenced benefits across all areas taught. So we will need to look beyond general Hawthorn effects to specific features of system design and use in order to explain how and why some systems give positive results some of the time.

Positive effects of educational intervention studies, computer-based or otherwise, typically wash out a short time after the period of active researcher involvement has ceased. The research reported here shows that this is not the case with one of the ILS studied. Evidence of maintained learning gains is presented for pupils a year or so after active intervention ceased. Whether one is philosophically for or against the principles underpinning the ILS, an obligation to explain such positive findings remains.

For me, one of the most attractive design features of the current research endeavour is the multiplicity of methodologies employed. Relatively large scale studies of learning outcomes, assessed using formal tests, are complemented by surveys of pupil and teacher attitudes and explorations of system use in a range of classroom settings. This variety of perspectives provides a rich and fascinating picture of likely costs and benefits associated with ILS usage in schools. It also starts to give some sense of different models which can help to guide schools and teachers in ways of integrating technology into the curriculum.

The latest estimate that I have read of the extent of ILS usage in the USA (the main pioneer of such systems) suggests that around a quarter of school districts make some use of them, mainly for academic low performers. Integrated Learning Systems are with us, and in a big way. There is currently an acute political interest in the future of ILS technology in UK schools. It is still too early to say whether or not systems of the types evaluated in this book will find large-scale application in UK education. However, it seems to me a fair bet that some form of large-scale, computer based, networked, adaptive technology, capable of adapting to the learner, will soon find its way into most or all of our classrooms. Whether of a technophile or Luddite tendency, anyone concerned about the future of education cannot afford to ignore current debates about the proper role of educational technology in that future. Nor should they feel free to ignore the evidence about the likely costs and benefits of technology presented and discussed in this important volume.

David Wood
The Director,
ESRC Centre for Research in Development, Instruction and Training
Department of Psychology
University of Nottingham

CHAPTER
1 # *Introduction: Why Integrated Learning Systems?*

Jean Underwood and Jenny Brown

The practice of education is a complex event but the goals of education are deceptively simple. Our main role as teachers is to promote useful learning. Teachers are involved in the social and moral development of the children in their care but they share these goals with many others such as parents, peers, social workers, youth workers and the police. The primary responsibility of the teacher is to encourage the cognitive development of the child, to ensure the retention, understanding and active use of knowledge and skills. As David Perkins (1992) asks, what is the point of acquiring knowledge if it is not to be retained? What is the value of knowledge if we don't understand it? What purpose is there to knowledge that can not be used in studying other subjects or in out-of-school environments now and later in life?

Propounding this view of the role of the teacher does not negate the importance of the social dimension to learning. There is a social as well as cognitive dimension to the reconstruction of knowledge by the learner. For the individual learner, all knowledge is context-dependent, and its understanding will be framed by existing cognitive structures that are themselves acquired in a social context (Brown 1990; Lave and Wenger 1991).

The seemingly simple goals of education have proved remarkably elusive, however. We seem often to fail to achieve even the rudimentary goal of knowledge retention over any significant period of time. Ask any student six months after they have completed their final examinations how much they retain of their course. They always display a frightening degree of information loss, whether through failed retention or an inability to generate an effective retrieval cue. The starting point of the project described here was the need to find effective strategies to promote, at least in part, sustainable and useful learning.

International comparisons

International league tables of student performance do not always present the UK education system in a good light. The reliability and validity of such league tables are the focus of much discussion. For example, it is widely accepted that there is a one hundred per cent literacy rate in Japan. Yet the Japanese threshold criterion of literacy, recognition of the 2,000 Kanji characters (pictograms equivalent to words) necessary to operate within that society, may be judged as a very low threshold for literacy in UK terms. Differences between Japanese and English schoolchildren are more likely to be accounted for by differences in the nature of the reading acquisition tasks rather than differences in innate ability or in schooling techniques. The criterion for literacy in Japanese is related to the learning of the 2,000 Kanji characters, whereas English readers have to cope with inconsistent spelling-to-sound rules. There are more than 200 rules needed to pronounce the most common 6,000 words used by nine-year-olds. The vowels alone require knowledge of 79 pronunciation rules, as is shown by comparing the pronunciation of three words — love, move, cove (see Underwood and Batt 1996). The number of rules to be learnt illustrates the difficulty of the task facing the beginning reader of English.

Nevertheless, studies do tend to show a disturbing level of illiteracy or poor levels of literacy in the UK.

'Fewer than one per cent of school-leavers and adults can be described as illiterate, but almost 15 per cent have limited literacy skills. An even larger proportion (20 per cent) of adults have limited literacy skills.'

Brooks, Foxman and Gorman, 1995, p.1.

Children in the UK have poorer basic numeracy skills than their counterparts in Japan or Germany although higher order mathematical skills are often comparable (Robitatille and Garden 1989; Blum *et al* 1993). There is evidence that this is a relatively new phenomenon. Current studies have shown that twenty to forty year-olds within the UK population are less competent at answering everyday practical mathematics questions than older age groups. Younger adults have failed to develop mechanical skills and so they were not able to apply those skills productively (Central Statistical Office 1995). This is a counter-intuitive finding if we base our analysis on time since formal schooling or indeed the research into the decline of mental abilities with age. It is less surprising to those who are aware of the *shift in focus from the acquisition of mathematics skills to the application of those skills* and to more problem oriented mathematics following the publication of the Cockroft Report (DES 1982). This perceived failure of the education system to deliver basic skills is clearly articulated in our national press as is exemplified by the following headlines:

'Why can an 8 year old Taiwanese child answer this question (*a simple shape sequencing question*) while a British child cannot? '

and

'Children worlds apart in success at school: Pupils in the Far East attain the highest standards.'

Judith Judd, The Independent, 7.4.95., p. 4.

As Brooks, Foxman and Gorman (1995) point out, current levels of basic literacy and numeracy within the UK are insufficient to meet the demands of many of today's occupations.

It is within this context of international league tables and growing public concern that members of the Department for Education, now the Department for Employment and Education (DfEE), and the National Council for Educational Technology (NCET) paid an exploratory visit to the USA. One outcome of that visit was an increased interest in Integrated Learning Systems (ILS). Such systems are well established in the USA and there is some evidence that they are an effective learning tool, although the findings do need to be viewed with care (Becker 1992). Teachers and students have reported considerable learning gains. The most consistent results have been in the area of remediation, where ILS have been found to bring under-achieving students up to normal levels of attainment, especially in the area of basic skills. Significant improvements have also been reported in attitudes to learning, leading to increased motivation (not only in the subject areas involved), and in some cases to improved school attendance levels.

It is not surprising that both DfEE and NCET should have responded so positively to a technological solution of a real educational problem. The UK government, and its associated agencies, have shown a strong commitment to the use of Information Technology in promoting learning, recognising:

'The potential for IT for enhancing the quality of teaching and learning across the curriculum — whether in traditional technology or traditionally non-technology areas — and to extend that benefit as widely as possible.' (DES 1987 p.1)

It is in this context of the need to resolve an outstanding educational problem and a belief in the positive benefits of IT on teaching and learning that NCET, in the spring and summer terms of 1994, conducted a national trial of two software packages in 12 UK schools. More detailed descriptions of the software are to be found in Chapter 2 of this text. The purpose of the trial was to assess whether the use of ILS would prove to be an appropriate and effective approach to learning in a UK context. A formal evaluation of the effectiveness of these two packages in promoting basic numeracy and literacy was undertaken by Leicester University. Within NCET a team was established to monitor the project in the schools and to look particularly at models of implementation and teacher development.

The outcomes of that trial, as in all good science, answered some questions but raised even more. Those outcomes, however, proved of sufficient interest to warrant a further trial of the ILS concept. Twenty-two schools took part in this second phase study. Leicester University again conducted the formal evaluation working with a core sample of 14 schools which focused on the sustainability of learning gains recorded in the first phase. In addition six further in-depth evaluation studies were commissioned to follow up issues raised by the first phase study. These issues included the role of ILS in the education of gifted children and of less able children.

What is an ILS?

The term Integrated Learning System (ILS) is an ill-defined and often misused term. It derives from the USA and is held to mean a system that includes extensive courseware plus management software usually running on a networked system (OTA 1988). ILS operates traditionally on the behaviourist model of learning which uses drill and practice to deliver a core curriculum content and skills, through individualised tutoring and practice, although more problem-oriented systems are now under development. There are three essential components to such a system:

- the curriculum content
- the record system and
- the management system.

Much of the subject specific software in the UK, and elsewhere, incorporates the first two components: that is a range of tutorial materials and assessment modules linked to a student record system. One dividing line between an ILS and many of these tutoring packages is that of scale. An ILS will have substantial course content and aggregated learner records.

A more fundamental difference between an ILS and a tutoring package is the management system of the ILS. The functionality of the management system may vary but at a basic level it will **update students' records, interpret learner responses to the task in hand and provide performance feedback to the learner and the teacher.** The individualised record system is, in effect, a model of the individual learner's knowledge, in that the system 'knows' about the abilities and performances of each individual user of the software. These data collected and interpreted by the system may also be used to provide an individualised pathway through the curriculum content. This ability of the system to provide a differentiated programme of work for individual children has proved to be a very important feature of the learning experience. The degree to which the locus of control over individual learning sequences lies with the machine, the teacher or the learner, is a key difference between the various systems now on the market and provides a demarcation line.

ILS is based on an old idea, that of programmed learning, but it is brought up to date through the use of the new multi-media technologies and more importantly through the availability of faster more powerful hardware to support the large data sets and many computations needed to monitor individualised work for students. This book traces the impact of this technology on children's learning, teacher development and the organisation and management of schools within a two year project throughout the UK.

How the book is organized

The book is divided into four sections. The first section describes the background to the project. Here we explore the concept of ILS and describe, in some detail, the software packages used in the national trial before setting the current project in the framework of previous studies into ILS usage. The reliability and validity of much of the research associated with ILS have been questioned and both the need for, and the issues in, conducting quantitative and qualitative evaluations of ILS in UK classrooms is examined.

Sections Two and Three present the key findings of the two year evaluation. The focus in Section Two is on the learners' response to the ILS while Section Three takes up the theme of teachers and tutors working with an ILS.

The first chapter in Section Two provides a summary of those factors identified as impinging on effective learning outcomes including teaching style, motivation, individual differences, domain knowledge and time of day effects.

The next chapter summarises the key learning outcomes identified over the two year period of the trial in the formal evaluation conducted by Leicester University. The key question here was whether the use of an ILS could enhance children's acquisition of basic skills in numeracy and literacy. Although the formal evaluation had a well defined focus on basic skills, questions were raised about the value of ILS in the promotion of a wider skills base. This question of going beyond basic numeracy is the focus of a small scale, in-depth comparison of children's mathematical development on and off the system. This study is one of many individual projects conducted by enquiring teachers stimulated by the impact of ILS in their own classrooms. The following six chapters monitor the response of targeted groups of children to ILS in the second year of the project. This targeting reflects current concerns about devising a curriculum for all abilities which develops the full potential of the learner and reduces learner disaffection in classrooms.

In Section Three we explore the relationship between the project teachers and the ILS. It has long been known that teachers are the key to the success of any education innovation. The attitudes and responses of teachers to the use of ILS in their schools proved generally positive. Here we present evidence to show that by encouraging the use of information technology for more effective management of learning, and through the use of diagnostic material provided by the system about students, the use of ILS can encourage the professional development of individual teachers. In Section Four we consider the management issues related to the implementation of ILS policy. Case studies implementation in distinctly different learning environments provides evidence of the widespread applicability of the ILS concept. These case studies review ILS use within a mainstream school already making considerable use of IT; and within two hospital schools and two pupil referral units (PRUs) whose pupils exhibit emotional and behavioural difficulties, managed by a central distant site. Such learning environments highlight a number of organisational issues for those intending to implement an ILS policy and these are documented here. The final chapter of this section represents three case studies which examine the costs of implementing ILS in schools. The studies take into account a number of variables including training, installation problems, system breakdowns, hidden costs such as extra cover, new furniture, health and safety implications, and the cost of upgrading both hardware and software. These studies will assist schools thinking about purchasing ILS and will provide useful guidance to manufacturers and suppliers on the needs of schools beginning to operate within different and more complex technology environments. The case study materials have been used to develop a costing model which summarises the various issues discussed.

SECTION 1
A framework for the evaluation

This section describes the background to the project and its relationship to previous studies of ILS usage. The general concept of an ILS is explored, and the software packages used in the trial are described in detail.

<table>
<tr><td>CHAPTER
2</td><td></td></tr>
</table>

| CHAPTER 2 | *When is a system an ILS?* |

CHAPTER 2 — *When is a system an ILS?*

Jenny Brown

Educational writers have been attempting to define Integrated Learning Systems (ILS) for some 30 years, an issue which Angela McFarlane discusses more fully in Chapter 3. McFarlane notes that these products are dynamic in nature and that current commercial products, which reflect the rapid development of the technology and changing curriculum content, bear little relation to those discussed in the early literature. Gerald W Bracey (1992) recounts his own severe reservations about the applicability of machines to learning in the 1960s and 70s. His attitude changed with the arrival of interactivity in the 1980s. Bracey makes the point that we are no longer in the 1960s nor is technology. The technology has improved and children who have grown up in the age of technology are ready to use it. This chapter does not document the history of ILS development but rather it attempts to bring together what has been learned about the nature of ILS throughout the two phases of the project *Integrated Learning Systems in UK Schools — an evaluation.*

Definitions of ILS

ILS can be defined in a number of ways:

- by straightforward description of the systems and the functions they can perform,
- by their curriculum content,
- through their learning objectives.

Most of the definitions found in the literature concentrate on the functional aspects of the systems and have much less to say about their curriculum content and learning objectives.

The functional definition of the software system and its component parts quoted below is taken from the report of the National Council for Educational Technology (NCET) on Phase 1 of its evaluation of ILS in UK schools published in 1994. This definition reflects the state of development of ILS at the beginning of the UK evaluation. It is based on information collected by NCET project staff on field visits to the US and Canada and from a study of the international literature.

Although vendors are currently exploring the potential for the delivery at distance of ILS over a range of communications technology and the greater use of multimedia within the systems, this functional definition of the component parts of the system remains accurate.

System features

In Phase 1 of the UK evaluation two ILS were evaluated:

- SuccessMaker which is produced by the Computer Curriculum Corporation (CCC) in the US and marketed and supported in the UK by Research Machines' Learning Divi-

An ILS is a computer-based system that manages the delivery of curriculum material to pupils so that they are presented with individual programmes of work over a number of weeks and months. The materials are often computer based, but not exclusively so. The system provides feedback to pupils as they work and detailed records which support the pupil and the teacher. Systems contain diagnostic elements that facilitate individual learning programmes. They usually have an on-line management system that enables a number of pupils to work on the system at the same time, at different levels, to receive immediate feedback on progress and, when needed, provide pupils with appropriate tutorial and practice sessions.

An ILS has three main components to facilitate the management of learning by teachers.

Curriculum content: this comprises an extensive range of tutorial, practice and assessment modules for a substantial part of a pupil's curriculum with coverage across a range of curriculum subjects and levels of ability.

A pupil record system: this maintains information on every pupil and records pupils' levels of achievement.

A management system: this links and controls the flow of data and may perform some or all of the following functions:
- Interpretation of pupil responses in relation to the current task
- Updating of pupil records based on individual responses
- Choice of pathways through the curriculum content
- Delivery of the appropriate sequence of learning modules
- Provision of feedback to pupils and teachers

Integrated Learning Systems vary in their ability to be linked with other resources. Some are structured so that their management systems only deal with the content provided within the ILS itself. Others have facilities for including other software, and sometimes for cross-referencing with other resources such as books and videos.

Usually an ILS runs on a set of computers networked to a file server which holds the content, the pupil records and the management system. Some systems can run on a single computer. Although other software can be run on the network most sites dedicate this network to the ILS use.

sion. It consists of extensive curriculum modules, managed and assessed by an automatic management system, to support the teacher's role.

- Global Learning Systems which is produced in the UK by SIR. It consists of extensive modules covering a range of curriculum areas including mathematics and English. Its management system is dependent on the teacher or pupil deciding which activities should be undertaken.

Towards the end of Phase 2 of the evaluation a third system became available in the UK. For this reason it was not part of the Leicester University quantitative study but was trialed in two schools.

- Jostens is a US company which produces an extensive range of ILS software. The management system has automatic capability but also allows for teacher intervention.

NCET was not asked to evaluate the individual software systems or to carry out a survey of ILS systems currently available but, because the three systems used in the study were very different, it was necessary to distinguish between the features they offered. This analysis of the main features of the three systems and their impact on learning has brought us much closer to a definition of what is a useful ILS. The following checklist of ILS features is reproduced from the Phase 2 report of the NCET project and encapsulates the key questions the project team posed in order to begin to evaluate the effectiveness of each system.

System features
Help features – Does the system offer students a help button to explain tasks?
Feedback – Do students get feedback on performance?
Pupil access to profile – Is this available for specific modules and for overall progress?
National Curriculum – Are there useful links within the software or through support documents?
Curriculum support materials – Can worksheets be printed off matched to individual needs or are there photocopiable worksheets on general themes?

Management system features
Topic routes – Can the teacher select units according to the topics which will be covered in class?
Individualised workplans – Does the system automatically present students with work of appropriate levels?
Can the teacher select an appropriate sequence of units for individual students?
Can specific sets of units be turned on or off within courses?
Can individual students be given menu access to specific sets of units?
Third-party software – Can the system launch third-party software?
Timed units – Can time on sessions be set on system?
Can response time be adjusted for individual tasks?
Can teachers ensure students complete tasks before moving on to the next unit?
Assessment – Does the system provide initial and summative assessment?
Reporting – Is a range of reports available: individual/class/group, to pupil/teacher/parents?
Monitoring and tracking – Does the system log pupil performance within specified set of units?
Can students check their own performance at any stage?
Are pupil responses to every task attempted recorded?
Diagnostic feedback – Does the system provide feedback on performance within a range of applications and skills?

Importance of the management system

It has become increasingly apparent that an effective ILS must include a management system which can contribute to the initial assessment of each pupil and then place them appropriately within the system. It must also offer feedback on performance to both pupil and teacher and from this information be able to produce an individualised workplan for each pupil. The provision of detailed diagnostic information for teachers is fundamental if they are to be able to plan both whole class and individual interventions and to integrate the work done on the system with that in the classroom. Research has been carried out in the US comparing the value of computer-based work with that of teacher-led work (Dalton and Hannafin 1988) which concludes that the most effective strategy is one which combines the two approaches.

The UK evaluation has shown that the teacher is a key component if an ILS is to be effective. The greatest learning gains in numeracy were found in schools where the teachers had become familiar with the system, its curriculum content and its management system. Knowing the curriculum content makes it possible for the teacher to integrate the work on the system with that of the classroom. Understanding the management system and being able to interpret the reports it provides enables the teacher to identify work that needs to be covered with the whole class. The reports on individual students bring to the teacher's attention students who need special support and who may need to focus on weaknesses or be brought on in areas of strength. It is the management system that distinguishes an ILS from other computer-based curriculum material.

This view is also reflected by Her Majesty's Inspectorate (HMI), who have studied the use of ILS in UK schools. In reports to the Steering Committee of the UK evaluation project they have offered the opinion that:

> 'ILS is an approach which critically depends on computer feedback based on performance and the management of the curriculum of the individual pupil. Learning systems which do not meet this description can only be described as computer-aided learning systems (CAL)' (HMI 1995).

User interfaces and learning models

The UK evaluation offered an opportunity to observe teachers and students using the three systems and to record their comments on the user interface features.

Need for consistency

Most users mentioned consistency as the most important factor in effective user interface. Buttons and icons need to be used in the same way in every module and operations standardised so that the user is left in no doubt about what has to be done to proceed. For example, students need to be given a visual clue which prompts them to enter data and this should be consistent throughout the system. Schools which devoted time at the beginning of the project to making sure that students were familiar with the styles of presentation used within the system and with the screen features designed to support the learner, found that students did well and gained in independence and confidence.

Value of feedback

An overview of research which looked at the effects of feedback on learning from computer based instruction was completed by Azevedo and Bernard (1995). This paper concluded that feedback improves student motivation by providing both encouragement and commiseration. Feedback can be simple, in other words it tells the student whether their answers are right or wrong, more elaborative, it offers correction, or adaptive, which it adjusts to individual learning needs. Adaptive feedback was found to be the most effective and this requires the computer to verify the correct answers and to identify underlying causes of error. This analysis of research also concluded that immediate feedback was more motivating than delayed feedback, a view supported by the UK evaluation findings where students suggested that instant feedback on their performance improved their self-esteem and confidence and led to greater motivation.

Current versions of ILS have few adaptive features. They are based on a model of learning which requires a specific student response and are not able to accept alternative answers. The UK evaluation project has shown that for some students this is unsatisfactory. Able students have articulated this dissatisfaction in terms of the need to ask more questions of the system so as to broaden their understanding of the problem being posed. As successful learners they resented the need to adapt strategies they have already developed and which they know will work in order to meet the response needs of the computer model. Less able students, who had come some way to understanding the process required to solve particular problems but who had failed on calculations or made small mistakes in their final responses, found themselves marked wrong with no further explanation. A teacher response in this situation would have been more encouraging and would have offered further support. During the course of this evaluation software vendors have listened to teacher and pupil comments on their systems and have made considerable improvements to them. Although there is still a great deal of room for development and improvement in the software, newer versions reflect moves towards more flexible systems able to respond to students within a common range of errors with more supportive and encouraging responses. The UK evaluation has also produced useful evidence of the system needs of specific groups of students. More visual materials are needed for students with little or no English. Optional reward systems which could be switched on or off according to the type of student using the system and more neutral graphics might make materials more age sensitive and suitable for adult learners.

The role of the teacher

Van Dusen and Worthen (1992) suggest that the reason why many ILS installations in US schools have failed to live up to expectations is that teachers had not been given adequate training and the models of use adopted were not effective. Students were not achieving anticipated learning gains, because in many cases they were not being given sufficient regular access to the systems. The models of use within these schools did not encourage teachers to become familiar with the curriculum content of the ILS or encourage them to integrate work on the system with the rest of the curriculum. Teachers were not familiar enough with the reporting system to interpret the diagnostic information it provided and to use this to inform their learning interventions. Expensive investments were being wasted because of the lack of proper planning by the school and inadequate staff development.

The NCET evaluation found these factors were equally important in UK schools. Whole school improvement had been observed in schools where planning had taken place involving the whole school and caused the staff to reconsider issues relating to:

- curriculum development;
- use of resources;
- teaching and learning styles.

Where class and subject teachers had been given the opportunity to become familiar with the curriculum content of the systems and had received some training in the interpretation of diagnostic reports, schools produced learning gains. In these schools teachers were able to make appropriate interventions for whole groups and for individual students.

Inefficient use of ILS is not a new problem. In 1990 the World Institute of Computer Training (WICAT) one US ILS producer financed researchers to go into a large number of classrooms and observe students and teachers using their systems to try to identify factors for successful use. The observers found that teachers rarely became proficient in the use of ILS in their first year of implementation. Some more persistent and interested teachers became proficient after two years, but most teachers never used the systems effectively. The researchers decided that in order to become proficient practitioners with ILS teachers needed to understand:

- the structure of the curriculum materials;
- how to place students within the system;
- how to interpret reports.

It was considered possible to develop a training programme to assist teachers in this development but researchers also realised that there was a need for development beyond this point so that teachers could begin to integrate the work they were doing on ILS with their curriculum aims. The paper resulting from this research (Schnitz and Azbell 1990) led vendors to change the emphasis of their development from materials to strategies to support teachers in ILS use.

Learning objectives

The brief of the evaluation was to look at ILS as a learning technology and to assess its value as an approach to learning. The evaluators were asked to focus on one particular learning objective, that is, the value of ILS to the development of basic numeracy and basic literacy. The main thrust of the quantitative study done by Leicester University was to measure learning gains in these two areas through standardised testing. But the systems may also be contributing to learning gains more widely within the mathematics curriculum and it is hoped to investigate this further in future research by applying different standardised tests.

The majority of use observed during the evaluation was of students using workstations individually. Depending on the learning objectives of the lesson, students were also observed using ILS in pairs, in small groups and on some occasions, via a large monitor or screen, as a whole class.

The three systems in the evaluation were very different. It became apparent that the ILS might be doing more than just developing basic skills, and that some ILS were more suited to this particular learning objective than others. During the evaluation, systems were seen to be supporting:

- basic skills development;
- reinforcement of prior learning and revision;
- use (often thematic) of computer based materials to support the curriculum.

Basic skills development

It is the use of ILS to develop basic skills which seems to be most controversial but it is in this area that the most dramatic claims have been made for learning gains. Many teachers view the use of this as little more than drill and practice and see the curriculum materials used as unimaginative and repetitive. The success of this learning approach does depend upon repetition and it is fair to report that whilst the majority of children in the evaluation enjoyed this style of learning, some children did not. However, sometimes repetition is necessary to consolidate learning whether it is done on a computer or by more traditional methods and one big advantage that ILS brings to students is that they are relieved of the chore of writing during the process. The teacher is also relieved of a great deal of repetitive marking and the immediate feedback on performance to individual students can identify potential areas of difficulty before frustration sets in. The evaluation found that most children using the SuccessMaker software said that working on an ILS was motivating. The instant feedback and positive response of the system raised self-esteem and confidence, concentration improved and children were able to work for longer at tasks. Students also mentioned the enjoyment they felt as they worked at their own pace and in private. Students said that they liked the variety of work offered by the system — within a session they would tackle a range of numeracy or literacy work rather than working within a single topic area as is often the style adopted in the classroom. This idea of keeping a whole set of skills in view and re-visiting them at regular intervals follows best practice identified in the work on learning and thinking skills done by Tony Buzan and others and is well documented in the literature related to study skills. SuccessMaker has a complex structure built into the system which can recognise that a pupil is lacking a particular skill needed to solve a problem and can take the pupil into a parallel activity to revisit and practice that skill. Teachers commented that sometimes students had covered new skills on the system before they had been taught in class. This motivated the teachers to become more familiar with the system content themselves and to be more pro-active in its use.

Flexible approaches to learning

In some project schools the use of ILS fitted into a flexible learning environment. Pupils spent no more than 30 minutes each day on ILS, working individually within a structured environment, and then moving on to other activities. These might have included working with other students in small groups on work which demanded a range of different learning styles or a whole class didactic lesson from the teacher. Research on flexible approaches to learning (Waterhouse 1990) has shown that students learn best when the teacher can draw upon a range of learning styles and can present each task within an appropriate framework for learning. Teachers in the evaluation reported a growth in independence in their students and this was particularly gratifying in students with special educational needs. An interesting point was raised by the principal of a middle school in Florida which was visited by the project team. She felt that the varied range of tasks offered by the software, particularly in mathematics, was useful to students in two ways. Firstly it gave them regular revision of skills and secondly it often covered topics which their teachers did not. The value of systematic revision of topics at regular intervals is well documented in the literature of study skills.

Through discussion with teachers working in the classroom it has been possible to establish what teachers and students find valuable in the current systems and how they would like to see them developed to be more useful in the future. The most important aspect of the use of ILS has been the provision of diagnostic feedback to teachers. This feature has sharpened professional practice and has contributed to more effective management of learning in the project schools. Teachers have reported that the detailed reports coming from SuccessMaker have provided them with an objective view of their students' performance. The reports have mostly confirmed their own assessments but in some cases have drawn attention to things which they might have overlooked and to students whose performance they had misjudged. Teachers in the evaluation project said that report interpretation was the one area in which they felt they needed more training.

Time on system

The time during which individual students spend on the ILS has also been identified as an important factor in effective use. Time has three facets in relation to ILS:

- Period during which students are given access to the systems. This could be, for example, over one academic year, or one academic term.
- Time on system for each session. This can be adjusted to meet the attention span of individual students.
- Response time, that is length of time allowed for the student to enter a response to individual questions or problems.

Because sessions are timed and students must respond to the system within a certain time period the work is very intense. The evaluation showed us that effective use of the system ceases if students work on it for periods much longer than 30 minutes per day. Some more able children enjoyed working relentlessly through the modules, improving their own individual scores. Less able children found the relentless pressing on of the system became too much for them after a while and needed to take a break, working on broadening and parallel activities to consolidate learning before returning to the system. Schools which took part in the evaluation are beginning to understand how the systems might be used to meet the specific needs of their students within differentiated learning programmes. Several teachers described an 'ideal system' which would provide initial assessment, give the student a learning experience and practice followed by further assessment, and then offer a range of optional broadening or extension materials which could be used before the student moved on within the system again. Newer versions of ILS software do offer modules with this variety of styles of learning and which would lend themselves to use by small groups or pairs or even as a teaching aid for whole class work.

Revision and consolidation

Within the evaluation Global mathematics offered a system which lent itself to use as a revision or consolidation tool. Arranged in the format of the National Curriculum it is easy for teachers and students to locate specific materials to support work on a particular topic. Where this software was offered as one resource option within a flexible learning environment it demonstrated some potential. The limitations of its use arose because of the instability of the software, for example students being told their answers were incorrect when they were not, and the lack of examples under any one topic to consolidate learning properly.

Both Jostens and SuccessMaker can be used for revision but the route is not so direct. It is possible to identify particular strands of work and to set up an individual learning programme to meet specific needs with both these systems. The producers of these systems have undertaken work and published documents which link their systems with the National Curriculum. The learning style of the programmed path of learning, which we have seen to work successfully in SuccessMaker but which is also available through Jostens, works towards consolidation of learning through regular revisiting and practising of skills. This method could be providing more effective ongoing revision and be preparing students better for examinations. This is an issue which needs further investigation.

Use of computer-based materials to support the curriculum

The ideal ILS for most teachers would be one that had the ability to use a range of computer-based resources, in conjunction with other materials to support learning, together with a management system which could provide diagnostic feedback on student performance to teachers. The ideal system would also carry provision to record assessment information and to produce pupil profiles. There is evidence that although this ideal is some way off system developers are working towards it. They are beginning to build searchable banks of curriculum materials which can provide specific or thematic support to the curriculum. The ability to draw in third-party software to some ILS is already possible. In one project school which operates a flexible integrated day for its students once a week, the Jostens software was used in conjunction with teacher input and practical learning experiences to support curriculum work in science and mathematics. In special support units using stand-alone machines with a limited range of Jostens software, teachers have been able to design individual learning programmes including computer work, classwork and individual off-computer work to support the curriculum.

Conclusion

The UK evaluation project demonstrated three learning outcomes from ILS: basic skills development, use in revision and consolidation, and the use of ILS to support thematic or specific curriculum work. A key factor in a successful ILS was found to be an effective management system. Diagnostic feedback on student performance was seen to be essential and where it was present was seen to sharpen professional practice and to improve the quality of management of learning. Time on the system was seen to be important in three respects, length of time during which students are allowed access, length of each session on the ILS, and the response time allowed. Systems were seen to be developing and working towards more adaptive feedback to students and modules offering a wider range of learning styles.

CHAPTER 3

The effectiveness of ILS

Angela McFarlane

This chapter presents the major findings of published research into the implementation, use and effects of ILS. The published literature relating to the use of ILS is vast and spans three decades. It is also of very variable quality and relevance to present day implementations of current commercial product due to the rapid development of the technology and content. This review, therefore, concentrates on independently disseminated research carried out or reported by authors who have produced significant work in this area over several years, and wherever possible on studies relating to versions of the ILS in question released in the 1990s.

Few published studies are comprehensive or long term. This chapter deals with independent studies, largely published in refereed sources, up to the end of 1994. It does not deal in any depth with the findings of Phase 1 or 2 of the UK evaluation managed by NCET, *Integrated Learning Systems in UK Schools — an evaluation,* the results from which constitute the rest of this book. No other individual study has equalled the scope of that UK based evaluation.

The material reported here concentrates on their use in schools, where a majority of the research data available relates to elementary schools.

The use of an ILS for subjects other than mathematics and language skills is extremely rare, and little evidence relating to this use is available. Many installations of an ILS have been made in an attempt to reverse poor pupil attainment in those basic skill areas, with little obvious success.

The influence on learning gains of factors such as pupil ability, gender and socio-economic status, time on the system, social interaction, the role of the teacher and degree of integration into the curriculum have all been studied and the overall picture is complex. Few if any of these factors operate in isolation and their influence is hard to predict. Perhaps as a result of this complexity, the outcomes of evaluations are variable. The majority of studies carried out to date show a mildly positive effect on learning outcomes, generally more evident for more able students. However, many evaluations are poorly designed and reported, with little or no information about the particular ILS, the teacher, the school or the curriculum the ILS replaces. Little information is given relating to control groups on the infrequent occasions they are used. No data exist on the success or cost of alternative computer-based or non-computer-based interventions aimed at the improvement of the same basic skills, when compared to an ILS.

ILS vary widely from product to product, and their impact is dependent on a multiplicity of inter-related factors. Any attempt to generalise from the particular is fraught with difficulty. Indeed, when some vendors choose to offer ILS data relating to other products to encourage purchase of their ILS, this can be positively misleading. There is, however, one possible exception; there is good evidence from sources in a variety of circumstances that the most benefit is obtained from an ILS when the system is manipulated by teachers who are fully trained in its management and use. These teachers then integrate the ILS fully into the curriculum and create effective learning scenarios for each pupil. Where the use of an ILS is divorced from mainstream lessons little positive value is evident. Further, when an ILS is used by pairs or groups as opposed to the individual users the vendors designed it for, greater gains are achieved (Mevarech 1994).

When is an ILS not an ILS?

When attempting to define an ILS most authors have confined themselves to the functional implementation of the system with no reference to the nature of the content, the media used for presentation of courseware, the user interface offered to students, or any learning objectives. Becker and Hativa (1994) offer the following definition:

> 'ILS are systems across computer networks that provide a comprehensive, multi-year collection of computer-assisted instruction (CAI), delivered primarily through a model of individual assessment and task-assignment, and which record and report student achievement'.

In the functional model they propose they also make it clear that task-assignment is automated and acts at the level of selection of each item within a session. This feature has been identified as a key element in producing enhanced test performance and is essential to any definition of a present day ILS. Maddux and Willis (1992) argue that large banks of computer assisted instruction (CAI) material which record student performance, and permit selection of the next lesson by a teacher or student using the report of previous performance for guidance do not constitute an ILS.

Any research data relating to the use of a true ILS cannot, therefore, be assumed to apply directly to such systems (and vice versa). However, authors are not rigorous in their use of the term ILS, and often fail to give a description which allows the reader to work out whether the product they refer to fits the Becker and Hativa definition.

A brief history

The first workers to develop a CAI system which included individualised diagnostic and prescriptive elements were Suppes and Atkinson in the late 1960s and early 1970s. They provided material for US elementary school mathematics and language arts which allowed a whole class of students to work on individualised programmes of problems. The selection of problems was based on the evidence collected by the system, which assessed what the children did and did not know (Suppes and Morningstar 1972). Sufficient evidence of improved performance in standardised basic skills tests (Ragosta *et al* 1982) led to the development of many commercial ILS based on the Suppes-Atkinson diagnostic-prescriptive algorithms, used under licence, or other algorithms generated by vendors. None of these algorithms have ever been published.

The concept of the teaching machine dates back to the 19th century (Saettler 1990). It has common antecedence with the paper-based programmed learning schemes based on operant-conditioning learning theory which were developed in the 1960s (Lange 1967). The most fully developed implementation model is one where individual learners are presented with a question, usually a multiple choice item or an arithmetic problem, and the response is recorded. The management software compares the learner response to the correct response stored in the system. The student is given instant feedback on the judgement and an automated selection of the next item is made (Becker and Hativa 1994). Not all products currently marketed as an ILS fulfil all of the functions described by Becker and Hativa. In particular not all have the diagnostic and prescriptive facilities offered by the systems which have evolved from the original Suppes-Atkinson model, or the individualised task assignment, and are therefore not ILS in the full sense.

ILS have been installed in up to 25 per cent of US schools, including an estimated two thirds of those elementary schools which have networked computers (Becker 1992; White 1992). In 1990 approximately US$200 million were spent on ILS (Bailey 1992).To what extent this level of installation is a measure of acceptance of the data relating to positive impact on basic skills enhancement, or the result of effective marketing by vendors, is unclear.

The theoretical basis of ILS

The development of ILS is grounded firmly in the behavioural school of learning theory. ILS have largely addressed mathematical and language material where the body of content is arranged hierarchically. Additionally, there are deemed to be identifiably right and wrong answers. The behaviourist approach taken by ILS designers precludes any element of social interaction. The systems are designed for use by isolated individuals, often wearing headphones. Learning is perceived as a solitary activity, a purely psychological interaction between the learner and the text or content to be mastered. It takes no account of the role of interpersonal dialogue, student-teacher or student-student, which can transform understanding. The role of social interactions can be seen as compatible with the constructivist approach, and both are at odds with the behavioural. Interestingly, when classroom implementation of ILS departs from the vendor promoted model to include social interaction, learning gains are enhanced.

Clearly further discussion of different learning theories goes beyond the scope of this chapter. However, one aspect to note is that ILS development is tending towards products which, it is claimed, will develop higher order thinking skills. No published, independent evaluations of these more recent developments exist. It is worth noting at this point a comment made by Bracey (1992) that until developers understand cognitive processes better, and design software which better supports the way people learn, ILS systems will be of limited value. Furthermore, the technology may have to advance beyond the recognition of correct mouse clicks or key presses to analysis of open ended responses (Hawkins and Collins 1992; Sherry 1992).

Sources of data on the impact of ILS

The main body of research evidence relates to the use of ILS for mathematics, particularly arithmetic, and less frequently language, particularly spelling and grammar.There are very few ILS which deal with other content and skill areas, and little or no independent evaluation of these is available.There is also a bias in the literature which favours evaluation of the use of ILS in elementary schools, where most implementation has occurred in the US.

Independent studies are often carried out by or on behalf of education authorities requiring data to inform decisions on investment in educational provision. Becker (1990 and 1992) has published two reports of a review of 32 ILS evaluations, including a mixture of vendor, school district and independently disseminated reports. He does not identify areas of the curriculum under study in each case, but refers to basic skills learning which may be in mathematics, language or both. He begins by pointing out that the selection of studies published is likely to provide bias; few researchers publish results which show no effect. This is especially likely when the funding agency is a commercial vendor or a school district which has invested large sums in a system for a number of schools.

A major independent study not covered in Becker's critique was carried out in US schools using Computer Curriculum Corporation (CCC) or WICAT (now owned by Jostens Learning Systems), and in Israeli schools using one of two Hebrew systems, (CAL) and (PWC). The study ran over a period of six years, from 1984 to 1991, and was undertaken by a team from the University of Tel Aviv (Hativa 1994). The PWC system was the most closely studied. It is a system where the arithmetic programme follows the design and implementation of the CCC system very closely. Many hundreds of students took part in the study as a whole, with some individual students followed for four consecutive years.

The Hativa studies concentrated exclusively on the use of ILS in teaching arithmetic, including number concepts and decimals, arithmetic technique and word problems. This study is of particular interest as it had a longer time frame than most other studies. The usual period of other studies has been one year, precluding any comment on long term effects. Hativa was additionally able to conduct studies where the characteristics of the ILS were manipulated and the resulting effects monitored.

Hativa's study sought to examine; 'a variety of cognitive, behavioural, sociological, affective, and instructional issues identified in the ILS work of students and their teachers, and the effects of a variety of ILS design issues related to hardware, software, and method of operation on students' and teachers' behaviour in the ILS environment', (Hativa 1994, p 81).

Additional evidence comes from the work of Roy Clariana. Formerly an employee of WICAT, an ILS developer and vendor, he now works for Jostens Learning Systems which took over WICAT. Although Clariana's work has been done under the patronage of a vendor, his research is well planned and reported and the outcomes, both positive and negative, have been published in refereed journals. He has looked at the use of ILS for development of skills in reading, writing and mathematics.

The problem of meaningful comparisons

Becker identifies some of the difficulties in interpreting published reports: poor evaluation designs compounded by inadequate data collection; poor data analysis and presentation of results; and inadequate description of the implementation and the conditions and environment where the program was used. Many reports have no controls or controls of questionable relevance. Furthermore, where controls exist they are not described further than saying the class followed a traditional or normal curriculum.

In any study published to date there is an assumption that the learning gains seen are due solely to the use of the ILS, often measured purely by the system's own management software. However, no known study has made any attempt to monitor the experimental or control group's non-ILS experience in the subjects under scrutiny during the study. There is an assumption that the selected control represented what the ILS users would have experienced if they had not used an ILS. Where the tests used to assess student progress are based on the curriculum covered by the ILS, and this differs even slightly from the curriculum covered by the control group, the small comparative positive gains seen in ILS users are inevitable.

Studies usually only report on the staff involved when the same teacher is teaching both experimental and control groups, which is rare. In a study published in 1990 Becker found no difference in test scores between ILS and non-ILS users in mathematics where the classes were taught by the same teacher. A school offering classes for ILS evaluation may select the more motivated and innovative teachers to lead those classes. Also teachers of identified control groups may alter their usual behaviour when targeted by an external evaluation. The resulting differences in learning gains may be as much influenced by teacher behaviour as by the ILS. Clariana (1992c) has identified teacher style as an important factor often overlooked in CAL research generally.

One marked aspect of ILS evaluations is the lack of consistency seen in measured learning gains, as in the 32 studies analysed by Becker (1992). In the UK Phase 1 study there are high levels of gain (average effect size 0.4) for mathematics with one of the systems under evaluation (Underwood *et al* 1994). The consistency of this result across schools and age ranges has been interpreted as evidence that these effects are due to the use of the ILS. The studies Becker reported did, however, involve larger numbers of schools and students. As Braun (1990) and Roberts and Madhere (1990) have pointed out, ILS is most effective when used as a supplement to, rather than a replacement for teaching, but any supplemental instruction improves results as 'increased time-on-task leads to increased achievement' (Balajthy 1987, p65).

Factors affecting the impact of ILS

A model of the effective intervention proposed by Slavin (1986 and 1987) and used to good effect by Becker (1992b) states that the level of instruction must be appropriate for the learner; who must have the incentive to learn, academic learning time must be sufficient and the instructional quality should be adequate. Moreover the relationship between these factors is multiplicative; the outcome can only be as good as the weakest component.

The great strength of ILS, it is claimed, is that the material presented is tailored to the individual, although Hativa's findings (discussed further on page 22) show this is often not the case. When a school has purchased an ILS pupils are given adequate time on the system to maximise possible return on the investment. The use of the computer is motivating and novel enough to give pupils incentive, although Becker offers data which suggest this effect declines when students have increased experience of computers in other contexts. It seems that Slavin's conditions for effective intervention are likely to be met.

For low and high ability students it is possible to show positive gains in some studies by ILS users compared to non-ILS users. Average ability students, as reported by Becker (1992b), do not show any such gains. Becker explains this by pointing out that pupils in mainstream classes receive the same experience: teachers rarely provide differentiated programmes of work. This work is most likely to be appropriate for the average students in the class, but too easy for the high end and too difficult for the low end. Average ability students therefore receive work appropriate to their needs on or off an ILS. It is interesting to note that in many cases pupils of low ability respond better to work of an inappropriate level which is teacher mediated than to more appropriate material presented through the ILS. This is believed to be due to the importance of personal support and intervention by the teacher for these students.

Another reason Becker believes that ILS prove less effective overall than might be hoped is that the quality of instruction they offer is poor. His reasoning for this focuses essentially on the behaviourist origins of ILS. Without the social interactions or meaningful interaction with the material required for personal knowledge construction, opportunities for genuine learning are reduced. He does go on to suggest, however, that different models of implementation where pupils work together in pairs or small groups, or room plans which allow discussion of current problems with surrounding peers, could be used to make the use of ILS more effective for all pupils. This is also supported by evidence from a study by Mevarech (1994) where students made much better gains in basic skills and cognitive processes where they worked in pairs, a model which contradicts the one planned by the developers and vendors of the system.

Implementation models

There is evidence that the implementation of an ILS as intended by the vendors is relatively uncommon (Worthen, Van Drusen and Sailor 1994; Van Drusen and Worthen 1994). Some authors suggest that closer adherence to vendor implementation models, and in particular the age and ability of the target students, would improve outcomes. However, there is evidence that the developers may often get it wrong; systems designed for remediation of low achievers have greatest impact on high ability students; systems designed to reduce competition increase it; systems designed for use by solitary individuals produce better results when used co-operatively.

Student type

Perhaps the greatest variability in implementation models used in ILS evaluations is the age and ability of the students. In the US particularly, ILS tend to be used in schools with Chapter 1 students, those identified as having a particular disadvantage due to socio-economic background (Mageau 1990). The reasons for this include the fact that such students attract additional educational funding so school districts can afford to buy ILS. The use of ILS for such remediation has no basis in research evidence. Even though the designers and vendors may have intended a system to be particularly effective with such students there is much evidence to show this is not the case. One such study is aptly titled *What you design is not what you get* (Hativa 1994).

Time on the system.

A conclusion frequently offered by studies of the time on system as a variable is that the more time spent, and the more frequent the sessions within the school week, the greater the gains. However, few studies actually give students more than 30 minutes in one session (Becker 1994; Hativa 1994; West and Marcotte 1994). During the time on the ILS it has been found that pupils spend more time on task than those using non-ILS activities. As more of the lesson is spent engaged with the material under study, there is a longer period when learning is likely to take place (Van Drusen and Worthen 1994).

West and Marcotte (1994) showed that time on the ILS did show a positive correlation with achievement in 9th grade (age 14) algebra. The maximum time allowed in their study was 40 per cent of teaching time, and they made (undocumented) corrections for effects due to gender and previous achievement in this subject. They suggest that with more time in the ILS laboratory students become more comfortable, and confidence and efficiency in working improved. It is possible that the errors in input seen by Hativa due to poor software design are reduced as students become used to the user interface (described further on page 28). In West and Marcotte's model students did not show signs of tiring of the computer, although Becker has data which suggest this is not so when students have greater overall exposure to computers (Becker 1992b).

Location of the ILS

The location of an ILS delivery network is inextricably linked to the scope for integration into the normal lesson, as is the nature of the cohort of students using the ILS (Mageau 1990). Where the ILS is in a special computer laboratory, classes must be relocated and the whole lesson is modified by its presence. Where the ILS is offered via a distributed network, with a small number of terminals in each classroom, integration into the curriculum and teacher support for learning essential to successful implementation of ILS are easier. Ross (1992) describes alternative placement models. Shore and Johnson (1992) state firmly that the future of the ILS is in the classroom not an ILS laboratory.

Where a whole class visits an ILS laboratory together and all the students use the system simultaneously, the ease with which a teacher can provide related follow-up work for all pupils will depend on the range of levels of current activity among students in the class. Where the whole class goes to the ILS laboratory together but only half the class use the system at once while the other half do related work with the teacher, students seem to benefit from the individualised attention they receive from the teacher (Underwood *et al* 1994).

Where groups are withdrawn from normal lessons to use the ILS they may be deprived of the teacher support identified as synergistic with ILS. The integration into normal lessons of ILS use, including relevant individualised follow-up work, is also very difficult for the class teacher to manage, again precluding complementary enhancement.

Learning gains measured by test performance

Evaluations seeking to find out whether the use of ILS systems by students leads to increased knowledge of basic skills in mathematics and language are plentiful. They have looked at a number of ILS products implemented in various contexts with differing objectives.

Published evaluations carried out by, or on behalf of, vendors are unequivocal — they show massive gains in all cases, in the order of one to two years learning in one year. The objective observer is bound to be sceptical of studies linked so closely to commercial interests. There are other reasons to question these studies, however. They use the commercially confidential assessment and diagnostic algorithms of the software management of the ILS to measure student progress. The original assessment of student performance is made by the system, and subsequent gains are reported against that base line. Without independent evaluation it is impossible to know how valid those initial placements are. In addition there is no evidence from these studies that student performance on the system can be replicated in other contexts.

To compare learning gains reported in different studies Becker uses effect size. He calculates that an effect size of +0.3 over one year is evidence of a significant gain in learning outcomes. Fraser and Teh (1995) reported that in 134 meta-analyses encompassing 7,827 individual studies the average effect size of any successful educational intervention is +0.4. It therefore seems that Becker is being generous to ILS.

It is interesting to note the difference between median effect size in studies disseminated through vendors and those disseminated through independent sources. Independent assessments of the SuccessMaker (CCC) system show a median effect size of +0.15 compared to +0.40 from the vendors. The figures are +0.33 and +0.0 respectively for Jostens.

Table 1: Summary of Effect Size Analysis of Integrated Learning Systems from Becker 1992

Program & source	Effect size Under +.15 (Negligible)	Effect size +.15 to +.30 (Moderate)	Effect size Over +.30 (Substantial)	Median Effect size	Effect size of randomised designs
WICAT through vendor	*******	****	****	+.17	—
CCC through vendor—	—	—	****	+.40	—
CCC: LEA or independent	**	***	—	+.15	+.17(2)
Jostens through vendor	*	—	—	+.0	—
Jostens independent	*	—	**	+.33	+.26 (2)
* represents each study.					

Becker goes on to add the caveat to these results: simpler analysis of the results taking only reported data rather than his corrected effect sizes would suggest a greater impact for ILS. The variation in results and the modest positive effects seen suggest to Becker that we should expect widely differing effects from ILS depending on the conditions of the study and the system used, as well as the methodology of the study. Students will do somewhat better with ILS than they would be expected to do without intervention; sometimes the results are substantially superior under some conditions, but on the evidence so far it is difficult to predict what these might be. Finally, and perhaps most importantly, he concludes that evaluation data considered in his critical study are 'too flimsy a reed on which school districts should base their acquisition and investment decisions'.

Hativa's study looked at the gains made by students using an ILS without reference to non-ILS users (Hativa 1994). There is a basic premise that a student should make progress at one grade level per year. In fact this study found that the quantity of material mastered by students in one school year varied from 0.3 to 3.0 grade levels. This variation in students' gain shows a marked correlation with student ability, the more able students making the greater gains. Students in the same year might be working with material of different degrees of complexity, that is a Year 4 child might be working on material from the Year 6 curriculum. A consequence of this difference in rate of progress which is maintained over time is that students in the same class showing a difference of one to two grade levels in Year 2, can vary by as much as four to six grades by Year 6 (Hativa 1988; Ben Dror 1991). Studies of the behaviour of students of different ability while using the ILS suggest possible explanations for these differences.

Performance related to student ability — the issue of individualised courseware

A great strength of ILS is the supposed ability of the management software to provide each student with an individualised programme of material appropriate to his or her learning needs based on an assessment of what a pupil does or does not know. Parr (1994, p34) claims that in the ILS she studied the management software may underestimate students' starting level during initial assessment on the system and that this could be a deliberate strategy on the part of the ILS developers so that initial learning gains reported by the system will always appear favourable.

Hativa claims that the management software's inability to determine the knowledge underlying students' answers accurately, and the erroneous responses to student input which occur as a result, inhibits students' learning and advancement. Students of all abilities may be provided with learning material inappropriate to their real needs. For example students may guess an answer through a lack of understanding, or click at random on an answer through boredom. The system evaluates this answer as the answer the student believes to be correct, assumes a particular misconception and presents new material accordingly. This leads to more guesses or random clicks and students enter a spiral of decline. This phenomenon was reported in all four systems studied by Hativa (Hativa 1988b and 1990; Hativa et al 1993) and occurs in the findings of the UK Phase 1 evaluation (Underwood et al 1994). Hativa concludes, however, that even low ability students do gain more from working with the ILS than they gain from regular class instruction. Since she also states that her studies did not involve comparisons with non-ILS users, the data on which this conclusion is based are unknown.

More able students in Hativa's study had a very different experience. All the exercises they received were new to them, as they performed well enough to avoid being trapped at one level. This often meant they were dealing with material well in advance of that taught in lessons and had to be very resourceful in finding multiple strategies for achieving goals in ILS work. This proved very challenging and led to the mushrooming of students cognitive and behavioural strategies. These differences were maintained for the three years during which these students formed a particular focus of study. Where students received explanations of concepts and procedures at home this reinforced their learning and made them less likely to forget. Students of low socio-economic status did not perform as well as students of high socio-economic status of the same ability level. This difference is attributed largely to the absence of this home based support and reinforcement.

Becker has also conducted studies related to learning gains and student ability. He too found that significant learning gains occur with more able students, and to a lesser extent with less able students. However, he found that for the middle 40 per cent of the ability range in mainstream classes, as determined using Californian achievement tests, there was no net gain or loss. His was a very well structured and balanced study using mathematics and language arts ILS with 16 classes from Grades 2 to 5 (ages 7 to 10) (Becker 1992b). This failure to impact on the average student is offered as an explanation for average gains in many studies being marginal. This highlights the importance of ensuring data on student ability are included in any evaluation, and supports the view that the gains in the UK Phase 1 evaluation were influenced by the ability profile of students which was skewed towards those of lower ability (Underwood et al 1994).

It is noticeable that the instructional element of the ILS did not apparently meet student needs in either Becker or Hativa's studies. A major difference between the less able and more able student was therefore their ability to develop self-support strategies.

Transferability

Transference of skills and knowledge gained through an ILS have been tested in separate paper and pencil tests relating to the same material (Osin and Nesher 1988; Perry 1990). This is taken to be evidence of transference of cognitive learning from the ILS environment to an alternative context. These studies found that a large proportion, from 50 to

90 per cent of students, actually performed well in paper tests on material at a higher level than the one they were currently assigned to on the ILS. Also pupils frequently performed less well on paper than on the ILS on material they have already completed on the ILS. A study by Mager (1989) found no transfer of skills practised on the ILS to paper tests. Discrepancies between paper and ILS based assessments of student performance found in four ILS led the authors to the conclusion that 'there is some level of inaccuracy in the computer's evaluation and management of students' work' (Hativa 1994). These evaluations are the core of the decision-making process in an ILS management system so inaccuracies here have profound consequences.

These inaccuracies in assessment of pupils' knowledge and understanding are not confined to ILS or any other computer-based scenario. They can also be found in teacher mediated instruction (Erlwanger 1973). However, the implications of such inaccurate assessments within an ILS may be far reaching. Decisions concerning the selection of material, based on inaccurate assessments, will inevitably lead to the presentation of inappropriate content to the student, although this may be true in the classroom as well.

Persistence of learning gains

Few studies have had the opportunity to follow up students after they have stopped using an ILS to see if the effects of any acceleration in learning persist. Ramey (1991) and Ross *et al* (1991) found that after one or two years of ILS use students performed as well as or better than students who had not used the system. However, during the year following the end of the ILS use the scores of the ILS students increased more slowly or even decreased. Hermon (1994) also reports what he refers to as 'fade out' when pupils stop using the system.

Gender differences

Overall results relating to gender are the most varied and unpredictable. Hativa's (1994) results relating to gender, using ILS in arithmetic, are inconclusive. In two studies she found no gender differences. In two other studies, the only gender specific finding was some evidence that girls do not make progress on the ILS at the same rate as boys of similar ability with the same level of access to the system. This was attributed to a lower level of competitiveness found in the girls, since other studies had established that competition, when students compare their results, was an important element in accelerated learning on the ILS.

Clariana (1992) looked at gender differences in reading and writing using WICAT programs. He found a marked difference related to gender, with girls gaining no benefit from the treatment, and boys showing significant improvements. This was based on equal exposure, and reading ability was assessed using the Stanford Reading Test. Clariana's data suggest that an ILS environment favours students who are aggressive or hurried, with the quantity of tasks completed being given more weight than the quality of the work done. This may favour boys over girls, who may work more thoughtfully, make more use of on-screen help, and generally read the on-screen material more thoroughly, but complete fewer tasks in the time allotted and be penalised with lower scores overall.

Clariana was looking at an ILS which aimed to promote effective writing. Presumably at this time the software can make assessments about the quantity of text produced by a child, the spelling and possibly grammar, and the time taken to write it. It is less obvious how it can assess the quality of the meaning contained in the text. This could mean the quality of girls' writing is not gaining due recognition on the system; they are not getting the positive feedback so vital to pupil motivation which correlates strongly with increased learning gains. Clariana suggests that teacher mediated encouragement might have compensated the girls, but the teacher was absent from the lab.

Clariana and Schultz (1993) looked at ability and gender in relation to achievement in ILS use for mathematics and language arts. They found that low ability females did not do well compared to high ability females, or males of any ability in mathematics. In language arts, however, the low ability females made the largest gains compared to the other groups. This apparently contradicts the earlier findings of Clariana (1992). They conclude that gender differences in ILS may be related to content.

Student attitudes

In studies in the US and Israel Hativa found that 70 to 75 per cent of students like to work with an ILS whereas 15 to 20 per cent do not. Correct responses from the ILS were identified as very motivating and the incorrect ones as discouraging. Clearly this has implications related to student ability: the more able the student the better the ratio of correct to incorrect responses. This is reflected in the finding that 92 per cent of high achievers like to work with an ILS, compared to 87 per cent of less able students (Hativa 1989).

Reports to students

Some systems produce regular on-screen reports to students. The expression of progress as a measure of gain, rather than the absolute level, give the achievements of all pupils strong credibility, not just those of the high achievers. These reports increase pupil pride, self-confidence and motivation substantially in all ability groups (Hoorvitch-Steimberg 1990).

Clariana (1993) conducted a comparison of behaviours of two cohorts of students of varying ability with varying levels of independence in their learning patterns attending a summer remediation programme in mathematics. One group received regular reports of their progress from the system, the other did not. Those who got regular feedback showed increased motivation as measured by attendance rate (a factor which was significantly greater with females); and did better on tests. Since other authors have shown that time on the system is a significant variable it is not clear from these data whether the reports or the increased attendance they fostered were responsible for the increase. Where pupils are using ILS as part of the school day, and have less choice about using it, the reports cannot be assumed to produce the same effect.

Competition v co-operation

Much attention is paid to cognitive learning consequences of ILS, with few studies considering social factors which can also have substantial effects on that learning. Interactions between pupils, whether they compete or co-operate for example, are rarely studied. Dissatisfaction with competition in schools has led to the promotion of individual or co-operative goal structures (Johnson and Johnson 1975). Computer-based individualisation of instruction was expected to reduce competition by making it difficult for pupils to compare their performance with others.

No attempt will be made here to make value judgements on the role of competition and co-operation in educational settings. This is a large and complex issue well beyond the scope of this chapter. Rather a report will be presented on the impact of certain ILS design features on these behaviours, and the consequences for the resulting learning. It is worth noting that neither of the systems studied here were designed to promote either competition or co-operation, rather the opposite. The PWC system used in Israel is implemented via terminals positioned to separate students and make it impossible to see other screens, specifically to reduce inter-student competition and, incidentally, to preclude co-operation (Hativa *et al* 1993).

ILS which report performance on screen to the student and produce hierarchical reports which are used by teachers increase competition between individuals in the class who compare their scores. In addition, teacher reports are frequently used by teachers to encourage comparisons and competition. In this situation students expressed a negative view of competition in attitude surveys. Where significant competition is present, disadvantaged students and low achievers showed greater negative feelings relating to failure.

Where students are not given on-screen summative reports, only responses to inputs in the context of an individual item, and teachers do not use reports to encourage comparison (often because the reports are hard to understand and therefore ignored) students behave more co-operatively. This does not mean that there is no competition. Students do observe each other's screens and can recognise when a peer is receiving easier material. However, this comparison is not formalised. In this situation students expressed a positive view of competition in attitude surveys, having been exposed to little pressure to compete.

In both scenarios boys were more competitive than girls and this difference was unaffected by the nature of the ILS. However girls perceived themselves as more persistent in their work with the ILS.

Role of the teacher

Maddux and Willis (1992) point out that the early teaching machines were marketed as replacements for teachers, and as such were developed and marketed as

> 'self-contained, automated teachers complete unto themselves. No attempt was made to build flexibility into the devices, since they were never conceived as supplements to teachers. Because they did not contain the flexibility to empower teachers, and because they could not replace teachers, we saw that parents, students, teachers, and eventually school boards....rejected the machines'.

They also suggest that if developers of ILS learn the lessons of the teaching machines and produce products which are flexible and form a supplement to teaching they may succeed and gain a permanent place in educational technology.

Research supports the view that teachers play a key role in the success of ILS use. Where ILS sessions are supervised by a passive supervisor who does not offer support, results, particularly of the low achievers, suffer (e.g. Clariana 1990; Taylor 1990; Becker 1994). Teachers who support and encourage students while they are using the system, and provide related follow-up work in class, assist students to make greater cognitive gains. This is closely linked to the integration of ILS work into the mainstream curriculum and effective use of ILS reports of student performance to inform classwork.

Work-load

In studies which take place over a short term covering the initial use of an ILS by teachers and students, it is commonly reported that teachers appreciate the reduction in workload which results from computer marking and selection of pupil work. However, in longer term studies teacher workload increases, often dramatically. This results from the need to produce differentiated programmes of work for a class in non-ILS lessons (Hativa 1994).

The ILS often reveals starkly the variation in ability levels within a class, which may have been ignored or unappreciated previously. All students are reported on individually, moreover their mastery of different strands is often shown to vary widely. Teachers respond to this by preparing schemes of work which will better address the needs of small groups of students in the class with similar requirements. As time goes on the variation in ability within a class widens, increasing the number of alternatives a teacher must offer.

As well as the extra administrative burden of preparing these schemes of work and marking the results, teaching itself becomes more demanding. Teachers must learn to respond to pupils working on a range of activities simultaneously. Teaching one thing to the whole class, and concentrating on one idea at a time becomes a forgotten luxury. However, teachers respond positively to the increased work-load as they recognise the value of the enhanced learning outcomes it facilitates (Hativa 1994).

ILS vendors can help with this problem by providing system generated worksheets and cross-referencing the curriculum of the ILS to materials from other sources (Hativa and Becker 1994). Some vendors also believe they will alleviate the problem entirely in time by offering the complete curriculum through the ILS. However, the importance of interaction with and support from a human teacher, even for high ability students, suggest this is unlikely to prove effective.

Reports to teachers

The information used by an ILS management system to make diagnostic-prescriptive choices about individual student task assignment may or may not be the data presented in teachers' reports. As mentioned earlier, the way in which management software analyses student input and translates this into a comment on performance or selects material for the student, is not known. These algorithms have been described as the *crown jewels* of the ILS vendors and are not made public.

Data reported varies from time taken to respond to an item or the time spent on an exercise as a whole, to a complete evaluation of an individual student's progress in terms of a score for each strand of work attempted. The ease with which teachers can access and interpret these reports has implications for the integration of ILS based work into the mainstream curriculum.

Where reports are confusing or difficult to format, teachers tend to ignore them. However, where they give easily interpreted student scores, in different skill areas for example, teachers will use them to help plan a more individualised curriculum for each student. Alternatively they will use a printout arranged in performance order to group children together for work at an appropriate level on areas of shared difficulty (Hativa 1994).

Teachers may discuss the reports they receive from the system with individual students, to help them monitor and understand their own progress and identify difficulties. Students may then use their own reports to identify areas of weakness and seek out help and appropriate teaching material, as reported by schools in Pennsylvania (McFarlane 1994).

Training

If teachers are to make best use of an ILS they need training on the management system of the ILS. Furthermore that system must present a logical, consistent and easy to use interface to facilitate this process. The manipulation of the ILS by teachers, for example to produce good curriculum matching, is essential if students are to gain maximum benefit (Schnitz and Azbell 1990; Blickhan 1992; Clariana 1992b; Robinson 1992; Shore and Johnson 1992). However, this process can be complex, especially where systems allow the integration of third party software into the management system, for example the WICAT system now owned by Jostens.

The issue of staff training is particularly relevant when the data on implementation of ILS are considered. Inadequate implementation, where teachers do not use systems as intended by the developers, frequently leads to underestimation of the possible impact of ILS in general (Worthen, Van Drusen and Sailor 1994; Van Drusen and Worthen 1994). This is exacerbated by the insufficiency of the research based theory for guiding both vendors and school users in how they implement this computer-based resource (Hativa 1994). It seems then that teachers and developers need a better understanding of the strategies which bring about effective learning, and they need more evidence from research to inform that understanding. (See also Bailey and Lumley 1991.)

Software design issues

Features of ILS design frequently identified as undesirable include time limits, the evaluation of each digit as typed, the impossibility of correcting an erroneous digit once typed, and the lack of an adequate explanation when students did not know how to solve an exercise. Imposing a time limit on students is associated with student irritation, decreased self-confidence and efficiency, and increased number of incorrect responses (Hativa 1986 and 1988; Hoorvitch-Steimberg 1990). These effects were greater with lower ability students (Hativa 1989).

None of the products evaluated in any of the studies analysed can be seen as uniform or static. The Educational Products Information Exchange (EPIE) published a report of the characteristics of 11 systems (EPIE 1990). This report is purely descriptive, relates to products as they were at the time of the study, and contains no evaluative material. Wilson (1990) published a survey of the products marketed under the term ILS by 12 companies. She compared philosophical approaches, curriculum areas, management systems, costs and company stability.

A casual observer, viewing an example of an ILS found in a school in 1988, and comparing it with the state-of-the-art ILS systems currently on the market in the mid-1990s might express justifiable surprise that the definition of an ILS has changed so little in eight years when the technology itself has apparently changed so much. In 1988 for example, the most common hardware implementation of ILS was a minicomputer serving terminals which did not support audio or high resolution graphics, with software which was text based and command driven. In contrast, present day systems can be run on networked or stand-alone microcomputers from a CD ROM or laser disk, and offer audio, text, high resolution graphics and moving images in a mouse-driven software environment.

The design of the ILS evaluated to date have all been based on a common view of the mechanism by which such computer-assisted instruction systems can impact on student learning. However, the change in the nature of the material which constitutes the courseware, and its presentation to students, is surely an important factor to be considered when considering the relevance of studies of the ILS of the late 1980s to those of the mid-1990s. It is reasonable to propose that these changes are likely to have an effect on student attitude, motivation and level of engagement, all of which can affect learning. However, no research which has come to light during this review considers these changes in the courseware as a variable. Even when different systems are compared in a study, the design, style, user interface, media employed, type of test items employed, curriculum coverage or indeed almost any other aspect of courseware are not given or even commented on.

Geoffrey Underwood and Jean Underwood

CHAPTER 4

Evaluating the educational impact of information technology on teaching and learning: the case against techno-romanticism

Research in education is a contentious affair. Controversy surrounds both the methods and the goals of such research. It is a politically sensitive issue because it is linked, through demands to evaluate the educational process, to the assessment of both children and teachers. Education is also a fertile ground for the development of arguments between humanists and empiricists in their approaches to the study of human behaviour.

Research in education is essentially directed towards evaluating the effectiveness of the educational process. This catch-all generalisation hides a multitude of issues concerning the goals of education, but as demands for accountability increase, evaluation studies have become more important and more complex. This chapter will review the case for evaluating any educational innovation, ILS included, with an empirical approach, and will consider the question of whether experiments can be conducted in classrooms.

Experimental method: an analogy

First let us consider a hypothetical case in medicine, a field in which most people have little difficulty in accepting the experimental method. Suppose you return from an exotic holiday with a dread disease that is rarely seen in this country. Your doctors have not seen the disease before, and they admit to not having read any reports of successful treatments. However, they are optimists and they have insight, and they believe that your symptoms look similar to others that they have read about. This being the case they recommend a course of treatment involving a new wonder drug. The risk involved is that the treatment will take time and if it is ineffective your disease will get progressively worse. What should you do? The wonder drug has not been tested, the treatment will cost valuable time, but your doctors' insight and beliefs tell them that this might be just the treatment that will solve your problem.

No doctor would make this recommendation of course, because experimental trials are necessary before a drug can be released for general use. The same should be true in education! The drug we are talking about involves the use of classroom computers. Is it a panacea for all ills? A simple treatment that can cure a national disease that is seeing the academic achievement in our classrooms fall behind in the international league tables so favoured by the tabloid press? In the hypothetical example of the wonder drug, the recommendation comes via the insights of an individual with a belief. The possible benefits may convince you that they outweigh the possible costs, but without evidence from clinical trials this would be an act of faith. If we adopt a classroom intervention such as an ILS, without the equivalent of a clinical trial, then we too would be acting in faith rather than in knowledge.

The costs of implementing an ILS are well known and considerable, but what of the benefits? Can an ILS help our educational goals? If so by how much, for whom, and under what circumstances? And how should we go about answering these questions? Should we perform a clinical trial, or rely upon the opinions of either the system designers or perhaps a user who has already been convinced? The opinions of an innovator are worth no more than those of an opponent, unless they are based upon evidence. The more people we poll for an opinion, the more opinions we will collect. Eventually we will have to collect some evidence to help us decide which opinion to believe. If we fail to do this, and accept perhaps the first opinion to be offered, or the opinion that is declared in the loudest voice, then we are not only fooling ourselves but we are also at risk of making a costly error. Evidence answers questions, substantiates belief, and allows us to make informed decisions. The need for evidence is indisputable, whether we are talking of education or medicine, and the only remaining question concerns the nature of the method for collecting this evidence.

Allow us to continue with the medical analogy for a moment. If we are to collect evidence, then how should we test the wonder drug as a treatment for our disease? It has to be tested on people who suffer from the disease, with a sample of patients assigned to one of two groups. One group will receive the new drug, the other will receive the normal treatment. (You might of course want a third group who receive no treatment at all — it might be that the body can cope better by itself — or a group given a placebo to counteract the Hawthorn effect). The two groups are compared, after a designated period of time, for level of improvement of health. If the improvement amongst those taking the new drug is significantly greater than for those receiving normal treatment, then we can say that the new drug is likely to be beneficial. Very few people would argue against the case for experimental research here.

Now let us return to our educational example. Can a course of treatment with an ILS produce brighter children? The evidence to be considered elsewhere in this book includes comparisons made with the aid of traditional experimental methods. In the simplest design children could be assigned to two groups, one group receiving the treatment (the experimental group) while the other group does not (the control group). The children would need to be pre-tested, to check that the two groups were scoring similar test results at the beginning, and then they would be re-tested to see if the experimental group scored higher test results than the control group. If the experimental group scored significantly higher than the control group it could be said that exposure to the ILS produces benefits for children's learning.

This example is likely to produce more criticism and questions about the interpretation than the medical example, yet are they really so different? One regularly heard objection is that it is impossible to control for every variable in education, but this is also true in the evaluation of a medical intervention. The patients in the disease study will vary in the environmental conditions in which they live (damp environments may be a factor for example) and in the levels of exercise taken throughout their lives, in their smoking and drinking habits, and in their other illnesses and injuries. There are ways of taking these additional variables into account, of course, and multi-variate analyses have been developed to determine the contribution of these uncontrolled variables. What is necessary, in the case of educational research and elsewhere, is that the potentially influential factors be observed and measured (even on a nominal scale of smoker versus non-smoker or large class versus small class) so that their effect can be taken into account. The differences between experiments in education and those in medicine are not so great as might be imagined. Treatments should only be prescribed after evidence has been collected. Some people believe that education can only benefit if children spend more time at computer keyboards, but this opinion, unsupported with evidence, can only be described as techno-romanticism. The alternative is to collect the evidence.

Investigating the impact of IT on teaching and learning

The early 1980s were dominated by a perception that classroom IT must be doing good and as a result little or no systematic evaluation of the learning outcomes took place. Richard Clark (1983) led the assault on this new faith, criticising those who 'knew IT did you good' but saving his most acerbic attacks for those conducting low-quality research. He argued that every positive effect attributed to IT would be better attributed to such factors as the quality of teacher input, novelty or motivation of the students. When we do observe effects, even if the effect is one of promoting enthusiasm, how should we identify the cause of the effect? Consider the following extract from a letter written by an 11-year-old and published in a national newspaper:

'I recently started an American spelling program on our computer at home, called *Spell It 3*, which has changed my spelling dramatically. It has lots of fun programs. Each game uses a different method, like one shows a sentence with a word highlighted. If it is spelt wrong, you delete it and type in the correct spelling. Each time you get five right, a frog appears and plays a tune. In another, you are a frog jumping on lily pads. If you choose the right spelling, a snake pops out and spins around and falls to the ground. It is brilliant. I suggest schools get it for their computers.'

(*The Independent*, 9 February 1996)

Let us suppose that we are conducting an investigation of the value of this program. The first point to make concerns the number of children to be tested. Can we rely upon the performance of the one individual who has written this letter or should we look for a group of children? The reason for testing a number of children is that even within a well-defined population there will be individual differences that cannot be controlled. By looking at a reasonably large sample from our population we can obtain an estimate of the confidence that we could have in declaring that the improvement in spelling can be generalised beyond the sample tested to the population as a whole. With a sample of just one program user we cannot say whether the improvement would be seen in other children selected from the same population. A study is necessary to discover whether the improvement produces a general effect in a selected sample. If it does, then we can conclude that the natural range of variation attributable to individual differences does not account for the improvement in spelling. In other words, we would be able to say that the spelling program works.

Appropriate sampling is critical, as can be illustrated with an example from the ILS evaluation. Our caution over the Global mathematics findings in Phase 1 of the NCET trial arose from our concern about the unrepresentative nature of the sample. All the children were drawn from single-sex rather than the more standard co-educational schools.

A simple experiment based upon the enthusiasm expressed in the above letter might find, for example, that a class performs better on a spelling test after using a frog-game spelling program. Such an experiment could not lead to the conclusion that the program produces spelling gains, because no control group has been used. The improvement may be a product of increased motivation, either through attention from the researchers (the Hawthorn effect) or through the games format of the spelling program, for example. A control group of children matched at least on the basis of initial spelling ability is necessary, with this group experiencing similar levels of involvement in research and use of a similarly motivating piece of software. And yet recommendations based on exploratory research abound. This hypothetical spelling game example would be a perfectly valid exploration of children's interactions with the program and its outcomes. Such a project would need no control groups, provided that the limitation is kept in mind and provided that the researcher simply wants to observe children's use of the program. Without control groups, however, we do not even know whether the improvement is a product of the computer game or of other activities undertaken in the interval between the two spelling tests. The value of the experimental method is in the control of influential variables.

Clark's criticisms have resulted in a more rigorous empirical evaluation of classroom IT. For example, our own work (Underwood 1985; Underwood and Underwood 1990) and that of groups such as Klahr and Carver (1988) and Johnson, Johnson and Stanne (1985) has shown that there are measurable learning gains though the use of IT. There is considerable evidence, however, particularly in the study of LOGO, of the ineffectiveness of IT strategies. Failures to confirm the education gains claimed for the use of IT have often been associated with inadequate methodological control. The contradiction in evidence sets up a research question to determine the conditions under which IT is beneficial to learning. For example, Jocelyn Wishart (1990) has investigated the relationship between cognitive demand, motivation and learning in computer simulations, and Robin Kay (1992) has conducted a detailed analysis of gender, attitude and IT competence. The general conclusions from this research are that IT can have beneficial effects on teaching and learning but that use of IT will not inevitably lead to educational gains.

What is the nature of the effect of IT on teaching and learning?

Under the right conditions IT can have an effect on teaching and learning, but what is the nature of that effect? Enormous changes were predicted following the introduction of computers into classrooms. The computer was and is still seen as a powerful learning tool partly because it can be used to support every style of teaching and learning. There have been a number of papers published discussing this question. Rushby (1979), after Kemmis (1978), established a categorisation of software which implicitly explored the cognitive activity involved in interacting with the various types of software. Two papers are of particular importance here. Gavriel Salomon and his colleagues (1991) have drawn our attention to the distinction between effects *with* and *of* the computer, and Roy Pea (1985) talks of the amplification of, versus the reorganisation of, mental functions. Essentially they are both saying that we can use the computer either to enhance our performance or we can enter into qualitatively new ways of thinking. Survey evidence shows that even good classrooms are using IT primarily as a tool to enhance performance — poor classrooms have not reached this stage at all (HMI 1995). There is little evidence of teachers or students working beyond the performance enhancement stage. Indeed, Ron Ragsdale (1991), working with Canadian teacher trainees, has shown that acquiring IT tools may be relatively easy but that gaining the wisdom to use them effectively may not! The general conclusions from this research are that good current use of IT in classrooms is directed towards performance enhancement, but that the use of computers as a reward rather than for enhancement is still rife. There is little evidence that the computer is being widely used to develop new thinking skills.

The use of IT as a catalyst for change

There is an awareness that the use of IT should be investigated in context. An exciting development has been the coming together of two research agendas: investigations into co-operative and collaborative learning and the IT agenda (Light 1993; Underwood and Underwood 1993). The focus has moved from mental states to the social context of learning in which the computer can play many parts including that of a significant other in the Vygotskian sense. This awareness of the importance of the social context in teaching and learning leads full circle back to Clark's criticism that it is not possible to separate the effect of the IT intervention from the other variables in the classroom. That may be so, but Gavriel Salomon (1990) in his paper *The Flute versus the Orchestra,* turns this criticism around by asking whether we should be attempting to separate out these potent variables. If the computer brings about a change in social organisation that in turn leads to educational benefits of some kind then perhaps we should be satisfied in achieving an educational goal. The understanding of the specific causes of change is a secondary issue, even if the causes are at all separable.

On a less optimistic but significantly cautious note Olson (1989) and many others have shown how resistant to change classroom settings are. It is in these classrooms we will see poor use of IT leading to few if any educational gains.

The nature of evaluation

Evaluation may take a number of different forms, depending on the reasons for that evaluation and the method of data collection. The nature of any evaluation is generally defined by a series of dichotomies: is the evaluation formative or summative; will it take the form of a controlled experiment or will it be a collection of observations over time? As Kemmis (1978) has pointed out, these different approaches to evaluation have arisen from the different views of the nature of generalisation, of the nature of explanation, and of the nature of social science itself.

The simplest summative evaluation looks at outcomes using the pre/post-tests design. Venezky (1983) suggests that an equally valuable approach is the time-series design. Here student outcomes following the onset of the educational treatment are compared with outcomes in the same context prior to the treatment, and not with the performances of a control group. Venezky argues that although the time-series design lacks the experimental rigour of the control-group design, it does have increased ecological validity. Both methods have a problem in attributing a cause to any observable change. An improvement might be due to other changes in the school, including changes to the teaching staff and the teaching environment, as well as to extraneous factors such as changes in nutrition and the success of the local football team. Both methods are rooted in the nomothetic tradition of the scientific method.

It is often the case that the researcher will want to go beyond the measurement of achievement through the use of teacher and pupil questionnaires and classroom observations. Venezky calls this the fieldwork additive model of evaluation and he suggests that such observational material adds significantly to the interpretation of achievement measures. This additive model is the meeting ground between the nomothetic and the hermeneutic approaches to evaluation. The methodology of such evaluations is observational case studies and its strength is its high level of ecological validity, but it lacks the rigour of the nomothetic approach and, importantly in the case of the ILS project, the ability to generalise from the results.

Empiricism: a controversial approach in educational research

To set out to conduct relevant and valid research in the classroom is a daunting task. The classroom is a highly complex environment, a seething mass of interdependent variables which, in many eyes, are uncontrollable in any formal empirical sense. It is this very complexity that has led to one of the deep rifts in studies in the classroom, between the empiricists on the one hand, generally operating from a base of logical-positivism, and the more hermeneutic research tradition on the other hand. Within Europe as a whole there has always been a strong hermeneutic tradition, in part due to the philosophical and sociological traditions of academic Europe, whereas, the US, and to a lesser extent the UK, traditionally followed the empirical approach to educational research.

In the last two decades the experimental approach to research in education has been the subject of much debate and criticism, especially from proponents of the case study, many of whom believe that information about children's learning must come from the people closest to those children, namely the teachers. It has been argued that the aim of empirical research is to explain, while that of the hermeneutic school is to understand the phenomena under investigation (von Wright 1971). This is exemplified by Piaget and Inhelder's (1947) argument that the results of the types of pre-post tests frequently used in the assessment of learning can only give an indication of the efficiency of mental activity while failing to illuminate our understanding of the mental operations themselves.

The first commonly-voiced objection is that empirical methods do not tell us why something works or happens, although a series of experiments that controls potent factors can aid in this understanding. What it certainly does is to indicate where there is an effect which is worthy of further investigation in order to gain a fuller understanding. What it can also do, working the other way round, is to find out if a one-off, casually observed effect is replicated in other situations. It is not that one research method is superior to another, but rather that each method has an important role to play, each providing a piece of the jigsaw to aid our understanding.

A second objection is that experiments in education are not true experiments because the classroom is complex, with many interacting factors. All investigations involving humans are complex. The argument is that empirical procedures are ineffective because they merely evaluate a treatment under a specific set of conditions, and this is a fundamental weakness of the approach. We have discussed the answer to this objection in our earlier comparison of experiments in educational and medical research and we see this as an argument for the observation and recording of all variables that may be relevant so that their influence can be assessed with multi-variate analyses. Briefly, it can be argued that this is its very strength: the conditions of testing are well defined and so the conditions of effective treatment are well-defined. Teachers can benefit from research information which tells them under what conditions an intervention is known to work.

A view sometimes voiced in defence of empiricism is that critics are unhappy with experiments because they, the critics, are unable to conduct experiments properly. There certainly exist many examples of poorly controlled evaluations which give rise to uncertain conclusions but we cannot reject a methodology on the basis that someone somewhere cannot use it cleanly. A poor experiment is arguably less use than no experiment at all, but are there no good experiments in the educational domain? Clark (1983, 1984) suggests that, for research on the new technologies and education, the answer is a decisive and blunt *no*. Becker (1992), in reviewing the past research on ILS, agrees there have been some poor investigations of these systems. These criticisms were that the interval between treatment and assessment of effects is generally too brief to know whether sustainable gains have been achieved, and that control groups are generally not matched to the experimental groups. This is not to say that experimental research in education is impossible, of course, just that acceptable experiments have specific requirements. To reject all experiments on the effectiveness of new technology would be to throw out the baby with the bath water, and these criticisms should simply be kept in mind when designing future studies. In particular, the ILS evaluation has made a point of looking for sustainable gains over several months, and has matched control and experimental groups on a number of performance measures that are not directly a part of the content of the ILS materials.

Further, Becker argues that different studies have used different measures, and so comparisons between them are at best difficult. He suggests that in addition to the traditional measures of central tendency we should report our results in terms of effect sizes (ES), and thereby gain comparability through this standard metric. The ES for ILS study was the difference in performance between the ILS and control groups, expressed as a proportion of one standard deviation of pre-trial scores for the combined ILS and control groups (after Becker 1992). Becker argues that an ES of 0.15 over a year is negligible as it can be accounted for by among other things, maturation. An ES above 0.15 is significant, however, as it cannot be accounted for by children's variation in natural increase in performance with age.

Clark's reservations about the value of new technologies to education have been noted above. Although the computer may have a brief novelty effect on improving learning, the change is transitory. In general, the well-prepared traditional teacher can do just as well. Reservations is too restrained a term, however, when we consider Clark's views on the quality of research in this area. In the two papers cited he has led a thoughtful, articulate and scathing attack on research purporting to show learning benefits from the use of various technologies in the classroom. He argues that careful re-analysis of published research data reveals consistent evidence of the failure of any new technologies to increase learning significantly. Further, where data do indicate performance or efficiency gains, the data could be equally explained by other hypotheses, so ill-controlled are the experiments. Clark suggests that the two most important problems with such an approach result from the confounding of variables in the experimental design and the failure to account for novelty effects in achievement gains. He concludes that performance gains from computer usage drop off dramatically after the fourth week of use but he reflects that few studies are conducted over even this brief time-scale.

Is Clark's message one of despair or one of admonishment tinged with guarded hope? Is he suggesting that no comparative studies of learning under differing teaching strategies can be valid, or are researchers simply being encouraged to tighten up their experimental procedures. In this evaluation the more optimistic view of Clark's work has been assumed, but his pertinent criticisms, along with those of Becker, have been used to develop the experimental procedures used here.

Evaluating the ILS intervention

The two key questions when evaluating this innovation are: how well does it work, and how can it be improved? In answering these questions we have at all times to keep in mind both the audience and the purpose of the evaluation. Less frequently evaluators may ask what practices emerge as the innovation is incorporated into different settings, and how the innovation can be recreated in another setting. These were important questions for the ILS evaluation at both Phase 1 and 2, as a prime objective of the project was the effective dissemination of the innovation across institutions should the summative evaluations prove positive. In answering these questions we had at all times to keep in mind both the audience and the purpose of the evaluation. The evaluation was to aid policy makers at national, regional and institutional levels in making decisions about whether to adopt this method of teaching or not; to support users of the system; and to provide feedback to developers of the systems.

How well does it work?

Summative evaluation is used to investigate the impact of an innovation as a whole on learning or some other outcome. It is concerned with the effects of using an innovation. In the case of the ILS project the outcomes would be learning gains in basic numeracy and literacy. Summative evaluation treats the technical details of the system as a black box. The data gained from such an evaluation are used in making adoption or continuation decisions and the audience is the end user.

How can it be improved?

Formative evaluation is used to monitor the innovation to ascertain how different features of the system work. This information is used in developing the innovation and the audience is the system designer. Formative evaluation can be carried out in such a way that it brings the users of the innovation (tutors and pupils) into the development process. This has been an important goal of the ILS project.

Summative evaluations typically yield quantitative results, such as performance gains. Recognition of the need not only to identify change but also to understand that change has led to an increased use of qualitative data to assess the usefulness of the innovation. At all times these qualitative methods maintain the goals and audience of summative evaluation, emphasising generalisations rather than contrasts between implementations of the innovation. Formative evaluations typically yield qualitative results, such as lists of changes to be made to the innovation. The boundary between these two types of evaluation is fuzzy and formative evaluation can be viewed as micro-summative.

Both summative and formative evaluations are valuable procedures but a shared limitation is the lack of provision for examining the interaction between the innovation and the situation in which the innovation is used. Implementing an innovation means introducing something new into an existing system. If the innovation is significant, it will trigger changes in the system, some of which will be predictable but others will not. It is important when planning the evaluation strategy for any innovation to develop tools that will capture not only the expected but also the unexpected events and outcomes.

The evaluation

In Phase 1 the evaluation was conducted by two groups, a team of researchers from Leicester University and the NCET project team. The core summative evaluation, used to investigate the impact of the innovation, was the responsibility of the Leicester team while NCET conducted qualitative observational studies of classroom management and organisation. The outcomes were numeracy and reading gains, together with changes in motivation and attitudes towards learning. The evaluation model was a standard pre/post testing paradigm with treatment (ILS users) and control (non-ILS users) groups of peers who would continue working in their normal classrooms. All children in both the pilot ILS groups and the control groups completed standardised tests of non-verbal ability, mathematical ability and reading ability at the start (pre-test) and at the end (post-test) of the six-month trial period. In addition, weekly aggregated attendance figures were taken over the period of the evaluation for each of the ILS and control classes as an indication of motivation for learning. Pupils' attitudes to core areas of study formed a further pre/post measure. The pre/post test data were supplemented by a range of qualitative data which are discussed more fully in Chapters 5 to 12. In Phase 2 the role of Leicester and the NCET remained much the same although additional outcome measures were taken. The major change to the evaluation was the introduction of four additional field researchers each conducting a small-scale qualitative study of a specific group of users.

In Phase 1 it became apparent that there was some level of user disaffection with the system. In Phase 2 John Gardner undertook an investigation of this thorny issue of disaffection and under-achievement in relationship to the use of ILS (Chapter 9). Colin Harrison, Ann Lewis and Susan Rodriguez respectively followed small groups of English as a second language, special needs, and gifted children. The evaluations by Gardner and Lewis have each applied rigour to their study through the technique of triangulation, the use of three separate data sources focused on and illuminating the research question. Harrison and Rodriguez have employed a descriptive case study approach. For each researcher, their role was to gain a fuller understanding of how each of these groups of children interacted with the system and to aid in our understanding of the quantitative measures of learning that were being produced by the core project.

There was one additional strand of research conducted by Carol Fitz-Gibbon and Neil Defty (Chapter 8). This operated a quantitative summative model. Here the mathematics performance of a small group of ILS pupils at GCSE was compared with a predicted level of performance in relation to a large nationally distributed population sample external to the school.

Collectively these evaluation techniques have provided a rich, but as yet, incomplete picture of the impact of the ILS intervention on children's learning. They have also provided much valuable data on how and when the intervention works, for example how long and frequent must exposure to the system be for beneficial effects to occur (Chapter 5). Earlier it was stated that any innovation of significance will trigger changes in the system. Here, as Chapters 5 and 7 in particular show, ILS are having interesting impacts on classrooms and schools in general.

SECTION 2 *Focus on learning*

This section looks at learners' responses to ILS, and includes details of the key learning outcomes identified over the trial period. The evaluation looked at whether basic skills in numeracy and literacy can be enhanced, and at the value of ILS in developing a wider skills base.

When and why do pupils learn from ILS?

*Sue Cavendish, Jean Underwood, Tony Lawson and
Sheila Dowling*

This chapter provides a summary of those factors which have been identified as impinging on effective learning outcomes, including motivation, teaching and learning styles, individual differences and time on the system.

Motivation

There is a wealth of evidence that use of a computer, often regardless of the quality of software, can be motivating to pupils. For example, the ImpacT study (Watson 1993) reported that computers were good motivators which heightened pupils' interest in and enjoyment of subjects and led to a raising of the status of the subject in which IT was used.

Other researchers have suggested that this motivating factor of the computer declines in time as the novelty wears off (Clark 1983). There was ample time for such a deterioration in interest to occur in the NCET project. Many of the pupils involved in Phase 1 and 2 of the project had worked for 30 minutes a day over an 18 month period with the ILS. Here then, one might expect the novelty factor to diminish and we can look at the long-term effects of ILS on motivation.

Motivation is a broad concept which encompasses amongst other things attitudes, needs, interests and incentives, all of which describe our enthusiasm and direct our behaviour. It is generally accepted that achievement motivation correlates with academic performance, but the measurement of motivation to achieve in the classroom is problematic. For the ILS study, our evidence for motivation is taken from school attendance rates, pupil interviews, questionnaires and observation of behaviour.

Attitude to school

In Phase 1 several schools were characterised by high truancy rates. Several reasons have been extended to account for this but by far the most influential was thought to be a negative attitude towards school. There is evidence from the US to suggest that use of ILS can lead to improved attitudes towards school and a significant reduction in truancy rates. Would similar benefits emerge in the UK? Many Phase 1 teachers reported improved pupil attitudes to school and to work as a result of working on the ILS system. But could the quantitative evidence support these claims?

Interviews with both ILS and non-ILS users showed positive attitudes towards school in general, although some level of disaffection was expressed by about 20 per cent of the children. It was argued that should the ILS succeed in improving attitudes of these disaffected pupils then attendance rates should also improve. Comparing attendance figures prior to use of ILS with those later in the school year when the ILS was well established there was no evidence of improvement in attendance figures during Phase 1. In Phase 2 improvements were only apparent in secondary schools using Global, where ILS pupils had higher summer term attendance than their control peers.

It may not be surprising that we failed to find measurable differences in attendance for primary schools as the opportunity for truanting is far lower for this younger age. For secondary schools these conflicting results are more difficult to explain but it might be that the culture of the school is playing an overriding part here, in particular the school's culture of achievement.

Analysis by school revealed some interesting patterns of attendance. One school using Global provided data for only three ILS pupils and three control pupils but the improved attendance over the school year for ILS pupils corresponded with a fall in attendance for control pupils. We would suggest that in this boys-only school the ILS has resulted in increased pupil self-esteem which, because of the culture of high achievement, has subsequently led to higher attendance rates. This concurs with other research which shows that peer pressure results in pupils in cultures of high achievement being proud of their achievements, while in cultures of low achievement they often feel the need to hide their accomplishments. However, improved attendance was **not** found in the secondary school using SuccessMaker with a culture of high achievement and it may be inherent differences between the two ILS systems which cause differential effects on attitudes towards school.

In a second school using Global we monitored three groups of pupils, one using ILS for mathematics only, one for English and one as a control. The ILS was in use spasmodically during the summer term. Attendance figures for these three groups throughout the year are shown in Figure 1.

Control pupils' attendance rates dropped gently across the three terms, and this appears to be the general pattern for all schools. Pupils using Global mathematics, however, kept a fairly steady attendance rate, with a slight but non-significant increase in the summer term, contrary to the decline one would normally expect. The biggest difference is with pupils using Global English, who show a steady decline from the Autumn to

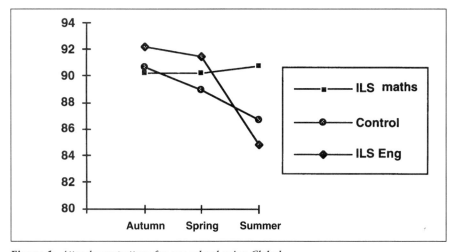

Figure 1: *Attendance pattern for one school using Global*

Spring terms, but a dramatic drop in the Summer term. Bearing in mind that the ILS was in place for the Summer term only, the figures appear to reflect pupils' feelings about the specific ILS modules. Of particular relevance here, is the repeated failure of the system when running the English module. Observations of some English sessions revealed the system going down for about 40 per cent of the time (as described on page 57). This was not true of the mathematics software, which was far more robust. So while the Global mathematics module appears to have had a positive effect on attitude to school, the English module appears to have had a negative effect as a consequence of the instability of the system.

In summary, for secondary aged pupils using Global mathematics there was a positive effect on pupils' attitudes towards school as measured by attendance rates, but the Global English software had a negative effect. There were no discernible differences in attendance for SuccessMaker pupils at any level.

Attitude to the subject.

Teachers in Phase 1 reported an improvement not only in the attitudes to learning of pupils using ILS, but also to their work in mathematics and English. However, interviews with Phase 1 pupils revealed that while they had more positive attitudes to English than their control peers, this was not true for mathematics. One reason expressed for this positive attitude to ILS English was the lack of writing. On the other hand classroom mathematics was liked when it was exploratory, that is active and doing things, as opposed to sums or book work. It is curious that in the case of SuccessMaker these attitudes towards English and mathematics are contrary to the performance gains made in these subjects. The relationship between positive attitude and learning gains does, therefore, warrant further research.

In Phase 2 teachers reported on the attitude, effort and achievement in mathematics and English of target pupils from the control and ILS groups. Pupils using SuccessMaker and new to ILS were reported to make more effort in the classroom than control pupils, and pupils who were on ILS for their second year were better than their control peers in terms of their attitude, effort and improvement in achievement. For one primary school using SuccessMaker, reports were obtained on ILS pupils from tutors in their new secondary schools. For both mathematics and English the former ILS pupils were perceived more favourably than their peers in terms of attitudes, effort, behaviour and in some cases achievement.

The evidence suggests that the SuccessMaker experience over a sustained period of time led to transfer of positive attitudes to both mathematics and English and that this benefit was sustained even after pupils had stopped using the system. This improved attitude was in both mathematics and English even though performance gains were found mainly in mathematics.

Evidence from schools using Global is less easy to interpret than that from schools using SuccessMaker. Many pupils new to ILS experienced disruption of their ILS experience, and some schools had elected to use the mathematics programme only. Generally though, attitudes towards mathematics were less positive for ILS pupils than for their control group peers. There was no evidence to suggest that the Global ILS experience resulted in improved attitudes to mathematics or English.

To summarise, experience of using the Global system appears in certain cases to influence attitude to school but not to the subject, whereas the SuccessMaker system influences attitude to the subject but not to school. There appear to be inherent differences between Global and SuccessMaker which have different effects on pupils' attitudes and learning. Further information on the factors involved here was sought from the pupils themselves in relation to their feelings about the ILS system they used.

Attitude to ILS

An ILS has particular characteristics which require considerable concentration by the pupils. Do pupils like this form of learning? What impact does it have on their attitudes towards learning *per se* and towards the curriculum areas involved? A study by Hativa (1989) suggested that pupils have a love-hate relationship with ILS - they like it when the computer tells them they have got something right, but not when they have got it wrong, so the ILS is both motivating and demotivating. It was also reported that positive attitude towards ILS varied according to the ratio of correct responses to attempted questions and we shall return to this issue again later as it is of particular relevance to the ILS evaluated in this study.

Pupils' attitudes towards ILS were investigated by means of interviews and short pupil questionnaires administered at the end of an ILS session. Overall, pupils showed a strong preference for work on the ILS rather than in the classroom.

The results from the end of Phase 1 are presented in Figure 2 and are illustrative of our findings over both phases of the study. In only one school did the pupils show a preference for working in the classroom. This particular school, using SuccessMaker software, had considerable difficulty at the start of using ILS in establishing a suitable starting level for the pupils. In addition, the pupils were withdrawn from normal classes and from the interviews it was apparent that they felt labelled as failures.

Interviews with early years pupils suggested that SuccessMaker had an important role in improving attitude towards basic number work, while providing a non-threatening way of testing their spelling. Spelling in the classroom was particularly disliked, yet spelling on the computer was deemed enjoyable alongside mathematics and English. The classroom, however, has an equally important role in providing enjoyment in the practical activities which are not provided by the ILS.

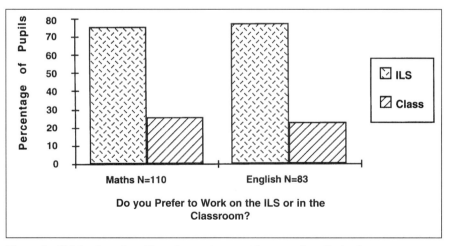

Figure 2: Children's preferred learning environment by group for all schools

All primary school pupils tended to show a positive attitude towards using computers and one might expect, therefore, that ILS work has an advantage over the classroom in motivating pupils. Indeed, the pupils interviewed who were using SuccessMaker were even more positive than their control peers and were unanimous in enjoying mathematics and English on the computer:

'It talks to you.'

'You know what to do the next time 'cos if you get it wrong the first time they give it you again slightly different.'

'You don't have to use a pencil.'

The control pupils expressed a strong dislike of doing sums, particularly long division. It appears that SuccessMaker ILS is suited to presenting tests and formal arithmetic in an enjoyable way leaving the classroom work for more practical and investigative mathematics.

Secondary school pupils were similarly positive towards SuccessMaker work with mathematics being favoured over English even though pupils thought they were doing better in English. In reality these pupils were achieving well in both subject areas. One of the few pupils to prefer working in the classroom commented that she felt she had been put on the computer because 'they think I'm stupid and need extra learning'. This effect is important and one which needs to be addressed when schools are considering selection of pupils for ILS use.

Our questionnaires showed some decline in enjoyment of ILS work over time, but the majority of both primary and secondary children were still positive about this mode of learning. This finding held even for pupils using ILS for their second year, and this positive attitude cannot be accounted for by the novelty of working with a new learning system.

Overall, pupils using Global were also very positive. Primary pupils particularly liked the games in mathematics, and they liked speaking into the microphone for English. There were some improvements they would like to the system, including more variety, clearer instructions and a saving facility so that the system would remember where they had got to in the program; 'I wish it would save 'cos in mathematics when you come back in you have to start again'.

Those children who showed disaffection with the Global system were often in schools which had experienced significant system failure. Children commented that the system tended to freeze, although at one school, where children were not supervised during their ILS time, this was viewed positively; 'Some people make it go wrong because they want to go back to their classroom'. These same pupils commented that they would like to discuss their ILS work with their teacher, but while that had happened at the beginning of the project, it had now ceased, partly due to the teacher's frustration with the system.

'Teachers used to read our comments but they don't anymore so it's a waste of time writing any.'

'We used to keep a diary but don't anymore because it took up too much paper to print out.'

'The teacher doesn't let us talk to her about it 'cos she doesn't want to know.'

'Teachers are too busy. I wish they would listen to us more.'

There were major problems in the running of the Global system and yet despite this many children were positive about their experiences. Our observations and discussions with staff confirmed that some children were fascinated by the technology itself. Those who were able to help their peers gained status. This finding might also provide some insight as to why the Global system appears to improve attitude to school but not attitude to the specific curriculum areas of mathematics and English. The pupils appeared to have an enjoyable time using the technology, for example the microphones, and this may have produced positive attitudes to the computer and hence made school more enjoyable. However, if the children were not doing any work on the curriculum then one would not expect the system to have any impact on specific subject areas.

Self-esteem

Mathematics is known to be a subject which is both difficult to teach and difficult to learn. As a result, many children experience failure with a subsequent loss in motivation and lowering of self-esteem in relation to the subject. This adverse reaction is often exacerbated by teachers criticising children for incorrect answers. Investigations into pupil attitudes towards mathematics show a strong association in pupils' minds between getting sums wrong and receiving criticism for behaviour (Cavendish 1988). This negative association appears to create apprehension in the minds of the pupils and leads to fear of failure (Holt 1982). It is important for tasks to be devised and presented in such a way that each child experiences success – a key objective of the differentiated programmes of work available through an ILS.

Alongside this individualised instruction an ILS provides instant feedback to students on the current task and access to progress reports which inform them of their rate of success during that particular ILS session. The term feedback is taken here to mean the indication of correctness or otherwise of pupil responses. This feedback can be presented in several forms: some give 'rewards' such as the appearance of rosettes, or of moving graphics; while others provide information as scores. These features should, according to Hoorvitch-Steimberg (1990), result in considerable benefits for the pupils in terms of increased pride, self-confidence and motivation as well as learning. But does this access to reports leads to unhealthy competition between pupils?

So how did the pupils respond to the feedback system of the ILS? While a few pupils disliked the reward system, with some saying that the pictures were too babyish, there was a generally positive attitude towards SuccessMaker and Global software. Pupils felt that it provided clear explanations and liked the immediate feedback whether right or wrong. Typical pupil comments about SuccessMaker were, 'it tells you your corrections quickly and easily,' and 'the wee pictures come up when you get them right'. In addition, the gentle nature of feedback following an incorrect response was viewed in a positive light; 'It doesn't give you a hard time, just tells you to try again'.

Feedback from the Global report system was not without its problems. A key issue here was that a child could achieve a perfect 100 per cent score after completing one question, but this dropped to 50 per cent if the pupil was unsuccessful in a second question. Pupils rapidly realised that it was better to complete as few questions as possible, particularly if the first questions were successfully completed. These reports may or may not have improved their standing with their peers or increased their self-esteem but it is unlikely that such tactics, which resulted in very little work being done, would result in learning gains. This strategy, employed by some children, may have been a contributing factor to the failure of the Global system to improve attitude to the subject area even though attitude to school is improved.

Some schools using SuccessMaker made use of rewards extrinsic to the system. For example, pupils who had obtained a score of 45 per cent or better in the ILS session recorded their success on the 45 club sheet on the classroom wall. Pupils were observed checking their score regularly throughout the lesson until their score was 45 per cent and then taking a relaxed approach in their pace of working. The impact was not one of inducing competition between pupils but of enabling pupils to work only as hard as they needed to reach an acceptable level, a form of mastery learning. Other schools avoided the risk of peer competition. Pupils entered their scores on to a personal log sheet and their performance target was set against their own previous performance.

In summary, pupils were receiving immediate feedback in a gentle way. Access to progress reports did not appear to induce unhealthy competition between peers but did enable pupils to see the fruits of their efforts. Pupils were unlikely to feel that they were failing and so less likely to develop a fear of failure than in normal class teaching. This more positive approach to learning might be expected to result in pupils feeling more positive about themselves and to have high self-esteem.

Burns (1982) defines the self-concept as composed of all the beliefs and evaluations an individual has about him/herself. All individuals have a belief about themselves – a self-image – and an evaluation of this belief – one's self-esteem. Schunk (1990) suggests that when dealing with self-concepts specific to a particular curriculum, programmes that include both instruction and opportunity to practise specific skills tend to increase pupils' self-confidence. In particular, positive feedback enhances these positive feelings. He points out, however, that this increase will be short-lived if pupils' subsequent efforts result in failure. We might conclude that working on an ILS, with its differentiated programme of work structured to induce success, will result in increased self-confidence and more positive feelings about oneself. Furthermore, many studies have found a correlational relationship between self-concept and academic success (Backman and Secord 1968).

All new Phase 2 pupils completed a standardised test of self esteem (B/G STEEM) both before and after the trial. There was an improvement in self-esteem for secondary pupils using SuccessMaker across all ability levels and interestingly, although self-esteem did not improve at the primary level, there was a tendency for initial self-esteem to be related to improvement in numeracy and reading. Those primary pupils using SuccessMaker described as having a normal level of self-esteem made greater gains than those with a high self-esteem. There were insufficient pupils of low self-esteem for analysis. There are two things to note here. Firstly, that the SuccessMaker ILS can lead to an increase in self-esteem for secondary age pupils. Secondly, that the primary pupils who make best use of the ILS are those who start with a normal measure of self-esteem. There is also some indication at the primary level that a well-established level of self-esteem has some effect on learning.

New Phase 2 pupils using Global recorded a deterioration of self-esteem over the trial period when compared with the control groups. However, given the difficulties encountered with system crashes and screen freezes, we cannot attribute this deterioration to use of the software as it may be due to frustration at being without a reliable working system.

When pupils in Phase 1 were interviewed most felt that the ILS experience had been beneficial. Only a few children felt that their performance on the ILS had declined over the period of the trial. In reality, learning gains were inversely related to children's analysis of their own progress, that is children who used SuccessMaker were confident in their English work and the children who used Global their mathematics work. However, it was in SuccessMaker mathematics where significant learning gains were found. We speculated that this mismatch could be due to the end-of-session scores. For example, some children on the Global system received scores of 90 per cent and subsequently would feel they were doing well even if their learning had advanced only a little. There is a fine balance to be achieved here. It is important to prevent a child experiencing repeated failure, but it is equally important to give a realistic message about their performance.

Pupil types and learning styles

An ILS is designed to be used by children working individually at a computer, yet many researchers (Kerry and Sands 1982; Biott 1987; Underwood and Underwood 1993) have argued that co-operative working is important for the development of learning. For some teachers the one-to-one experience of the ILS may be seen as atypical of the normal way of working, but research evidence shows that the present day practice of seating children in groups does not necessarily lead to co-operative work (Galton *et al* 1980; Mortimore *et al* 1988). For example, Galton's Oracle study of classrooms reported that while pupils were seated in groups for nearly 80 per cent of their time, the children worked alone on individual assignments, particularly in mathematics and English. There were, however, high levels of distraction with pupils talking about non-work matters. This social interaction is considered by some educationists to be an important element in children's development. Working in groups has an important effect on a person's social identity or self-concept (Brown 1988; Turner 1982).

It can be argued that a range of learning tasks requires a range of teaching and learning strategies. Equally children have preferred styles of learning. Galton *et al* (1983) identified several types of secondary pupil behaviour some of which were more prevalent than others in specific curriculum areas. For example, in mathematics the majority of pupils were what the Oracle study termed *Easy Riders,* while in English not only were there *Easy Riders,* but there were also those described as *Hard Grinders.* Similar pupil types were identified for the primary age range but analysis of this data was based on the accumulated observations across all curriculum areas. However, these data were re-analysed by Cavendish (1988) to reveal primary pupil types by curriculum area comparative to those for the secondary age group. So are these pupil types apparent in the ILS situation? Could it be that ILS favours one particular style of learning or pupil type over another? Table 1 presents a summary description of Oracle pupil types found in the mathematics and English classrooms.

In Phase 1 pupils were tracked in lessons before and after their ILS session and during their ILS session. Observations of group and individual pupil behaviour were made. For Phase 2, pupils were observed during ILS sessions and immediately following the sessions.

At the start of the study in the secondary schools using SuccessMaker and in those using Global the majority of pupils behaved like *Hard Grinders.* Pupils' attention to task and level of behaviour was far higher than in classroom-based lessons. At the end of the Phase 1 trial there was some evidence of transfer of this good behaviour and high level of attention to the classroom. There were, however, some pupils who appeared to be disaffected with school generally; when working on the ILS they behaved like *Solitary Workers.* For example, in one school using SuccessMaker one boy spent a great deal of

Table 1: *Percentage of pupils with different behaviour characteristics*

Pupil type	Main behaviour characteristics	Mathematics		English	
		Primary	*Secondary*	*Primary*	*Secondary*
Easy Riders	Work at a leisurely pace, doing just enough to avoid the teacher's attention. Some interaction with peers.	0%	82%	41%	52%
Hard Grinders	Work on task for most of the time. Little interaction with teacher or peers.	32%	6%	0%	35%
Intermittent Workers	Work while talking to peers about non-task matters.	28%	0%	16%	0%
Solitary Workers	Little interaction with teacher or peers. Appear to work hard but spend most of the time avoiding work by sharpening pencil, etc.	20%	0%	19%	0%
Fusspots	Busy being helpful while achieving very little.	21%	7%	24%	1%
Group Toilers	Work hard on task but collaborate with peers.	0%	5%	0%	12%

time swinging on his chair, glancing around, avoiding eye-contact with the screen. In the classroom his level of concentration was similarly poor but he was also disruptive. ILS appeared to contain his behaviour to the benefit of other pupils, but did not succeed in engaging his attention. Negative behaviour in one school using Global took a slightly different form. Here pupils who appeared to be on-task were in reality acting out their fantasies as pop stars and sports commentators. The children were also seen to switch frequently from one work task to another, making extensive use of the menus and icons available. When pupils were faced with an activity they could not do or respond to, they tended to quit it and return to the menu, thus making little or no progress in their learning. Pupils did report they liked having their own choice of modules, but the observations show that the effect was not always positive.

Where secondary pupils were using the ILS for their second year the behaviour of pupils continued to be good for the majority of pupils; this demonstrates the long-lasting effect on motivation. There were some changes in the patterns of behaviour. Pupils in secondary schools using Global showed an increase in the number of task-related interactions with other pupils and moved into a pattern similar to *Group Toilers;* that is, the one-to-one nature of ILS did not prevent peer collaboration.

In one group using SuccessMaker there was a polarisation of behaviour. The group divided into those who remained well focused on their work and those who did very little. Pupils in this latter group were observed abusing the system by entering totally inappropriate answers in order to access the help function. This provided answers more quickly and with less effort than if they had to do the work for themselves. These pupils also frequently checked their scores to see when they had obtained the score required to enter onto the class achievement record sheet. The pupils in this group were behaving either as *Hard Grinders,* the on-task workers, or as *Solitary Workers,* appearing busy but actually doing very little.

Only one group of pupils using SuccessMaker recorded negative attitudes towards ILS but these pupils were negative about school generally. All reported preferring the class-room to their ILS time as they could talk to their friends in the classroom whereas they had to be silent for ILS sessions. They were *Intermittent Workers* who viewed the Suc-cessMaker way of working unfavourably. This negative view does not, however, appear to have affected performance as the SuccessMaker groups of pupils were found to make accelerated gains compared to their control peers.

Observers of primary pupils using SuccessMaker were similarly impressed by the con-stant on-task behaviour of the ILS pupils. The working atmosphere of peace and quiet can only be described as astounding. This contrasts with the pre and post-ILS sessions where more non-task interactions took place. Pupils who were continuing with ILS for their second year asked for help from the teacher more frequently than was observed with the new pupils. Whether this is a result of increased pupil confidence in the teacher's ability to help or a shift in teacher attitude in that they now felt they had a use-ful role to play in the ILS experience is an open question.

At one school using SuccessMaker a significant number of primary pupils behaved as *Solitary Workers.* The pupils at first appeared to be busy, but when observed more closely were not working purposefully. It is interesting to note that the level of achieve-ment of these pupils did not match the gains reported in other primary schools. The pupils were not working on their task but remained quiet so that the teacher, who was out of sight working in a different area with other pupils, could not hear them. The neg-ative effect of lack of teacher supervision was also evident in the primary schools using Global. Here there was a great deal of off-task behaviour related to helping each other to manage the system, to using keyboard skills or to responding to the screen. Adequate supervision of pupils new to ILS is essential if the children are to engage in their work.

Evidence showed that early years pupils, with the low concentration level associated with this age, require a much longer period of time to respond to the computer than that required by the older groups. Early in the study pupils were observed to be well focused on their task and there were few recorded interactions with the teacher or other pupils. There were some noticeable differences at the second visit to the school, with a high incidence of peer interaction, much of which can be accounted for by the pupils' ten-dency to help each other with hardware issues such as adjusting headphones. The pupils also showed curiosity in each other's progress. These pupils behaved like *Fusspots.* There was some shift towards a more focused approach to the ILS by the end of the study and this may either be due to general maturation or to experience with the ILS. This length of time required for familiarisation may account for the absence of measurable learning gains in these children.

Tables 2 and 3 summarise the pupil types at the beginning and end of the study.

In summary, there were individual preferences in learning styles; one girl, for instance, liked writing essays because she preferred working alone. Pupils who prefer solitary work appear to be suited to ILS work, while pupils who like group interaction appear to be more suited to classroom work. However, given that greater learning gains were made by the SuccessMaker ILS group than by the control children, it might be that group inter-action is detrimental to learning gains in the basic skills of numeracy and reading. We might postulate that ILS provides a useful environment for learning basic skills, while other classroom activities should include more socially oriented activities to cater for the needs of all pupils. The social aspect of school life is of greater importance to the sec-ondary age pupils than it appeared to be for the younger age groups.

Table 2: Summaries of pupil types for SuccessMaker and Global

	Beginning	End
Early Years	Hard Grinders	Fusspots Group Toilers
Primary	Hard Grinders Solitary Workers (unsupervised)	Group Toilers Solitary Workers
Secondary	Hard Grinders Solitary Workers (negative attitude to school generally)	Intermittent Workers/ Easy Riders Solitary Workers

Table3: Global pupil types

	Beginning	End
Primary	Fusspots	Fusspots
Secondary	Hard Grinders	Group Toilers (continuing pupils) Intermittent Workers (New pupils)
	Solitary Workers	Solitary Workers

Teaching style

The teaching style adopted by the SuccessMaker and Global ILS was not investigated in any depth for the evaluation and remains an issue for further research. Here we shall describe some of the factors related to teaching style which were raised by teachers or students throughout the study.

The organisation of the ILS in each school determined whether or not working on ILS meant a change in the learning environment, with some pupils working in ILS designated areas while others worked in areas where other teaching was going on. Even so, the majority of pupils reported that use of ILS led to a change from the more boisterous nature of the classroom to a quiet and calm atmosphere where the individual could work privately with other pupils being unaware of how well or how poorly they were doing. Many pupils liked the peace and quiet but, as discussed earlier, one group of ILS pupils expressed a dislike of this enforced peace and quiet as 'talking to friends is not allowed'.

From the pupils' point of view one of the major benefits of working with ILS was the enjoyment of being able to work at their own pace yet still having the benefit of a teacher equivalent, feeling that they had a teacher all to themselves. As one child put it so succinctly 'it doesn't go off to help someone else'. The benefit of being able to work at one's own pace was particularly valid for faster pupils, some of whom stated that they preferred English work on the computer because 'the teacher takes too long to explain things'. Pupils who preferred a more leisurely pace, however, expressed some frustration at the SuccessMaker system because of the limited time allowed to respond to a question. This was particularly so for questions involving US money, as pupils had to refer to a conversion chart before they were able to complete the task. This conversion was usually long enough for the computer to time-out the pupil on that particular task and pupils wished that there was a pause button they could use.

In Phase 1, many pupils expressed a dislike of the US nature of the SuccessMaker material: both the American accent and the context of some written work, such as the Vietnam War. This strength of feeling was not so apparent with new pupils in Phase 2 or with continuing pupils, some of whom viewed it in a positive light, 'You learn different things on it. American money for example', going further to suggest that it taught them about a different culture, and even prepared them for a future holiday in the US.

The colourful graphics and the games format of some tasks were particularly liked. While they were not unanimous, most pupils new to ILS in both phases of the project felt that SuccessMaker provided variety in the material, changing style or content of presentation just at the time they felt that boredom would set in. Secondary pupils who had been working on ILS over the extended period of 18 months remained positive about ILS generally, but some began to feel the English software was repetitive. A greater choice of subject areas, such as science, was requested, and so too was more algebra and problem-solving. Both new and continuing pupils on the Global software criticised the system for not providing enough variety or enough examples to work through for each topic.

A few pupils were not happy with the organisation of the SuccessMaker sessions, saying that when they had finished they just had to sit there with nothing to do. Some schools recognised this problem and responded by managing the system in such a way as to provide extra games which the pupils could play while the others completed their designated time. Where half the pupils worked on ILS and half on classroom work followed by a changeover half-way through the lesson, some pupils commented that this changeover 'interferes with what you're doing'.

Individual differences between pupils

A key question for the study was to establish whether identifiable groups of pupils were differently affected by their time on the system.

Ability level

Becker (1992) stated that high and low ability students perform well on ILS while average students perform least well. This could be explained, he suggested, by the teachers teaching to the norm and failing to provide individual programmes of work to stretch the high ability or support the low ability students. The benefits of ILS to more able students have been reported to be substantial by Hativa (1989). More able students improved in relation to several factors including, amongst others: motivation to succeed, concentration on task, competitiveness, persistence, responsibility for self-learning and the development of helpful cognitive strategies. The ILS study investigated this issue of ability level.

For Phase 2 new pupils, three groups were identified: those of below average ability, average ability, and above average ability. The level of ability was determined using the Raven's standardised scores.

For early years pupils, the above average pupils faired best and the average pupils performed least well in their performance in both the mathematics and the English tests, but this finding held true for both ILS and control groups; that is the system did not benefit any one ability level more than another.

For primary pupils, in both the SuccessMaker and the Global schools there was no difference in terms of performance gains according to ability and no effect according to the group they belonged to. That is the ILS system did not preferentially benefit one ability group over another other than might be expected from any teaching intervention.

At the secondary age, there were no ability effects with the SuccessMaker schools, and in Global schools while the more able pupils made greatest gains and the below average pupils made least gains, this was true in both the ILS and the control groups. The findings, then, concur with Becker at the early years age only, and generally give support to Hativa's statement that high ability pupils benefit most from ILS when compared with other ability levels.

Gender differences

Given that girls are often seen as less confident than boys in both the use of IT and in mathematics, one might expect an ILS system to benefit boys more than girls. Alternatively, the absence of competition in the ILS environment provided could benefit girls more than boys. Gender differences were investigated by Clariana (1992, 1993) but the results of the two studies were contradictory. In our evaluation, no significant gender differences in performance were recorded for either the SuccessMaker or control groups.

For pupils using Global there was a tendency, though not reaching significance, for girls in the Year 3 ILS group to perform less well than those in the control group and less well than boys in either group in the post-test of numeracy. While for secondary pupils, boys from the ILS group performed less well in the numeracy post-test than any of the other groups. Given the instability of use of the Global system it is difficult to come to any reliable conclusions about any different effects of the system according to gender.

Age

The SuccessMaker mathematics program has proved to be generally effective at secondary level and in the later primary years. Contrary to the finding for older pupils there is no evidence of the ILS treatment proving differentially effective with youngest pupils other than for spelling. Our observations of early years children showed that for a substantial part of the study they behaved like *Fusspots* in that they spent a great deal of time fussing about headphones and other hardware, and showing curiosity in other pupils' progress. It was towards the end of the evaluation that the children started settling down to more focused work on the ILS. The findings from Phase 2 suggest that the very youngest pupils may be at a stage when gains are behavioural rather than cognitive.

Time effects

The evaluation has been conducted over two phases of time, with some pupils spending six months or less working on the system, and others a period of up to 18 months. The identification of the impact of time on an ILS system is complex. Not only can the length of time of each working session vary, but so too can the number of sessions per week and the period of time over which exposure takes place. Slavin (1986, 1987), in presenting a model of effective intervention, includes the importance of learning time. The level of instruction must be appropriate for the learner, who must have the incentive to learn. Academic learning time must be sufficient and the instructional quality should be adequate. How long is sufficient? Researchers have suggested that generally the more time spent on the computer the greater the learning gains (West and Marcotte 1994) but still the question remains as to whether it matters how frequent and regular the time is, or how long each session lasts for, and whether there is a minimum time on system required for learning gains to be measurable.

Watson (1993) suggests in the ImpacT study that some minimum threshold of IT access, experience and use was necessary for the contribution to pupils' learning to be apparent. That also appears to be true in this ILS evaluation. While further investigation is needed in this area, some of our data suggest that a minimum of nine hours of ILS work is required for gains in numeracy to be measurably greater than those for pupils working in their normal classrooms. In addition, the sustainability of motivation is vulnerable over long periods, with one secondary pupil remarking that she liked the SuccessMaker ILS for about 18 months and then she began to get bored.

Time on system has proved to be an important controlling variable of differential learning gains from the system, although there is evidence that the time on system must be quality time, that is the learner must be focused on the task in hand. In the few cases where task orientation is low, there were null, and in one case negative results.

While the regularity of use of ILS varied considerably in our study, there was some observational evidence that in general children work constructively on the ILS for about 15 minutes at a time before requiring a change of activity. Lower ability levels may find even this length of time beyond their attention span. Added to this limited concentration span, a few pupils commented that the time of day they went on to the ILS affected their work. Working in the mornings presented no problems, but Friday afternoons, in particular, led to headaches and suffering from tired eyes.

Conclusion

A number of factors have been discussed in relation to the impact of ILS on learning. The picture is complex in that different ILS systems have different effects. There are clear indications that use of these systems has had many positive effects on pupil attitudes as well as on learning.

Further research is essential if our knowledge is to progress from the findings of this study so that we can optimise the use of ILS for all children.

CHAPTER
6

A study of sustainable learning gains in UK schools

Jean Underwood, Susan Cavendish, Sheila Dowling and Tony Lawson

The context of the evaluation

The NCET national trial of Integrated Learning Technology in UK schools spanned an 18-month period from January 1994 to July 1995. There were two phases to this pilot trial, which was designed to assess whether the use of ILS would prove to be an appropriate and effective approach to learning in a UK context. The key question for the formal evaluation was whether use of an ILS could enhance children's acquisition of basic skills in numeracy and literacy. This summative evaluation of learning gains was conducted by the team at Leicester University.

In this formal evaluation at Phase 1 and 2 we investigated the effectiveness of the SuccessMaker and Global mathematics and English programs. Small scale qualitative evaluations of two other systems were undertaken by colleagues in other institutions; these did not contribute to the main evaluation but they are described in subsequent chapters.

It rapidly became apparent that these two trial software packages had as many differences as similarities. Although ostensibly covering similar curriculum areas and using structured practice and fine grained steps through that content, they differed in the scope and function of the management system. Both systems were able to provide continuous updating of pupils' records, to interpret learner responses to the task in hand and to provide performance feedback to the learner and the teacher. Such data, collected and interpreted by the system, could also be used to provide an individualised pathway, a differentiated programme of work for individual children, through the curriculum content. Management of learning in this way produces a closed system. The curriculum content and the learning sequences are not designed to be changed or added to by either the tutor or the learner.

SuccessMaker is such a closed system although later versions of the package are predicted to be more open. This closed structure does not reduce all learners to taking the same pathway through the material. The management system, within the bounds of preset algorithms, will produce a differentiated teaching sequence for each learner based on his or her previous and current performances and teachers can disable one or more curriculum strands or re-enter children at a new level on the system should they need to.

The Global Learning Systems software is a more open system. Although there is a prescribed content, the routes through that material and the level at which children are to work, are controlled by the teacher and not the management system.

The degree to which control over individual learning sequences lies with the ILS, the teacher or the learner was the key difference between the systems. For Global Learning Systems this control lay with the teacher and in practice to a lesser extent with the student. For SuccessMaker the control lay largely although not exclusively with the system. As we worked with the schools over the two phases of the evaluation it became increasingly apparent that this factor, locus of control, had a pivotal impact on many aspects of the educational experience, including learning outcomes and curriculum integration.

Evaluating the performance outcomes

The formal evaluation of learning outcomes followed a standard summative pre/post testing paradigm. Here the outcomes were numeracy and reading gains, together with the change in motivation and attitude towards learning *per se* in Phase 1 with the addition of measures of spelling and self-esteem in Phase 2. Descriptions of all the test instruments are available in our evaluation report (Underwood *et al* 1996).

Table 1: *Distribution of schools for the two trial phases*

	SuccessMaker		Global	
	Phase 1	Phase 2	Phase 1	Phase 2
Early years primary		1		
Later years primary	1	3		2
Secondary	3	4	3	4

Six of the 12 trial schools in Phase 1 agreed to allow the evaluators to test not only those pupils who were to use the ILS system but also a control group of peers who would continue working in their normal classrooms. This was increased to 14 out of 22 schools in Phase 2 (Table 1). The need for control groups is convincingly argued by Becker in his critique of previous evaluations (Becker 1992) and by Underwood in Chapter 4 of this book. The evaluation team was unable to select control groups. We worked in schools which could provide us with at least two comparable age and ability groups within the school.

The sample population in Phase 2 was selected to correct a number of deficiencies in the sample from Phase 1 and also to overcome the inevitable data loss that occurs when working in real-world situations.

In Phase 1 all children in both the ILS groups and the control groups completed standardised tests of non-verbal ability, mathematical ability and reading ability at the start (pre-test) and at the end (post-test) of the six-month trial period. In addition, weekly aggregated attendance figures were taken over the period of the evaluation for each of the ILS and control classes. Pupil attitude to core areas of study formed a further pre/post measure.

The pre/post test data were supplemented by:

- Observations of both the whole class and targeted individual pupils in their normal classroom activities immediately before and after their ILS session and working on the ILS;
- Pupils' perceptions of their ILS work;
- Subject and class teachers' comments on selected pupils' attendance, effort and achievement over the period of the evaluation;

- Tutors' initial expectations, and their mid-term and end of project perceptions of the ILS in their schools;
- Comparison of models of ILS use within the pilot schools.

As with the data collection, we endeavoured at all times to complete comparable analyses of results for the data from both our ILS interventions. This was not always possible because we were unable to extract data of equivalent detail from the two systems. However, the core analyses were consistent across the ILS interventions and across the two phases of the evaluation.

The natural definition of change is the difference between initial and final scores but such a simple measure is unsatisfactory for a number of reasons (see Youngman 1979). Specifically, it cannot be assumed that two children with different starting abilities and performances will progress at the same rate or indeed follow a simple linear progression of development. We employed an analysis of co-variance to ascertain whether or not the post-trial numeracy and reading scores for the ILS and control pupils were significantly different. An aptitude-treatment interaction such as this measures differential change in relation to the initial abilities and performance levels of the children. That is, the analyses of learning gain conducted both at the end of Phase 1 and 2 took cognisance of the initial starting abilities and performance levels of the children, with pre-trial mathematics, reading and non-verbal ability scores being entered as controlling variables in the analyses.

The outcomes of the Phase 1 evaluation were substantially different for the two ILS under review. We felt at the outset of Phase 2 that we had sufficient data from the SuccessMaker schools to begin to investigate the long-term educational effects of the program. We did not, however, have sufficient quality data to track long-term gains for the Global schools. There was no Phase 1 baseline for the Global ILS from which to compare learning outcomes in Phase 2. As a consequence we conducted separate evaluations of the two ILS and this is reflected in the separate discussions that follow. The key goals of measuring the impact of each system on basic numeracy and literacy remained the same, however, as did the evaluation tools for the two investigations. For this chapter we are confining our comments to the core issues of learning gains in basic numeracy and literacy.

Throughout this chapter we use the terms Phase 2 Old School and Phase 2 New School. A Phase 2 Old School is a school which took part in the Phase 1 evaluation and has continued to work with the evaluators at Phase 2. A Phase 2 New school is a school joining the project at the start of Phase 2.

Performance outcomes for Global Learning Systems

In Phase 1 of the evaluation we conducted trials in three single-sex secondary schools where pupils used the Global mathematics program. Global English was still under development at this time and formed no part in the trial. Performance outcomes from this Phase 1 trial were not encouraging. The performance gains on our basic numeracy test were significantly higher for the control pupils than for children in the ILS treatment groups. There were severe limitations in the sample population, however, and these results were deemed inconclusive. All parties agreed that a new trial of the Global software was required in order to answer the key question of whether or not the software enhanced childrens' learning. The Global schools sample needed to be larger, to include a wider range of ability, to be drawn from a wider range of geographical locations and to include co-educational schools. In addition, the age range for testing was expanded to include primary school children.

To establish this more balanced and representative sample two new primary schools and two new secondary schools were inducted into the formal evaluation programme at Phase 2, and one of the Phase 1 single-sex secondary schools was removed. This school remained an important member of the overall project but played no further part in the formal evaluation. Care was also taken to ensure a better match between the ILS treatment groups and the control groups. This was achieved by negotiation with the schools. However, the schools remained the final arbiters of the sample to be made available to the evaluation team. Further details of the structure of the sample population are available in our evaluation report (Underwood *et al* 1996).

Our Phase 2 data provided no substantive evidence that Global mathematics and English modules were more effective than traditional classroom techniques in promoting children's learning in basic numeracy and literacy. Too many system failures led to sporadic use of the ILS in many cases. Where the material was being used consistently there is no doubt that the mathematics package proved to be more robust and generally more usable. We observed a number of classes working diligently with the mathematics software but the willingness of children to quit the system or a particular module when the work becomes challenging has been a continuing worry.

We are reluctant to comment on the content of the English modules. In some instances the content was made irrelevant by children's inability to ascertain what it was they were to do, their difficulty in carrying out the tasks at a pragmatic rather than cognitive level, and the ease with which children could subvert the task if not closely monitored by staff. Only the spelling, self-esteem and attendance measures are robust. It should come as no surprise that children operating on a system with serious operational failures should feel frustrated and this may well have led to the differential fall in self-esteem recorded by secondary school pupils. In the one school which had a fully working system and for which we have reliable data, from a small sample, the ILS appears not to contribute with differential effectiveness to children's learning.

Individual differences were investigated both for ability levels and pupil gender. The ILS system did not preferentially benefit one ability group over another: the higher ability pupils made the greatest gains in mathematics, and the lower ability pupils made least gains for both the control and the ILS groups. There were, however, differential effects according to gender. At age 9, girls in the ILS group made lower gains than the ILS boys and also made lower gains than both the control boys and girls. At secondary level (ages 11-14), it was the boys in the ILS group who appeared to be adversely affected by the ILS experience.

A comparison of end of trial attendance for ILS and control groups showed that children working on the Global ILS in secondary schools had higher levels of attendance at the end of the trial compared with their control peers. The positive comments from the secondary age pupils working with the ILS make this finding readily understandable. There were no differential effects on attendance for primary pupils.

For the Global trial, Phase 2 was beset with problems. Equipment arrived late into those new schools which we had identified as crucial to the evaluation. This meant that teachers, despite the best endeavours of the system trainers, were unable to gain familiarity with the system before going live with their pupils. Also, hardware and software incompatibilities further reduced children's effective time with the system. This was particularly true for Global English. From the SuccessMaker evaluation, time on-system proved to be an important contributing factor in performance outcomes, but we could not recover appropriate data from the management system to allow us to complete comparable analyses for pupils involved with Global software.

Our results conflict with the views of the teachers in the Global schools and are also not supported by the differential learning gains for mathematics recorded by our fellow researchers Carol Fitz-Gibbon and Neil Defty (Chapter 8). Can we explain this disparity? It is easy to say, as many have, that we were measuring the wrong thing: that the content of our tests and the learning experiences provided by Global are ill-matched. Our counter argument has always been that we are not looking for learning gains for specific curriculum content, although this is a worthwhile question; rather we are asking whether the ILS impacts on basic numeracy and literacy. Professor Fitz-Gibbon was asked to investigate a very different question, that is, does the use of Global mathematics have beneficial measurable effects when used as a revision tool. She and her team do report a significant positive impact on pupils' performance at GCSE level from the use of this package.

There are a number of important differences between our evaluation and that of Carol Fitz-Gibbon and the Newcastle team. The first is in the mode of use of the system for revision rather than as a tutoring tool. A second is that the children involved in using the system elected to do so. The third is that in looking at expected versus actual GCSE performances the focus has widened from basic numeracy. It is for a Phase 3 evaluation to investigate the breadth of learning provided by any of the systems under discussion, but here are our reflections on the first two differences between our two studies.

Alongside our measures of children's learning we conducted extensive observational studies of children using the system. In these we observed a number of children working diligently with the system but there were as many occasions when children worked to subvert the system. This took the form of failing to log-on as a work avoidance strategy, developing their own goals such as using microphones to act out fantasy roles rather than completing set exercises, and flipping between modules if and when encountering a challenging question. Quite often this resulted in pupils logging on to higher level modules before they had completed the lower level ones, leading them into further difficulties as they had not acquired the requisite skills from earlier work.

The pupils in the Newcastle evaluation were a small self-selected group, working to a clear personal purpose shared with their parents. In addition, the profile of these children showed that they had a preference for working alone and were more likely to express dissatisfaction with classroom experiences than their peers because they perceived such experiences as holding them back. We would suggest that such learners were unlikely to be involved in the less acceptable behaviour we had witnessed elsewhere. They were their own control mechanism managing the learning experience to full benefit.

Performance outcomes for SuccessMaker

In Phase 1 of the evaluation we conducted trials in four schools, of which one covered the later primary age range and three were at secondary level. Each school agreed to trial the SuccessMaker programs of work for mathematics and English and to provide the necessary control groups for our investigation. The results from the Phase 1 evaluation were encouraging. Children working on the SuccessMaker mathematics program performed significantly better than children working in the control groups. The differential gains made by the treatment group were equally strong at later primary and early secondary level. The effect size was substantial (+0.4). Taking the control group's progress as a baseline for six months' gain, the ILS mathematics group made the equivalent of up to 20 months' gain in that six months period. This finding concurs with CCC's own studies and with Becker's evaluation of other competitor systems (Becker 1992).

Are ILS's of greater benefit to low attainers?

A key question for this study was to establish whether identifiable groups of pupils were differentially affected by their time on the ILS. At the start of the pilot project both the teachers and the administrators involved in the project had expressed a view that the lower ability pupils would gain most from using the system. The view that tutoring packages are of greatest value to low-ability pupils is a widely and long-held one, as has been clearly articulated by Amarel (1984) for example, but it did not prove to be true in this case. The pupils who made most gains in mathematics were those who had a higher starting point – a case of to those that have shall be given (Underwood *et al* 1995). This was true for both ILS and control pupils. The ILS software did not benefit one ability group over another any more than one would find in normal classroom teaching. In a wide range of discussions with schools, administrators and other researchers this has been the result that proved least acceptable. If we look directly at the SuccessMaker reporting system there is evidence that the least and the most able pupils are differentially benefited by the system but this reporting system has a crude measure of the pupils entry level performance and does not take any account of more general ability. When the system places the children at a low entry level it is not possible to tell whether this is because they are of low ability or underachieving.

The limited learning gains made by the lowest achievers concur with the general observations of both teachers and evaluators. Although many teachers had an initial expectation that the least able would benefit most from working with the ILS, observation of their pupils using the system showed that this was unlikely to be so. There are a number of possible reasons for this. Certainly these children found it very difficult to maintain their span of attention and a number of schools argued for a shorter contact time with the system. Anecdotal data also suggested that the lower ability children were prone to guessing when faced with multiple-choice questions, particularly in English, as in the case of nine-year-old Jamie:

SCENARIO 1: JAMIE
Male – Year 5-Special Needs
SuccessMaker Reading Readiness

Jamie achieved a score of 6 out of 20 on his Reading Readiness work for the day. All of his correct answers were achieved on questions which forced him to interact with the system. For example, Jamie was successful with a problem requiring him:

to complete a sentence using the information in the preceding sentence:

Joan is travelling with her mother by bus to Derby.
Joan travelled on the bus with her _____ .

Jamie worked hard to solve such problems, selecting a word from the first sentence, typing it in and then rereading the second sentence to see if it had meaning for him. He changed his answer as many as four times before confirming that he was happy with it.

Faced with multiple-choice questions Jamie appeared to give little time or thought to the problem, quickly clicking on an answer and often making the same erroneous choice if wrong the first time.

In our interviews with children a number expressed a dislike of multiple-choice questions because they were 'cheating' or 'not proper work'. Other pupils, however, liked this type of question because it reduced the amount of writing!

The positive outcomes at Phase 1 for numeracy were not matched for reading. We identified no discernible differences between the ILS and control groups. This was not surprising. Becker's review of the evidence from US schools suggests that a small effect might be found over a full year and these children had worked for less than two terms on the system. The lack of any finding over a six-month period is, therefore, not surprising.

Questions for Phase 2

A number of core issues were identified from Phase 1 which influenced the Phase 2 evaluation. The positive gains in numeracy had been overwhelming. Were the findings replicable? If the results were confirmed in Phase 2 new, critical questions would need answering. In particular we needed to know whether the Phase 1 gains were sustainable over time both for pupils continuing to use the system and those who were no longer using the system. Was this simply a quick fix which would disappear once the children no longer had access to the system, or a lasting benefit? If children continued using the system would the learning curve reach a plateau or even begin a downward trajectory?

Our finding for basic literacy had established that overall children did neither better nor worse when using the system as opposed to working in a traditional classroom setting. Becker's review indicated that this result might be simply a matter of length of exposure to the system. Our own analyses showed that there was greater variation in learning outcomes across schools for reading than there had been for numeracy. There were therefore, questions to be asked about individual pupil responses to the Success-Maker English program. Our observations and interviews had shown pockets of disaffection among pupils working within specific elements of the English program. Further, we noted that there was greater variance in the ways teachers used and thought about this software. We needed to establish whether differential reading gains would occur with an extended period on the system and also to investigate further the tutor role as a manager and learning support agent in an ILS environment.

Finally, as for the Global schools, we wished to fill gaps in the population sample available to us in Phase 1. This meant increasing the number of primary pupils and schools involved in the evaluation. There was also a need to assess children working in a culture of academic achievement, children from more affluent backgrounds and children at the higher end of the ability range. As a consequence, one early years primary, two later years primary and one secondary school were inducted into the evaluation programme at Phase 2.

Results from Phase 2

The results of the Phase 2 study for SuccessMaker were complicated by the models of usage and by varying project start dates. The schools from Phase 1, having gained confidence with the system, embarked on a process of tailoring the ILS experience to fit their own specific requirements. Thus for some pupils the ILS experience lasted as little as ten minutes once a week, while other pupils worked for a full half-hour each and every day, split between mathematics and English. In addition some children were continuing users from Phase 1 and others were new to the system. By the end of Phase 2 there was a range of experience from those children who had worked with the system for 18 months, five times a week to those with ten minutes experience, once a week for approximately six months.

The new schools presented a more coherent sample with the standard five sessions per week regime. However, for the very youngest pupils the daily time on system was modified during the trial. There was also a problem with the starting of the project. The schools which were to start work in January did not receive the necessary hardware and software until February. Although the technical problems were less extensive than for Global, there were some delays which meant that a six-month trial to match the Phase 1 conditions was effectively reduced to four months.

The effects of these variations in system use meant that we could not conduct one overall analysis. Instead the data had to be inspected school-by-school. This necessarily reduced the sample numbers for any one analysis. In effect most analyses are conducted on a class (approximately 30 pupils) or half-class (approximately 15 pupils) comparison.

The details of all analyses are to found in the full evaluation report. Here we can only give the main thrust of our findings. If we once again look at the numeracy gains we found that where conditions of time and overall usage matched those of Phase 1 the result was replicated both in size and direction. That is the ILS treatment group made significant differential gains compared with their control peers, recording an equivalent substantial effect size of +0.4. However, only one school provided us with such a situation.

The results from the new schools, which had been included in the evaluation specifically to test the reliability of the Phase 1 result, were more mixed. The children had worked for only four months with the system and we were concerned that a number of them would not have sufficient time on system to produce measurable changes in performance. To allow for the late start of the project, therefore, pupils with minimal exposure to the system were removed from the analysis. This was possible because the system monitors cumulative time on system for each individual child. To maintain the integrity of the data this was done by removing pupils who fell in the lowest quartile of time on system as measured by the system records.

With the low users of the system removed there was no advantage in numeracy of the ILS treatment over the control treatment for early or later years pupils but the secondary ILS group significantly outperformed their peers in the control group as shown in the mean post-trial adjusted mathematics score. The effect size was + 0.1. Becker has pointed out that this should be rated as a weak and inconsequential effect if recorded over a full year but should be viewed as significant when recorded over this very short timescale of four months.

This beneficial effect of the ILS treatment in the secondary group is interesting for two reasons. It is a clear indication that such systems can aid children's learning in schools that are well endowed and are sited in a community in which educational success is valued. The second point of interest is that one of the ILS groups in this school had a negative attitude to school, despite the overall ethos of the school. This lack of motivation – the children expressed little interest in working with the ILS – does not appear to have differentially impacted on their learning.

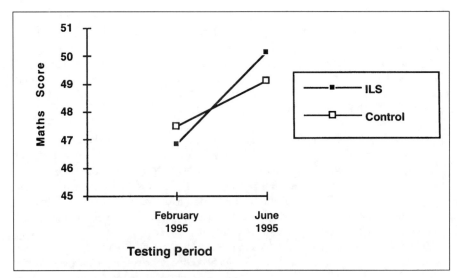

Figure 1:   *Mathematics performance by group*
Phase 2 New Secondary School

Our early years primary was also identified as a school with a culture of achievement but the ILS treatment proved to be neither more nor less effective than classroom practice in this school. The children tested here were very young (aged 6–8), and here and in other schools where we tested the youngest pupils we were unable to identify differential learning gains. Several explanations may account for this. It may be that such young children take a longer period of time for gains to become measurably different from those of children doing normal classwork. Or, as shown by the observations, the children may have spent so much time sharing their experiences with their ILS peers, and in

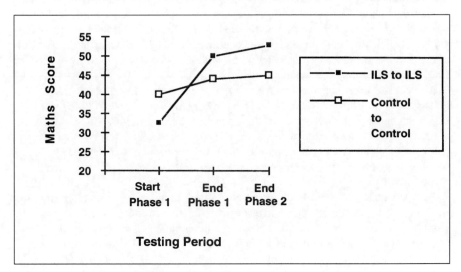

Figure 2:   *Mathematics performance by group over Phases 1 and 2*
Phase 2 Old Secondary School

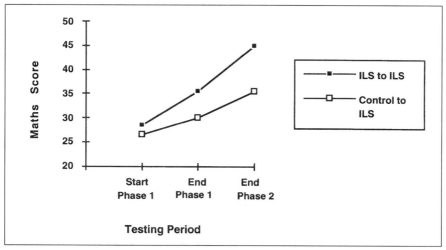

Figure 3: *Mathematics performance by group over Phases 1 and 2*
Phase 2 Old Primary School

attention to the novelty of the technology, that concentration on task was insufficient for the potential benefits of the system to have effect. Further investigation over a longer time span is required to gain a fuller understanding of the effect of ILS on this age group.

Analysis of the performances of those children in the schools continuing from Phase 1 showed that the accelerated gains in numeracy made by the ILS groups as compared with the control groups apparent in Phase 1, were largely sustained over time. That is, pupils who continued to work with ILS for a second year continued to outperform the control pupils in numeracy. Further inspection of the numeracy scores for the ILS and control groups in one secondary school show that much of the advantage exhibited by the ILS group over the control group was gained during the Phase 1 period. Although

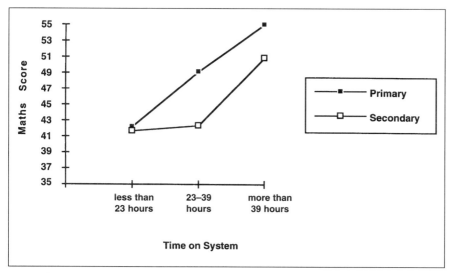

Figure 4: *Primary and Secondary schools by time on system*

the ILS group is still showing differential gains in Phase 2 the pace of change has slowed. It is difficult to comment on the rate of gain, however, for two reasons. The first is the change from a six-month, five sessions a week exposure to the system to a nine-month (full academic year), three sessions a week regime in this school. It is not possible to tease out the differential impact of period of time versus frequency of use in this case. Secondly as the ILS pupils had outperformed their peers in the control group at the end of Phase 1, the ILS and control groups were no longer matched. The ILS groups' mathematics entry level for Phase 2 was significantly higher than that of the control group, a reversal of the situation in Phase 1. The ILS children are more likely to be performing at an optimal level as measured by scores on the non-verbal test baseline in comparison with their control peers, that is we may be recording a ceiling effect of the mathematics learning.

There is an issue here of time on system which needs to be explored further. The evidence suggests that there is a minimum time on system necessary before gains can become apparent in numeracy and that increasing exposure to the system has beneficial effects on learning, as is clearly shown in Figure 4.

Regularity and period of time over which the ILS is used may also prove to be important variables although there was insufficient data in our study to investigate fully the impact of models of use.

Although samples were small we monitored the performances of two groups of children, one at primary and the other at secondary level, who were no longer using the ILS system to compare them with their control peers (Figure 5). There was no significant difference in the relative performances in numeracy of the primary ILS group, which now no longer had access to the system, and the control group during the Phase 2 trial period. This is a positive benefit of the system in that the advantage the ILS group had gained by the end of Phase 1 was still apparent at the end of Phase 2. The ILS group continued to progress at the same rate of change as their control peers but, for this small sample, the gains made in Phase 1 were maintained.

The secondary ILS group, which now no longer had access to the system, outperformed their peer control group in numeracy over the period of the Phase 2 trial, with a substantial effect size of +0.35. The old ILS group had, therefore, not only maintained their advantage over the control pupils after coming off the system but were also still

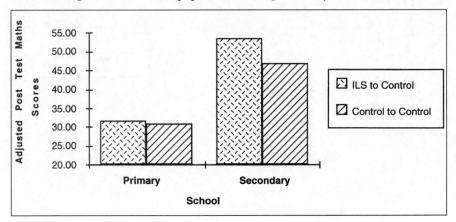

Figure 5:   *A comparison of mathematics scores one year after the ILS groups stopped using the system*

making differential gains compared with their peers. This finding suggests that the accelerated learning that had taken place by the end of Phase 1 was having a beneficial effect on learning in Phase 2.

The two key questions concerning the reliability of the Phase 1 findings and the sustainability of learning gains, at least in the medium term, have both provided positive outcomes for the mathematics intervention. We now need to ask to what extent this was also true for the English program. In Phase 1 we recorded no differential gains but there were indications that this finding was school specific. The Phase 2 results do little to clarify the picture. Indeed it might be said that they raise more questions than answers. In two of the test sites children working on the SuccessMaker English program performed significantly better in reading than children working in the control groups. These findings were not consistent across the schools and appear to be related to increased teacher intervention in the use of the system. There was one instance where differential gains favoured classroom teaching. This result was puzzling in that this school has much in common with the primary school recording benefits of the ILS treatment for reading. Factors which might explain the differences between the outcomes in these two primary schools include the reduced period in which the children worked with the system, but perhaps of greater significance are the model of use and the pupils' attitudes to the system. In the school recording negative gains for the ILS treatment group the children worked with minimal supervision. Also a greater proportion of children expressed reservations about using the system than we found in other schools. Our observations of the children in this school when working on the system showed a very low level of engagement and much quiet time wasting.

In summary, for SuccessMaker, while many of the analyses are based on small group sizes and although the results are not universally confirmatory, the weight of the evidence shows that the mathematics program is effective in improving the level of basic numeracy. This adds weight to the findings of Phase 1. There is no evidence, however, of the ILS treatment proving differentially effective with younger pupils other than for spelling. In Phase 1 we debated why the least able pupils were not gaining significantly from the system, and we came to the conclusion that they were in the process of developing good work habits, for example increased attention spans, that could lead to future gains. We concluded that for these most vulnerable children the computer room model was probably not beneficial and a distributed resource model would be more in keeping with their normal work patterns. The findings from Phase 2 would suggest that the very youngest pupils may also benefit from a less formal regime and that they too are at a stage when gains are behavioural rather than cognitive.

Time on system has proved to be an important controlling variable of differential learning gains from the system, although there is evidence that this must be quality time, with the learner focused on the task in hand. In the few cases where task orientation was low there were null results and in one case negative gains.

The results of the SuccessMaker English program have proved to be less consistent. We have recorded some benefits of the language program at both primary and secondary level in Phase 2 but no consistent pattern has developed. We had argued in Phase 1 that it was too early to expect differential performance gains in reading and this argument was supported by the research literature (Becker 1992). Earlier findings predicted smaller effects on reading would occur after a 12 month trial of the system. We predicted, therefore, that any reading gains would occur in the Phase 2 old schools, but this proved incorrect and the positive findings occur with new pupils to the system. Equally the one negative finding we have recorded for the language program is in a new primary school.

Summary conclusions

- The results for Global mathematics and English programs remain problematic. Although the data sample was deemed to be valid, problems in the use of the system render the results less than satisfactory. No differential learning gains were recorded for either numeracy or for reading from the ILS pupils.

- This evaluation confirmed the robustness of the Phase 1 findings for the Success-Maker mathematics program. Where conditions closely matched those of Phase 1, ILS groups outperformed their control peers.

- Differential performances noted in Phase 1 are still apparent in Phase 2 indicating sustainability of learning. Indeed there is some evidence that the differential benefits of SuccessMaker mathematics impacted on post-trial learning.

- Where the conditions did not closely match those of Phase 1 there was some variability in the findings for SuccessMaker mathematics. Part of this variability can be attributed to the reduction from Phase 1 in the frequency and length of time pupils worked on the system. Overall, however, the preponderance of significant effects and the weight of the evidence confirms that there were beneficial effects on learning.

- Within the limits of the test data we can confirm that the learning gains in numeracy for children using SuccessMaker apparent in Phase 1 were sustainable over time both for pupils continuing to use the system and those who are no longer using the system.

- The data do not present a consistent picture on the maintenance of the rate of learning for SuccessMaker mathematics although the ILS pupils continued to be advantaged.

- There was conflicting evidence of the value of the SuccessMaker English program. In the main the Phase 1 results were confirmed and no difference was recorded between the ILS Groups and their control peers. In several schools, however, there were differential reading gains by the ILS pupils compared with the control groups and in one primary school the control group outperformed the ILS group. There is some evidence that the effectiveness of the English language system is dependent on effective teacher intervention.

CHAPTER
7

Beyond numeracy

John Barrett and Jean Underwood

The formal evaluation of ILS by Leicester University focused on basic numeracy and literacy but questions concerning a wider mathematics curriculum were raised. This chapter starts by charting one school's progress in integrating the ILS experience into the wider curriculum. Specifically it presents the initial impact of making data from the ILS report system available in a comprehensible and usable form to teachers. The chapter goes on to report the outcomes of two case studies of children's mathematical development on and off the system. These small scale investigations developed from one tutor's growing appreciation of the value of the data held by the system and his informal observations of children working in both test and standard classroom situations. The school in question used the SuccessMaker software and was a Phase 1 school that continued into Phase 2.

The school

The school, located in a small town in West Cumbria, is on the edge of a large housing estate and is housed in a 1960s building. The catchment area is mixed, drawing pupils from both public and private housing. A high percentage of the parents are unemployed and a large number of the pupils are entitled to free dinners. The parent body is very supportive of all developments within the school. The school has 196 pupils organised within seven classes which are vertically grouped with each class teacher being responsible for two age groups. These teachers operate within two teams:

Year 3/4 team which has four parallel classes aged 7-9;
Year 5/6 team which has three parallel classes aged 9-11.

The school also has a special needs team which operates out of the development unit. The unit is open every morning and withdraws children who have been assessed and had their educational needs for special support statemented.

The school is a technologically rich environment which few other UK primary schools can match. The information technology resource base has expanded from four BBC machines to more than 120 in the last six years, the majority of which are high grade PC 486 and PC 386 portables. A variety of applications are used by both staff and children to support the curriculum. Care has been taken to ensure that staff and pupils' IT capabilities have developed in parallel to this increase in hardware and software provision.

The start of the project

In the autumn of 1994 the school became one of the 12 pilot schools in the Phase 1 evaluation. The school entered the project with an open mind as to the benefits of ILS for children's learning. The consensus of feeling was that such a system would add further breadth to the school's already extensive use of IT. In addition staff were hopeful that it would prove a useful adjunct to the development of mathematics and English language skills.

A 13 station network composed of ICL 486 multimedia computer systems was developed. Eight of the systems were provided as part of the project and the school decided to buy five additional machines to facilitate the proposed organisational structure that they had elected to put in place. The network was sited in a resource area away from the classrooms but with easy access for all the classes. The initial organisation of the system has remained basically the same throughout the project with only minor changes made to accommodate more children.

The network is run by a resource manager who operates in the resource area. The children are brought down to the resource area by the manager and she also provides front-line support during their time on the system. This support is generally at the operational level although she can and does step into the curriculum area on occasions, if she feels able to. She also monitors the children's behaviour. A key role is to liaise with and keep teaching staff informed about both behaviour and curriculum issues that have arisen when their children are using the system. At the end of the session the children are returned to their classroom and the resource manager then collects the next group of children.

The school has employed the same basic organisation in both Phase 1 and 2 of the project. The children work on ILS for half an hour each day. Twelve minutes of their time is spent on mathematics and 15 minutes on the English program. Three minutes are available for movement in and out of the resource area. The five additional machines were essential to the overall organisation of the ILS experience although the extra resource still did not allow for a full half-class to use the machines at any one time.

During the first phase of the project there was little real evidence that the learning gains recorded by the system were being transferred into the classroom, although occasionally children would identify things they had already done on ILS, or use terminology that they had acquired from the ILS. However, staff did note the high concentration and positive motivation that the system was generating amongst the pupils whilst they were working on it. The evidence of the Phase 1 formal evaluation proved so positive for mathematics that the school felt it needed to take as much advantage of the system as possible. In particular the school wanted to be able to send half of any one class to the ILS room at a time. Thirteen machines did not allow this to happen. An expansion of the network became imperative to allow all classes to have complete year groups on the ILS and so allow the teacher to concentrate on an individual year group within the classroom. The problems that arose in Phase 1 if a machine malfunctioned were also resolved by this additional resource base. The year group use of the ILS allowed the teaching staff to work with the remaining half of the class. This has proved invaluable in mixed age group classes as it has allowed teachers not only to be involved in small group teaching but also to focus on specific National Curriculum targets appropriate to that age group. One teacher has commented that it has been very beneficial, enabling her to organise experiences appropriate to her two age groups in curriculum areas such as science and history.

Getting to grips with the report system

The management system (described in detail on page 69) is capable of automatically producing 60 or so reports on an individual child or on a group of children. This wealth of data was an enticing prospect for tutors in the school. As they embarked on the project they set about using the report system as had been recommended in the initial training sessions conducted by the staff of the Computer Curriculum Corporation (CCC), the publishers of SuccessMaker. In these sessions trainees were encouraged to track the progress of individuals by means of the reports. The information recovered would then allow teachers to provide children with support and intervention when they needed it to consolidate their work and overcome any difficulties. To this end staff spent a large amount of time, thought and energy developing strategies to use the available reports.

Initially the school focused on three out of more than sixty reports which were felt to be of central importance. Even with this reduction in output the act of simply interpreting the reports proved extremely difficult. Staff felt overwhelmed by the task of sorting through the mass of paper produced for a class of 30 pupils. It soon became clear that it was an almost impossible task for a class teacher to make effective use of the information contained within the reports to the advantage of individual children. Although good quality information was produced, retrieving it in a meaningful form was incredibly time consuming. Teachers would frequently identify a problem and prepare material to support a child in difficulty, only to find that the computer had already reviewed the child's work and overcome the problem. Teachers were unable to predict those problems the system could rectify and those needing vital teacher intervention if the child was to continue to progress through the scheme. This was discouraging for all concerned.

The school's targeting of a small number of reports from the system was a sensible strategy but this alone was not sufficient. A simpler format of report that would provide an initial generalised summary of the child's progress was required as a starting point for all teachers. From information gained in staff discussions a simplified single page report using a spreadsheet format was developed. The report was based on what teachers considered the most important basic general information provided by SuccessMaker reports. This information consisted of:

- number of sessions,
- sessions completed that month,
- Initial Placement Motion Level (IPML, the individual start point for each child based on initial assessment by the system.),
- previous month's average performance,
- present month's average performance,
- monthly gain,
- total gain since IPML.

This newly designed report was updated monthly by the resource manager having first collected the information from the computer management system. The teachers used this report as the first stage in identifying individuals or groups with problems. They could then use the management reports to gain a more detailed understanding of any one child's difficulty. All teachers felt able to use this basic data.

At the end of Phase 2 some teachers were still expressing caution and concern over rudimentary tasks such as accessing performance reports themselves. They were able to identify what information they needed but had to ask the resource manager to provide them with a printout. This was the preferred mode of operation for Teacher A who used not only the monthly reports provided by the resource manager but also had additional reports run off for 'two or three children each month so I can do an in-depth analysis on their progress'. Other teachers had developed a high level of confidence as exemplified by Teacher B's comments: 'Yes, I feel confident with the system. I use the system reports that the co-ordinator provides for me but I also like to pull the course reports off the system for myself'.

The easily accessible data provided by the spreadsheet encouraged some teachers to explore the reporting system. The level of detail was now seen as valuable rather than overwhelming by these staff. Teacher C acknowledged that the level of detail reported by the system was far greater than he himself could achieve. For example, he knew 'Lydia has word skills problems but I was identifying the wrong skill – the ILS sorted that for me and I could direct my efforts to solving the child's problem'. He acknowledged that the diagnostic support from the system had allowed him to operate at a new level of competence. Observers noted that the insights he was achieving from using the system were now showing benefits in other areas of his teaching.

One of the main difficulties for the staff was visualising the type and level of material being presented to each child working on the system. Without this knowledge it proved very difficult to intervene successfully and to any significant degree in the child's learning. To overcome this difficulty it became essential that the teachers were able to observe the children working on the system regularly. Once a week the school developed formal opportunities for teachers to plan or to observe a child or group of children using the system. Initially the observation time was largely seen as a mechanism to allow teachers to familiarise themselves with the type of work and material the pupils were encountering. As this process continued the teachers began to focus on individuals and small groups of similar ability children enabling them to build up a more detailed knowledge of material being presented at any given level. The initial unfocused observation time was extremely important and a necessary stage for all the teachers. From these observations teachers gained confidence in their knowledge of the system and began to understand how and when teacher intervention might prove beneficial. In the spring term an observation sheet was developed to support teachers and further non-contact time was provided for the teachers to give them the opportunity to use a combination of assessment materials available to them.

Over the two phases of the project the school developed and expanded its in-service training to meet the growing needs of the staff. Detailed report booklets and information documents were produced on the use of each course. Not only did the booklets provide information that the staff were able to use but they acted as starting points for in depth discussions that helped to guide them through the coming year. Key to this work was the development of the staffs' ability and ease in using the ILS management system, particularly to collect information on individual pupils.

Numeracy and other skills

The Assessment of Performance Unit's (APU) 1982 and 1987 surveys recorded a decline in the computational skills of 11-year-olds (APU 1989). This was most apparent when computational skills were not set in context. It was suggested that this decline might reflect the impact of the Cockcroft Report (1982) which recommended less stress on computation, and hence led to a change in curriculum emphasis in the classroom. It was particularly noticeable, therefore, at the beginning of Phase 2, that some Year 4 children were dealing extremely efficiently with class work on addition and subtraction at a level and speed the author had not expected. This observation was repeated when invigilating the testing of ILS and control pupils for Leicester University. The ILS pupils appeared to be working through the computation tests with greater speed and efficiency than the control pupils. The latter appeared to be working slowly and only seemed willing to tackle questions that were familiar to them. The ILS pupils not only operated at speed but also appeared to be attempting a much wider selection of questions as is clearly shown in Table 1. These were informal observations but they raised questions which needed to be pursued.

Table 1: *Average number of questions completed for sections 5-7 of the standardised mathematics post-test*

Number of Questions Section 5	Section 6	Section 7	
Possible	28	28	36
Attempted by ILS pupils	25.2	23.3	30.5
Attempted by control pupils	19.1	16.2	14.5

To test those informal observations the author conducted a series of small scale tests to compare speed and accuracy in basic computation skills between the Year 4 ILS and control groups. At the time of testing ILS users had been working on the system for longer than a year. Both groups of children were of mixed ability but of the same age. Although formal matching of the children was not possible, the groups contained equal numbers of above average, normal and below average mathematical ability pupils based on teacher judgement. There were 14 children in each group. The children were given three teacher-generated tests as follows:

Tests two and three were designed to investigate both the child's ability to compute simple numbers and to follow the procedures involved in the subtraction and addition of larger numbers. The children were timed as they worked on the test. Individual completion times were recorded to the nearest half-minute. The results from each test are recorded below.

Test one
An addition test using number bonds up to 30 of increasing difficulty

Example: 3 + 12 =

Test two
A hundred, tens and units addition test with initially only simple addition, however, as the test progressed the children had to use procedural skills to carry numbers greater than ten.

Example: 356
                  + 243

Test three
A hundred, tens and units subtraction test starting with simple subtraction of numbers which became progressively more difficult, involving the decomposition of a single column followed by the decomposition of two columns.

Example: 478
                  – 234

Test one: **Number bonds to 30**
In the first test the children answered 57 questions gradually increasing in difficulty as they progressed. The results of this first test were striking: the graph shows that 11 of the ILS users completed the test within five and a half minutes whereas only three of the control group completed the test in the same period of time.

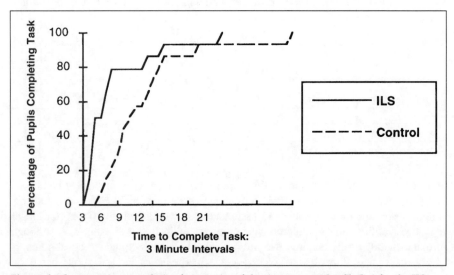

Figure 1: Comparative cumulative frequencies of the time to complete Task 1 for the ILS and control pupils (Group N = 14)

Only three of the ILS users took longer than five and a half minutes. Of these three children, two are of below average ability and have difficulty with mathematics. The third child has a number of behaviour problems that make his academic progress extremely

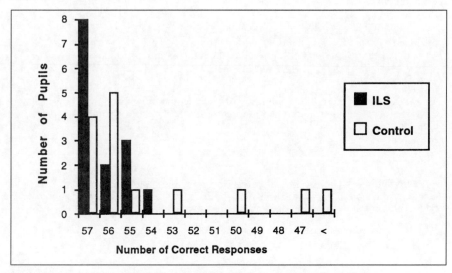

Figure 2: Comparison of success rates for the ILS and control pupils on Task 1

variable, and his work fluctuated from day-to-day in terms of quality, speed and presentation. Although the three pupils worked slowly compared with the rest of their group they were extremely precise. All three pupils answered all the questions correctly (Figure 2).

Within the control group those children taking the longest time to complete the activity also registered the most errors for their group. Two of these children would be classed as below average ability. Unlike the lower ability children within the ILS group, reducing the speed at which they worked did not have a great impact on their response – they each made more than ten mistakes. Five able pupils from the control group also worked relatively slowly, completing the test in longer than seven minutes. One child observed closely began the test extremely well but as the level of questions became more difficult the speed of answering fell and his error rate increased.

Test 2: **HTU addition**
The children had to complete 20 computations gradually increasing in difficulty. In many respects the results were very similar to the first test. Eleven of the ILS users finished within five minutes while only three of the control group finished in the same time:

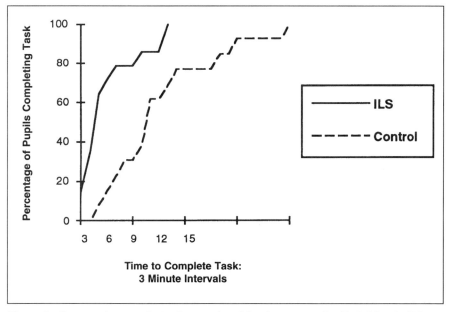

Figure 3: Comparative cumulative frequencies of the time to complete Task 2 for the ILS and control pupils (Group N=14)

Those ILS children who had been slowest in Test 1 again took the longest time on this test. Again, although two of these children were slow in completing the test they worked precisely and made very few mistakes. The third child worked correctly until he reached the level where he was required to carry numbers; he then began to make procedural mistakes resulting in incorrect answers.

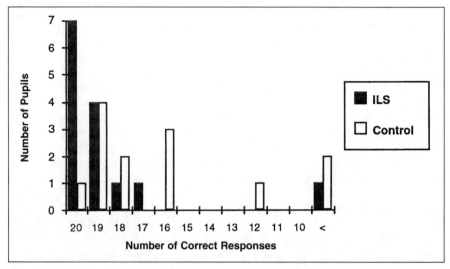

Figure 4: Comparison of success rates for the ILS and control pupils on Task 2

The control group did not follow the same pattern as in the first test. The more able children worked at a much faster pace than in the first test although they still did not match the speed of the more able ILS users. The initial part of this test is conceptually simple and the improved performance of the more able children is not surprising. The three children taking the greatest time were those considered the least able by their teacher. These children also made more errors than other members of the group.

Test three: **HTU subtraction**
This graph shows the comparison of time taken to complete a HTU subtraction test of 20 computations for the two groups. The test increased in difficulty as it progressed.

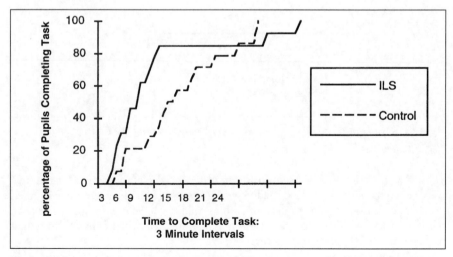

Figure 5: Comparative cumulative frequencies of the time to complete Task 3 for the ILS and control pupils (Group N=14)

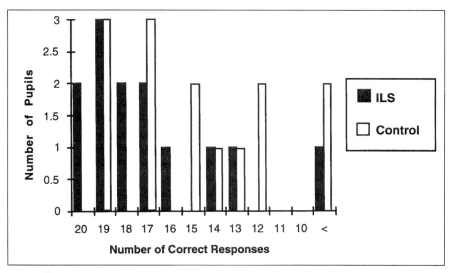

Figure 6: *Comparison of success rates for the ILS and control pupils on Task 3*

Initially the sums were straight take-aways, they then developed into tens decomposition, hundreds decomposition, and mixed decomposition.

There was less coherence in the pattern of completion times for children from the two groups. In general terms the children appear to have found the subtraction work more difficult and hence time consuming. Eight of the ILS group finished within seven and a half minutes but only three of the control group finished in this time.

Fewer children were able to complete this test without error and the number of errors per child also increased (Figure 6). In the first two tests only one child from the ILS group had more than three incorrect answers; in this test the number had increased to four children. Within the control group the increase was from six children to eight. Although the results are not as decisive as Tests 1 and 2, the control group did appear to be under performing compared with their peers.

These tests were conducted on a small scale and without the rigorous controls of the formal evaluation but the differing performances of the two groups of children do raise questions which need to be answered. It can be argued that the ILS children, through variable skills practice on the system, have developed an automaticity of skill that has not only resulted in increased speed of performance but may also have released cognitive processing capacity that those children can bring to bear on the problem to hand. The importance of procedural skills practice is well established (see Underwood and Everatt 1995) so we should not be surprised by the findings here. However, they do require full-scale replication.

Able pupils

It has always been the school's policy to provide for the individual needs of all its pupils and provide opportunities to develop their full potential. During the spring term of 1995 it became apparent that some children working on the ILS had developed a high level of competence in numeracy skills. The evidence for this came both from teacher assessment and from the ILS reports. On examination of the mathematics ILS results a number of children were shown to be working at a much higher level than their peers. For example, a small group of 8 year old pupils were working above the average level of the 10 year old pupils. These high performing children, of which we identified four 10 year olds, three 9 year olds and seven 8 year olds, were selected to form a cross-age-range enrichment group.

The staff wanted to ensure that these children had opportunities to use these skills in practical and investigative situations at an appropriate level but felt that it would prove difficult and time consuming to deliver this type of stimulating situation for an individual child at the required level within the average classroom. To provide for these children we put in place a weekly Maths Investigation Group. As well as enhancing their mathematical skills through a variety of investigations, we hoped that the group would provide the vehicle for mathematical discussions of a high level and, through participating in these discussions, help them see alternative ways of looking at solutions that might not occur in the class where the majority of children would be working at a lower level. The work was based around the National Curriculum Attainment Target 1 for mathematics. This target - Using and Applying Mathematics - focuses on the child's progress in making and monitoring decisions to solve problems, developing mathematical language and communication skills, and on developing mathematical reasoning. There were a number of areas that we hoped to develop through this work:

- Numerical/pattern investigations where the child is looking to establish a pattern within the context of the work;
- Practical investigations that would focus on real life situations;
- Discussions to help individuals with problems in some area of ILS;
- A forum for discussion of mathematical investigations allowing the children to verbalise their work and improve their ability to use mathematical terminology in the context of real life situations.

Some activities, such as work on averages, were a direct response to the children's current experience on the ILS. They were provided with an opportunity to apply their system developed knowledge of averages to new contexts. The work was skills based and all the children coped well in the new situation, working in sub-sets of the enrichment group.

In a later session the children were asked to design a new car park for the school. It was to hold 20 cars and had to take up as little space as possible. This task required a problem oriented approach with the application of ILS taught skills and more general problem–solving skills being used in combination. The children needed to work out the information they would require, collect and apply it, and then revise their idea in the light of group discussion. A number of the children were unable to work out how to organise themselves and found it difficult to apply their mathematical skills to the problem.

There was, however, a small group of children who appeared to relish the challenge of the problem. The APU reports that 'Girls appear to be better at identifying tasks, investigations and appraising ideas, whilst boys seem better at generating and developing ideas', (1991, p205). This differentiation of role was clearly visible in this group in which a girl led the attempt to solve the problem. She was readily able to grasp the realities of the problem, including the need to provide space for both car doors to open, should there be a passenger. This is not surprising as the APU has shown that girls do tend to outperform boys when the context focuses on people as it does in this car park problem.

This group immediately set to work in an organised way measuring the length and width of a car. They also took into account factors such as the space needed to open the car doors. They were able to give a detailed reasoned account of the completed work and then explain their next developments in an extremely mature manner. They produced scale plans of their car parks and worked out the area of land needed.

During later discussions all the children evaluated their work in small groups and were able to comment on the other groups' attempts and then revise their own work considering suggestions and ideas provided by the other children. The children who had originally found this task complex were able to complete it having listened to the ideas and seen the work of the others.

The children who appeared to enjoy this type of task were all those that were working at the highest level on ILS in comparison with the rest of their own year group within the investigation group. The other children, although working at a higher level than their peers within the classroom, were working at least half a year below (ILS average level) the most able children who had enjoyed the real life problem-solving activities.

As part of the Maths Investigation Group's work the children completed the *Practical Maths Assessment Test* (Foxman, Hagues and Ruddock 1990). This diagnostic test has four sections:

Number problems: Squares and counters
Handling Data: Length
   Use of a calculator
   Work with dice

The results of the Practical Assessment Test are shown in this table:

Table 2: *Practical Maths Assessment Test scores for selected enrichment group pupils*

		Squares and counters	Length	Calculator	Dice
Year 5	Student 1	10	8	2	10
	Student 2	10	8	6	7
	Student 3	7	7	9	9
Year 4	**Student 1**	10	10	10	9
	Student 2	10	8	9	10
	Student 3	10	7	9	8
	Student 4	7	10	5	8
	Student 5	5	2	8	8
	Student 6	10	3	7	7

Those pupils who performed well on the car park problem are highlighted in bold. Overall their work in the tests is far more consistent than the other pupils'. The calculator section investigates the use of pattern in number; all four of these pupils scored well in comparison to the other children in the group. The two children that scored reasonably well, pupils 5 and 6, took a much longer time to complete the section on calculators than the other children but were determined to find the pattern.

Table 3: *Comparison of the ILS Performance Level and NFER Pupil Profile Test for selected enrichment group pupils*

		ILS Level	NFER Test
Year 5	Student 1	6.1	75.5
	Student 2	6.2	78.7
	Student 3	**6.6**	**65.4**
Year 4	**Student 1**	**6.3**	**81.9**
	Student 2	**5.7**	**70.7**
	Student 3	**6.4**	**77.7**
	Student 4	5.1	61.2
	Student 5	4.5	56.4
	Student 6	4.6	59.6

All four of the pupils who performed well in the car park investigation were working at higher levels on ILS than the other pupils (Table 3). The Year 4 pupils also performed better in the NFER *Profile of Mathematics Ability Level One Test* (France 1991) that was used by Leicester University as the prime tool of the research. This relationship between the test scores and good performance on the car park task did not hold for the Year 5 pupils.

As the work continued it became apparent that although the children were all working at a high level on ILS and could apply their numeracy skills in a logical order to problems, some of the children were much more able to apply their skills in problem-solving work.

Conclusion

In this school, as in others within the project, there has been a growing realisation that there was a rich resource trapped within the report system. The question was how to make the resource readily available to all teachers. This was achieved by reducing the key data into an easily and rapidly digestible form that could then be supplemented from the report system as needed.

As teachers became more confident in that data they began to consider the significance of the information for their classroom practice. For example, were there other aspects of improved performance not being measured by the system? This led to a small scale classroom trial of basic number skills, which indicates that the children using ILS have gained an automaticity of skill not achieved by their classroom peers. There are also indications of a shift in attitude as these children were willing to take more risks and tackle unfamiliar material.

One further outcome was the formation of enrichment groups for high achieving pupils. Observations of these pupils showed a ready ability to apply ILS gained numeracy skills to the classroom tasks. However, there was no correspondence between high ILS performance and the ability to solve real world problems.

CHAPTER 8

Using value added data to investigate ILS materials

Carol Taylor Fitz-Gibbon and Neil Defty

Year 11 Information System (YELLIS) is a broadly based monitoring system which collects data on some 44,000 Year 11 (aged 14) pupils before they sit the General Certificate of Secondary Education. From this data the effects of specific changes can be measured.

Schools that are using such a system have a built-in method for investigating the effects of a wide variety of changes they might make.

The changes investigated could be in the methods of teaching, how classes are organised, homework policies, the adoption of cross-age tutoring and so on. In the present case, the YELLIS data were used to explore the use of Global mathematics material for revision. Using only the YELLIS questionnaire data it was possible to answer a number of questions. Which students took advantage of the availability of the materials? How did these students achieve in GCSE mathematics compared to their performance in other subjects? What attitudes did these students express towards lessons and computers?

Schools in the YELLIS Project give a baseline test in Year 11 (the YELLIS Test) along with a basic questionnaire which picks up students' aspirations (specifically how likely they are to stay in education beyond the compulsory years of schooling) and a measure of *cultural capital,* an indicator of the support for education in the home. The cultural capital measure is illustrated for an anonymous school in Figure 1.

In the second term of Year 11 the students complete an extended questionnaire covering their attitudes to school in general, to teachers, English, mathematics and science

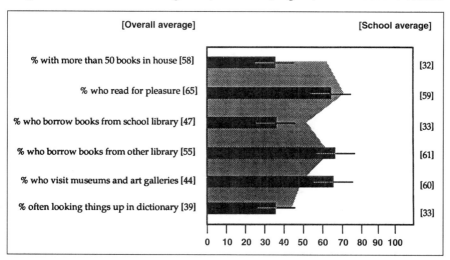

Figure 1: A YELLIS comparison graph

and including their responses to computers. These items can be used to compare the attitudes in ILS schools with the attitudes of students in similar schools not taking part in the ILS project. The full YELLIS sample in the school year 1994-1995 consisted of more than 44,000 students.

School X characteristics and value added

School X was participating in the YELLIS Project and had collected data on the extent to which 201 students in Year 11 used the ILS software.

The National School Performance Tables (league tables) produced for the Department for Education and Employment (DfEE) encourage unfair comparisons between schools, such as those based on the percentage attaining five grades A to C. The results a school

Table 1: *Relative ratings and value added for School X (YELLIS feedback for 1995)*

		Mean of pupil residuals	0.4
Art	0.3	Art	1.2
Biology		Biology	
Business Studies		Business Studies	
Chemistry		Chemistry	
Computing		Computing	
CDT	0	CDT	0.4
Economics		Economics	
English Language	−0.3	English Language	0.1
English Literature	0	English Literature	0.3
French	−0.1	French	0.4
Geography	−0.2	Geography	0.4
German	−0.6	German	0
History	0.3	History	0.9
Home Economics		Home Economics	
Information Technology		Information Technology	
Integrated Humanities	0.1	Integrated Humanities	0.4
Maths	−0.1	Maths	0.6
Media Studies		Media Studies	
Music		Music	
PE & Sport		PE & Sport	
Physics		Physics	
Religious Studies		Religious Studies	
Single Science		Single Science	
Double Science	0.1	Double Science	0.6
Sociology		Sociology	
Spanish	−0.9	Spanish	0.2
Urdu	0.5	Urdu	0.5

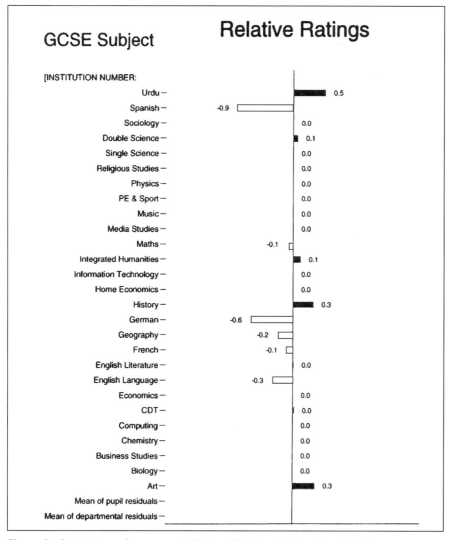

Figure 2: *Comparison of success rates for the ILS and control pupils on Task 1*

can obtain will be affected by the kind of students it is teaching. A fairer question is the value added question: did students at School X obtain GCSE results as good as those obtained by similar students in other schools? That is, did School X's students make reasonable progress? By comparing School X's performance on the YELLIS test with that of 44,000 other students, the relative progress made in Years 10 and 11 could be estimated. The value added is positive if School X's students made more progress than similar students elsewhere. The value added is negative if School X's students made less progress than similar students elsewhere.

The YELLIS test consists of vocabulary items and mathematics items. The important feature is that it predicts GCSE results very well, indeed as well as GCSE results predict A-levels, with correlation of about +0.7.

Table 1, an example of feedback to schools participating in the YELLIS project, shows that School X had positive value added scores in all the subjects indicated. This means that the students were, on average, achieving higher grades than would be predicted from their YELLIS test scores: their relative progress or value added was positive.

The value added scores provide fair comparisons, answering for each department the question 'How does this department's examination results compare with departments in other schools teaching the same subject to students with equivalent scores on the YELLIS test?' The difference between the GCSE grade a student obtained and the GCSE grade which was predicted for that student on the basis of the analyses of 44,000 YELLIS test and GCSE results is called the residual or value added for that student.

residual – value added score = actual grade – predicted grade

The student-by-student residuals are of use in making numerous comparisons within the school and were used in this study to assess the possible impact of the use of ILS materials in mathematics.

According to the YELLIS test, School X appeared to have a below average aptitude level in Year 10. From the YELLIS results for 1995, however, the GCSE results appeared positive in that students exceeded predictions made from the YELLIS test in practically every subject. In other words the value added in each subject was greater than average, indicating that students had made better than average progress from their Year 10 starting points.

We were looking, therefore, at a school with a low average aptitude intake but one in which students made commendable progress.

The Relative Ratings measures shown in the table and bar charts, compared the departments *within* the school *with each other*. The procedure, developed in Scotland (Kelly 1976), takes account of levels of difficulty between subjects. It will always be the case that approximately half the departments will have negative Relative Ratings.

Use of Global ILS software for GCSE mathematics revision

A dataset was provided by the school showing the extent of ILS use per week based on an eight week period from March to May 1995. Only 25 per cent had used Global mathematics for revision, and these students had used it to different degrees. For 75 per cent of students no time was spent using Global mathematics software, but some 51 students (25 per cent of Year 11) used the software for revision for at least a quarter of an hour per week. Twenty two of these students used the software for up to half an hour per week and four students used the software for three quarters of an hour or longer, per-week. This represented a light amount of use although the total hours would mount up over the eight week period.

The characteristics and attitudes of students who used the ILS Software

In Table 1 correlations are shown to indicate the extent to which those students who used ILS were different from those who did not. It appeared from the test scores that the Global software was used by the more able students and that there was a tendency for these students to come from homes with higher reported cultural capital. Perhaps this

Table 2: Correlations with ILS use:

Characteristics	Item	Correlation r	N	p<
Test scores	YELLIS Test	0.56	180	0.000
	Vocabulary Test	0.48	180	0.000
	Maths Test	0.56	180	0.000
Home background	"Cultural capital" – support for education in the home	0.22	179	0.003
Aspirations for education	Self-reported "likelihood of staying in education"	0.31	177	0.00
Attitudes:				
to computers	"I enjoy working with computers"	−0.08	167	0.29
to school	"I really like school"	−0.005	165	0.95
	"I am normally happy when I am at school"	0.04	165	0.59
to lessons	"I always do my best in lessons"	−0.14	166	0.06
	"I wish teachers would spend more time explaining things"	−0.19	165	0.01
	"I feel that teachers notice and recognise when I have worked hard"	−0.14	165	0.08

represented self-selection by able students who had computers at home and were therefore attracted to the software more than others – but this is only a speculation. The students who used the software also had stronger educational aspirations. With regard to attitudes to computers or to school in general, there appeared to be no differences between those who used the software and those who did not use the software. The correlations were all of the order of zero.

It was a different picture regarding attitudes to lessons. Those using the software tended to be pupils who did not feel that they did their best in lessons. They were not the ones who wished the teacher would spend more time explaining things; nor did they feel that the teachers noticed and recognised their work. These findings were fairly weak relationships but may have suggested that the students who used the software were those who were somewhat bored with lessons and independent about their learning and that they selected the software in preference to remaining with the activities of the normal classroom.

Tables 2a and 2b show that the majority of Year 11 students (the non-ILS group) in School X were more positive towards English and mathematics than students in YELLIS in general, but were less positive towards science. The ILS users were particularly positive to mathematics, more so than to English.

Effects on achievement

Can we use YELLIS data to assess the impact of the use of Global mathematics software on achievement? Given that more able students had used the ILS software it was not surprising to find that in every subject their GCSE scores were significantly better than the

Tables 3a and 3b: *Attitudes of three groups of students: those using ILS, those not using ILS and the YELLIS sample in general*

Percentage answering 'True' or 'Very true' to
'I look forward to lessons in...'

	Maths	English	Science
ILS	62	44	33
Non-ILS	42	55	27
YELLIS	33	53	40

Percentage answering 'True' or 'Very true' to
'like doing work in...'

	Maths	English	Science
ILS	73	60	53
Non-ILS	62	76	47
YELLIS	49	65	57

GCSE scores of other students. The important question was whether the *progress* that had been made compared favourably. This question was answered by looking at the value added or residual scores, that is the grades achieved taking into account the starting point of the student.

In Figure 3 we see the residuals in the five core curriculum subjects. These have been averaged for four groups of students: the 75 per cent who did not use ILS software and whose averages are shown as above the X axis label for zero hours, and three other groups formed according to their amount of use of the ILS materials.

The pattern in mathematics was quite striking, with significantly higher residuals for those using ILS. This means that *even taking account of the fact that more able students selected or were assigned to use ILS*, their achievement in GCSE mathematics was still, on average, about 0.9 of a grade higher than would have been predicted from their YELLIS test. They had made better than average progress to the extent of, on average, almost a whole grade. The residuals for those who had not used the ILS materials for revision were also positive.

The four students who had used ILS materials more extensively had not made such progress and were equivalent to those who hadn't used the material at all, with a residual score of 0.5. In other words there appeared to be an optimal amount of time for use of the materials beyond which effectiveness was not enhanced. Whether this was a self-selection effect (some students chose to waste time on the computers, spending longer than necessary and making less progress) or a distraction from other work of importance for GCSE results or required some other explanation could not be determined without further studies designed to consider such issues.

It must be remembered that this school in general had positive residuals and this can be seen in the graphs for the other four curriculum subjects. However, the only subject which showed a similar pattern to the mathematics residuals was double science. Whether this was due to some spin off effects in which the use of the mathematics software enhanced interest in science or whether this was simply a characteristic of these students is not known, although the Tables on this page showed they answered the YEL-

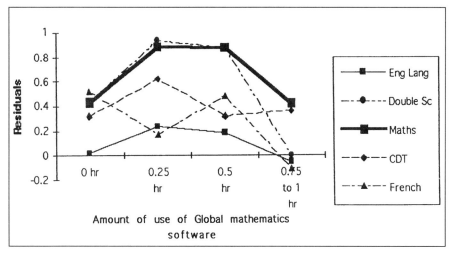

Figure 4: Residuals (value added) in core curriculum subjects

LIS questionnaire in a way which indicated greater attraction to science than other students in the school. Perhaps those students most interested in mathematics and science were more likely to make progress in these subjects and had also chosen to work with ILS materials.

Table 4 shows that the differences between the average residuals for ILS students and non ILS students were statistically significant at the conventional level (0.05 level) in mathematics and at the 0.06 level in double science but the differences were not significant in English language, CDT or French. In other words, in English language, CDT and French, students made better than expected progress (as they did generally in this school) but there were no differences between measures of the progress made by ILS students and those made by non-ILS students. This equivalence, linked with the fact that in mathematics and double science the ILS students had made more progress than non-ILS students, could be seen as lending support to the hypothesis that ILS had a beneficial effect.

Table 4: Correlations between ILS-use and YELLIS Raw Residuals:

Subject	Correlation	N	p<
English Language	0.06	171	0.467
Double Science	0.15	158	0.062
Maths	0.16	164	0.045
CDT	0.02	151	0.796
French	−0.11	76	0.328

The problem in interpreting the data lies not in the results themselves but in the self-selection. To find out if students who are *assigned* to work on ILS materials benefit – that is if the materials *cause* improvements, controlled experiments are needed, comparing equivalent groups of students.

A feature of the manner of use of the materials which could well be explored by randomised trials would be the amount of time per-week allocated to various ILS materials.

It may be that there are optimal amounts of time or it may be that student-self-selection is optimal in terms of effectiveness and efficiency.

Conclusions

This study suggested the presence of a positive impact due to the use of ILS materials in School X, with moderate amounts of time being optimal. However this finding could be explained by the possibility that well-motivated students had self-selected ILS materials and their good performance would have occurred anyway.

Designs incorporating deliberate allocation of differing amounts of time to using the ILS materials could rule out the self-selection explanation and possibly provide clues as to the optimal way of assigning time to the materials. In a school using YELLIS this kind of investigation would be easy to arrange and given that value added measures will soon be available for all schools (Fitz-Gibbon 1995) analyses of residuals will provide evidence regarding progress. The questionnaire items raise other issues of importance regarding non-cognitive outcomes, such as enjoyment and satisfaction with school.

In short, this small study highlights the need to know exactly how software comes to be used by students as this affects the interpretation of the outcome data. The outcomes of the use of learning materials are best assessed by residuals but even residuals cannot be interpreted with confidence in the absence of controlled designs.

The findings from this small study in one school are summarised here.

Summary

- Global mathematics was studied in one school which enrolled students in Year 10 with low aptitudes compared with the overall YELLIS sample but which generally produced better than expected progress amongst students in all subjects (that is, a school with positive value added in almost every subject).
- This limited small scale study simply provided an illustration of the use of a few items from YELLIS. The most important item available from the system was the residual or the measure of progress relative to that made by similar students in a large sample – greater than 44,000 students. The term value added is now applied to residuals and will soon be in widespread use.
- The use of ILS in the school studied was light and 75 per cent of students were not using it at all. The remaining 25 per cent used it for revision in mathematics generally for a quarter to a half an hour per week (as measured in an eight week period from March to May 1995).
- Those students using ILS were more able than others, and tended to come from homes in which there was more support for education and to have firmer intentions to stay in education after compulsory schooling.
- ILS users showed no significant differences in their attitudes to school or to computers, when compared with non-ILS students in the same school.
- When compared to non-ILS students in the same school, ILS users showed on average slight but statistically significant tendencies to be less positive about their lessons in general and possibly more inclined to work independently.
- When compared with the YELLIS sample, ILS students in this school obtained almost one grade higher than expected in their GCSE mathematics and double science examinations.

- When compared with non-ILS students in the same school, ILS users obtained significantly better grades in mathematics and double science but were equivalent in other core curriculum subjects.
- The better achievement of ILS students could be explained in several ways. Perhaps the ILS materials were effective for revision or perhaps those students choosing to use the materials would have made particularly good progress in any case.

ILS and under-achievers

John Gardner

This study investigated the proposition that an ILS enables under-achieving students to perform at a level approaching or matching their capacity. A number of schools were asked to identify known under-achievers who were using an ILS and were now considered to be achieving. Perceived impact on behaviour in the classroom was also of interest.

The schools

The chosen schools, two primary and two secondary, were all using the SuccessMaker system and were able to offer a variety of students whose performance was of interest to the study.

Study design and methods

The study was necessarily small scale, with a small sample and short timeframe, and much of the evidence was subjective. A multi-source approach to gathering evidence was therefore a crucial feature of the design. If a number of sources of information support the view that a particular student has been or is an under-achiever then this gives weight to that view. Similarly if a number of sources indicate increased achievement on the part of that student, some form of intervention has caused the turnaround. Unpicking the possibilities to discover if the ILS had influenced the turnaround was the central aim of the study. Ultimately the reader's judgement must rest on the balance of probabilities that all of the evidence might suggest.

The primary evidence source was the perception of the teachers involved and the rationale of the study required that their judgements be corroborated by as much collateral evidence as possible. Secondary sources therefore included the perceptions of the students themselves, attendance records, classwork and ILS-generated reports of the students' progress. The researcher also observed the students in class and, where appropriate, in the social context of the corridors or playground during break times.

The analysis involved the conventional categorisation and reduction of the data with the primary aim of ensuring that the results could be made as valid and as reliable as the constraints of the evaluation would allow. In this manner, and once the students were identified and had been visited, the measures and judgements relating to them (for example of under-achievement) were examined in the light of all available evidence.

Defining and identifying under-achievement

The initial stage of the study involved corresponding with the schools to set out the aims and conditions of proposed visits. The researcher's intention was to ask teachers if they could identify students who were on an ILS programme and whose:

- performance on the ILS and/or in normal classwork had improved in comparison with their previous history. The underlying achievement may be attributable to their teachers' low expectations of them, in which case the teachers express surprise about their relative success on ILS. Alternatively, it may be due to motivational or dis- affection issues, in which case the teachers are not surprised – having been well aware of their previously untapped ability.

- behaviour in normal class has changed in comparison with their previous history. Examples of a negative behavioural impact would be relatively surprising but a posi- tive impact may be reasonably expected as a consequence of any developing interest and success in learning, that the ILS experience might provide.

- performance on the ILS is not reaching the levels the teachers would expect, based on their previous history. This type of under-achievement may be attributable, in part at least, to the design or working context of the ILS.

Behavioural change has high visibility and immediacy for the teacher, whether it be a trend from usually bad behaviour towards good (or vice versa) or the increased partic- ipation of a previously withdrawn student (or vice versa). Evidence for such changes tends to be unambiguous and relatively easy to corroborate through observation. Impact on learning in the normal classroom is usually less tangible and much less easy to attribute partly or solely to the effect of ILS usage.

Academic under-achievement can have a variety of causes, often operating in combi- nation. Many will derive from the home experience while others will have a school or even class focus. Illness may cause prolonged absences which in turn may prevent a stu- dent performing to their true potential. Students with poor motivation to learn or who are disaffected with the subject, their teacher or their school are also likely to under- achieve academically. Some of these students may have disruptive tendencies. Students with specific learning difficulties will inevitably slip below their potential if the prob- lems remain unaddressed. Similarly, students who are less social and more withdrawn than the average student, and therefore not benefiting from classroom interaction and participation as much as they might do, may also under-achieve. All such under-achiev- ers can benefit from a tailored, personal approach to their tuition and a raising of their own academic self-image. An ILS, such as SuccessMaker, is a personal learning environ- ment offering structured tuition and a guarantee of success-on-task to build confidence. As such it is reasonable to expect SuccessMaker to have some degree of impact on such students.

The main confounding factor in attempts to attribute an ILS effect is the teaching. The quality and nature of the teaching and the teacher's relationships with the students must have a prominent influence on change. In most aspects of the study it was possible to focus on students who shared the same teacher, thereby increasing the focus on the ILS experience. However, it has not been possible to rule out the possibility that the patient and dedicated effort of a teacher over time is the main factor in any under-achiever's turnaround. Other external factors, which singly or in combination might also have a considerable part to play in turning round an under-achiever, include:

- an increased parental interest in the student's progress;
- a previously disturbed domestic environment beginning to stabilise;
- a growing acceptance of the school (settling down);
- or indeed, simple maturation.

The identification of appropriate subjects for the study was based on teacher judgement. Such a judgement arises from the many ways in which teachers know the potential of the students in their charge. It might be informed by class tests, specific types of class-work, or reports from previous years including, in some cases, reports from feeder primary schools. Often it will be the assessment of a teacher whose experience enables them quickly to develop a feel for the ability of the individual student from the complex mix of indicators such as motivation, self-confidence and level of achievement. Most teachers are aware of the self-fulfilling prophecy associated with attributing perhaps unwarranted negative personal and performance characteristics to students. It was only to be expected then, that the teachers in this study qualified their assessments of their students with cautions on the early-days nature of their relationships with the classes.

Validating the teachers' judgements of student achievement

Students who start using SuccessMaker do so at an enrolment level allocated to them by their teacher. The teachers in the study did this either by judging a level from existing test results – for example National Curriculum-related Cognitive Ability Test scores (CAT) – or simply by allocating an arbitrary score for all students. The data from two sets in one school were used to examine the correlation between these objective tests and the students' eventual Initial Placement Motion Level (IPML). The two classes were in Year 7 (Set A) and Year 8 (Set B) respectively and the correlations of interest are presented in Tables 1-3.

Table 1: *Illustration of the correlation between CAT scores and ILS measures (Maths Concepts and Skills – Set A, N=28)*

Time			
	CAT		since
	Quantitative	IPML	IPML
IPML	0.74 **		
Gain since IPML	0.67 **	0.59**	0.59**

Table 2: *Illustration of the correlation between CAT scores and ILS measures (Maths Concepts and Skills – Set B, N=26)*

Time			
	CAT		since
	Quantitative	IPML	IPML
IPML	0.73**		
Gain since IPML	0.38	0.47	0.54*

Table 3: *Illustration of correlation between external test scores and Reader's Workshop Measures (Set A, N=28)*

Time				
	CAT Verbal	Spooncer Test	IPML	since IPML
Spooncer Test	0.59**			
IPML	0.80**	0.64**		
Gain since IPML	0.28	0.45*	0.38*	0.28
(** indicates p <0.01, * indicates p<0.05)				

Tables 1 and 2 indicate a good correlation between the students' CAT (Quantitative) scores and their Mathematics Concepts and Skills (MCS) IPML scores (0.74 and 0.73 respectively). Teachers using CAT scores to allocate enrolment levels for students in these classes would therefore have made relatively reliable judgements. The Reader's Workshop (from SuccessMaker) IPML scores and the CAT (Verbal) scores in Table 3 are also quite strongly correlated for Set A (0.80). Again teachers using the CAT scores to judge enrolment levels would have been reasonably accurate.

The first stage of validating the teacher judgements is therefore accomplished with corroboration that the ILS settings were in good agreement with external test scores. Students with low IPML scores at the beginning of their ILS work could be deemed weak with some degree of reliability. In the context of this study, if such students began to show much improved scores, it could be argued that they had earlier been under-achieving and that the ILS was turning them round. To investigate this argument it is necessary to find a means of identifying and if possible charting any such improvement. Again the teacher is a crucial source of evidence, but one approach to validating their judgement is to use the data provided by the ILS itself.

As students use SuccessMaker they progress through achievement levels based on the number of questions they show mastery in. As they progress, the system charts their progress as a gain defined by the difference between their current average score and their IPML (their starting point). It is tempting to see this as a pre-test/post-test system (that is IPML scores versus current average scores) and to use techniques associated with gain score analysis. However, this approach would immediately run into problems if it were strictly adhered to, owing to the success-oriented model that the ILS uses. Gains in a normal pre-test/post-test model should not correlate positively with the pre-test score. For example, a student with a high pre-test score (such as 75 per cent) can expect to have a smaller gain (maximum 25 per cent) in the post-test than someone with a low pre-test score (such as 40 per cent) who has a larger gain potential (maximum 60 per cent). However, the gain in SuccessMaker is not assessed by the administration of two identical or similar tests over an interval of time. The nature of the progression in SuccessMaker is that everyone gains (success is built in) and the gains made are simply stages along the progression. It is therefore reasonable to propose that an able student should progress faster than a weaker student. Put another way, an able student should advance further along the progression than a weaker student in the same time-frame.

Tables 1 and 2 above suggest that the IPML is a reasonably grounded measure of a student's ability and should therefore be a reasonable predictor of the progress of a student.

A student who is misdiagnosed, that is who is actually at a higher or lower ability level than suggested by the IPML, can be expected to progress at a different rate than might be expected based on the IPML. An under-achiever who begins to achieve should therefore have a progression different from that which would normally be expected from their IPML.

Matching the teacher's views about a student's progress with evidence from the ILS data is one method of validating the view that an under-achiever is achieving but it relies on the IPML being a good predictor of progress. Tables 1 and 2 suggest that the original MCS IPML scores and the time spent measures (Time since IPML) are moderate predictors of the students' gains in ILS scores (0.59 and 0.59 respectively for Set A and 0.47 and 0.54 respectively for Set B).

Table 3, on the other hand, suggests that there is little relationship between Gains since IPML for the Reader's Workshop and any of the measures including the original IPML and the time spent on the ILS. However it is difficult to identify the algorithims underlying the Readers Workshop model and so the data makes very little sense (Time since IPML). Analyses of other Reader's Workshop data sets indicate the same low correlations and this is actually more in keeping with a normal pre- and post-test pattern. However, there are no grounds for arguing that the Reader's Workshop data actually do operate in a conventional fashion and the rest of the analyses will be confined to mathematics concepts and skills.

Tables 1 and 2 indicate a reasonable correlation between time spent on the ILS and the gain achieved. Although most students in a class will spend approximately the same amount of time on the system, for various reasons some students will do much less (for example absence through illness) or much more (working during lunch-times). Variation in the gain scores will therefore have a time dependence and for this reason it was decided to use the Rate of Gain (extent of gain per unit time) to chart progression. The Rate of Gain details how fast the student is improving and takes care of variations in time spent on the ILS. Figure 1 presents the standardised Rate of Gain scores, plotted along with the standardised IPML scores, for the top half (by IPML) of a whole year group in one of the schools. The data are standardised primarily to allow inspection of the extent to which the students' scores vary from the mean and partly to enable the two sets to exist on the same axes. The correlation between the Rate of Gain and the IPML is a relatively high 0.62.

How to read these figures:

The drop down lines between each pair of points are not indicative of a decrease between the two; they are there to assist the reader to examine the points in pairs. Each series of points is independently plotted against the standardised mean of their scores as a group; that is, both sets are plotted against the same standardised mean of zero. Taking Student 15 as an example, the IPML score is well above the group mean for IPML (by around one standard deviation) and the Rate of Gain in the MCS scores is well below that of the group mean for Rate of Gain (around 0.75 of a standard deviation). The Z scores are the standardised scores based on a mean of zero for each set of raw scores. In raw scores, Student 15 had an IPML of 4.53 (above the mean of 3.97), a gain of 1.27 (below the mean of 1.67) and a time spent of 949 minutes (below the mean of 1047 minutes).

Figure 1 shows that most of the students with IPML scores above the mean for the whole group also progress at a Rate of Gain above the mean for the group. As the IPML falls closer to the mean (for example from Student 29 onwards) there is a change in

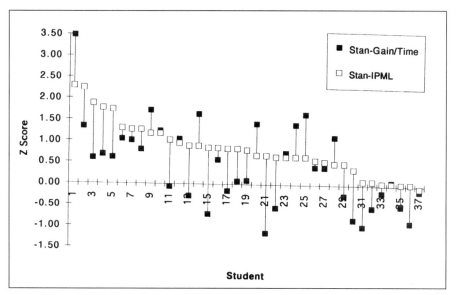

Figure 1: *Rate of gain vs IPML for Maths Concepts and Skills - top half of Year group*
(Plots of Standardised Z Scores for IPML and Gain/Time)

pattern in which the Rate of Gain begins to fall below its mean. This corroborates the earlier proposition that more able students (defined by high IPML) will generally exhibit higher rates of progress. Obvious as this may seem, it would not generally be the case since opportunities for able students to excel in conventional learning programmes usually become attenuated by the very difficulty that the progression in their work introduces. SuccessMaker appears to enable rapid progress, in its own context, by

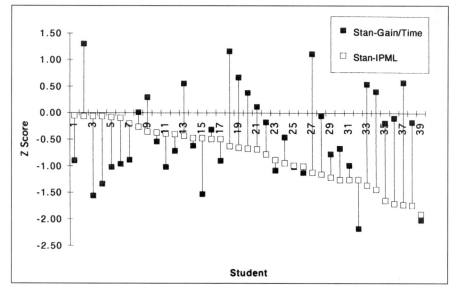

Figure 2: *Rate of Gain vs IPML for Maths Concepts and Skills - bottom half of Year group*

guaranteeing success on task. It would appear that the more able student is able to continue forging ahead at a high rate by virtue of this design feature. If this proposition were to hold generally for a variety of student groups, and this remains to be examined, instances of high IPML students not progressing at rates above the mean would suggest some level of disaffection or misdiagnosis.

An examination of the data for the lower half of the group (Figure 2) reveals further interesting results:

For the lower half of the group, the correlation between the Rate of Gain scores and the IPML scores is -0.06; much more like a conventional gains/pre-test correlation. In a continuation of the pattern shown in the previous graph, the mid-range students, with IPML scores up to around 0.5 standard deviations from the mean, are showing a pattern of Rate of Gain scores which fall some way below the mean. At the same time some of the weakest students, with IPML scores far below the group mean, are exhibiting Rate of Gain scores that are relatively high above their mean. These results suggest that mid-range students do not benefit from the ILS work to anything like the same extent as either the most able or the weakest students. The figure also indicates that the weakest students are achieving at rates that compare with or exceed the average for the class; thereby supporting the proposition that ILS has helped under-achievers to achieve. It must be emphasised that the achievement attained is in an ILS context and cannot be presumed to follow through to other learning and classroom success.

Analysis at a student level

At this point it is worth beginning the analysis at a student level. The four schools providing the bulk of the data offered 25 students of interest to the study. In this section of the report, a selection of these students is used to illustrate the types of findings that arose. Ten students of interest were offered from the whole year group illustrated in Figures 1 and 2.

Table 4: Maths Concepts and Skills data relating to a group of perceived under-achievers

Student IPML	Spooncer	IPML	Gain since IPML	Time since Now	Rank Rank	Original Rank Movement	
1	5.48	117	2.42	832	2	1	- 1
2	4.42	115	2.77	1293	4	20	+16
3	3.45	73	2.00	1300	41	59	+18
4	4.81	121	2.19	1103	8	7	- 1
5	3.01	88	1.75	996	63	71	+ 8
6	5.14	114	1.29	693	15	4	- 11
7	3.13	<80	0.83	1057	75	67	- 8
8	3.22	100	2.10	1038	49	63	+14
9	4.42	99	1.22	1037	31	20	- 11
10	3.73	85	1.98	1154	30	46	+16
Mean	3.97		1.67	1047			
S.D.	0.66		0.43	178			

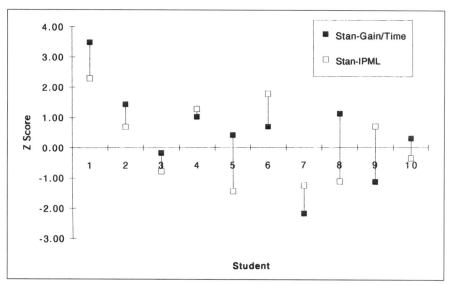

Figure 3: *Rate of Gain vs IPML for the group of under-achievers in table 4 Maths Concepts and Skills (Plots of Standardised Z Scores for IPML and Gain/Time)*

Table 4 presents the data for ten of the students from the whole year group above and their Rate of Gains versus IPML data is plotted in Figure 3.

Each of these students is a perceived under-achiever in some respect and a report of their specific cases follows. For conventional reasons the students will only be identified by a number and a gender. References to 'ability' relate to their IPML score.

Student 1 Summary

Student 1 is not an obvious under-achiever, indeed the data suggest that he is a top student. In the whole year group his original IPML ranked him as top student but his teacher had become increasingly worried that he was beginning to 'go off'. Up until his introduction to ILS his work and attitude has been deteriorating; he was falling into an under-achievement pattern. The ILS work then captured his motivation and he has sustained a high rate of progress since (see Figure 3). His teacher considered that using the ILS has improved his attitude to school and that this has impacted positively on his work in the classroom. (He is Student 1 in Figure 1.)

Student's view

Student 1 was reluctant to speak to the researcher as the maths exercise he was engaged in had a time penalty. Although he was clearly pleased with his 80s and 90s in MCS scores he preferred working in the Reading Investigations. He felt that the most important thing for him in the ILS sessions was the ability to work on his own.

Student 2 Summary

Student 2 has shown a major change in his ranking on ILS scores in the year group. He is easily distracted and although an able student (in the teacher's assessment and corroborated by his primary school report) he had fallen in with two much weaker boys who had disruptive tendencies. When together, the group perceive work as uncool and he had slipped into an under-achievement pattern. Classroom observation confirmed his propensity for being distracted and for distracting others although there was never any major disruption. The impact which ILS had on him was not immediate and his initial progress was relatively slow. However, it was soon clear that something of a rescue was underway as he became amenable to being grouped with able students for certain work. His progress also accelerated and he quickly topped out of Reader's Workshop into the more creative Reading Investigations. In recent times he has regressed a little in English, drawing closer to his cronies again and becoming less inclined to the extended writing which Reading Investigations seeks to promote. However, as Table 4 and Figure 3 show, he is still clearly progressing at a rate well above the average. (He is Student 20 in Figure 1.)

Student's view

Student 2 expressed a clear preference for ILS work instead of classwork – '...would do an hour no problem ... wouldn't even need a break .. would do it all day!' He alluded to the quietness of the ILS sessions – '...no asking for rubbers or pens .. no messing .. get work done'. He is well aware of the level he is working at in ILS in relation to one of his cronies (Student 3) and considers that he is doing more difficult mathematics.

Student 3 Summary

Student 3 has shown a major improvement in his ranking on ILS scores in the year group, moving up 18 places (Table 4). However, his Rate of Gain is not quite on a par with the average for the year group (Figure 3). He is a member of Student 2's potentially disruptive group and remains behaviourally difficult (as corroborated by classroom observation by the researcher). His teacher reports a marked improvement in some aspects of classwork, for example in grammar and in writing in complete sentences, but also points to some indications of maturation and settling in effects. In addition to the impact on basic skills, his teacher has noted increased confidence in his classwork. (He is Student 22 in Figure 2 and the third member of the group is Student 29 in the same Figure.)

Student's view

Student 3 also expressed a clear preference for ILS work instead of classwork and preferred mathematics to the English work. He was much less articulate than his friend, Student 2, and did not do much else other than agree with him.

Student 4 Summary

Student 4 is a student who is deemed quite able, ranking seven on the original IPML and with a high Spooncer score of 121. However, she is difficult to keep motivated in normal class, becomes bored easily and is reluctant to learn. Clearly vulnerable to slipping into under-achievement, her teacher considers that ILS Reading Investigations has offered her a challenge that has managed to hold her interest. She now periodically writes extensive creative pieces stimulated by the ILS. (She is Student 7 in Figure 1.)

Student's view

Student 4 expressed the view that she works better in the ILS class because she can work on her own. She described working alone as more fun.

Student 5 Summary

Student 5 is a low achieving student whose Rate of Gain is above the mean for the group.

She works intently on the ILS and regularly scores 70 per cent in sessions, earning a half-year certificate every two months. In class she exhibits spatial co-ordination problems leading to very poor handwriting, drawing and physical measurement skills. Her teacher considers that her success on the ILS has translated to the classroom where she has become more confident in several areas including mental arithmetic and other numerical work. (She is Student 34 in Figure 2.)

Student's view

The researcher did not have an opportunity to speak with Student 5 but observations in the ILS context confirmed the level of concentration. In class she did contribute but was inclined to drift; sometimes attending and sometimes daydreaming.

Student 6 Summary

According to her teacher, Student 6 shows little interest in the ILS and although quite able (original IPML rank was 4, Spooncer score 114) has slipped some 11 places down the ILS scoring rank. She is an example of a student who is considered to be under-achieving on the ILS since she works well in class at levels higher than the work she is tackling on the computer. Clearly she had not spent the same length of time on the Maths Concepts and Skills (her time spent was 693 minutes against an average of 1047, see Table 4) and it transpired that she was taking up too much of each ILS session on Reading Investigations work. However, Figure 3 shows that her progress rate, as measured by the Rate of Gain which corrects for the time factor, is still some way above the mean for the group. This is likely to improve further now her teacher has asked her to ensure she gives the Maths Concepts and Skills sessions their due time. (She is Student 4 in Figure 1.)

Student's View

Student 6 contradicted her teacher's view to some extent by saying she liked working on the ILS. Some aspects, for example the long division, were frustrating but she appreciated the variety of questions and '... different stuff every day'. Although her mathematics does not come up to the classwork levels, she did consider she was doing better in ILS than in class. It is possible that this is the case for her English classes.

Student 7 Summary

Student 7 is a low achieving student whose Rate of Gain falls some way below the mean for the group. He claims to have no problems in his learning but his behaviour is described by his teacher as often being strange. Earlier in the year he had appeared to begin to settle and to improve his performance but the improvement was not sustained. His teacher suggested that the noticeable improvement may have been due to his earning a half-year certificate or it may have been linked to his mother attending a parents' night. There has been some measure of improvement in his demeanour; for example, he was less negative, but he remains very difficult to motivate. Figure 2 (Student number 32) shows that his performance stands out among the weakest students in that his Rate of Gain is far behind that of his peers. It is tempting to conclude that the ILS is doing little for him but his teacher had evidence that poor as his ILS mathematics achievement was, he was working with a higher level of mathematics than he had managed to accomplish in his classwork.

Student's view

The researcher was unable to speak with Student 7 but did observe him in class. He spent a great deal of time seeking attention, putting his hand up to suggest silly answers and making loud groans when he considered his hand was up for too long. The school had allocated him a special assistant in an effort to deal with his behaviour and lack of achievement.

Student 8 Summary

Student 8 began the ILS work with a very low IPML (3.22) but Spooncer at least gave some indication of latent ability (Spooncer score 100). As Figure 3 shows, his progress on the ILS has been extraordinary, ending up a full standard deviation away from the mean for the Rate of Gain for the group. His progress mirrors that of a number of the weakest students as Figure 2 demonstrates (he is Student 27) and the results for him and the students below him on IPML score (for example Students 28-39 - bar number 32 above - in Figure 2) are strongly suggestive of under-achievers turning round.

Student's view

Student 8 really exudes pleasure in relation to ILS. He enjoys the speed games and '...getting fast at doing things like maths questions, adding, times, fractions, divisions...' He openly states that he feels more confident in mathematics and that he is now a good speller. He attributes much of his success to the ILS but is unable to articulate any particular reasons why ILS may have helped.

Student 9 Summary

Student 9 is a relatively able student with an IPML a good 0.5 standard deviations above the mean. However, her Rate of Gain shows the opposite trend, lying more than one deviation below the mean (Figure 3). This student, like Student 7, is considered to be under-achieving in ILS, having slipped some 11 places on the IPML ranking. Her teacher considers that she doesn't like computers and this includes working on the ILS. Her classwork mathematics level is much better than the level of work she is completing on the ILS and she seems to get great satisfaction from doing good work on paper. (She is Student 21 in Figure 1.)

Student's view

Student 9 confirmed the teacher's view that she prefers classwork. She also enjoys completing work in an exercise book which the computer obviously didn't facilitate. Observation revealed that she attended well and was a willing contributor to classroom activities.

Student 10 Summary

Student 10 is a very reserved student who sits passively in class, often with her coat still on and almost other-worldly in her manner. Figure 3 shows she is a little below the mean in her IPML but her Rate of Gain is a little above the mean. It is perhaps reasonable to suggest that her withdrawn manner would tend to keep her at an under-achieving level while the ILS allows her to move forward at a pace more in keeping with her ability. (She is Student 9 in Figure 2.)

Student's view

It was difficult to get information from Student 10 owing to her extreme shyness but she did admit to liking the privacy of the ILS learning environment, for example in getting several goes at spellings without anyone looking on. Observations of Student 10 in the corridors at break time and lunch time revealed that she remained withdrawn socially, not speaking or associating with any other students at any time during the short observations.

Several other students, from Classes A and B above, are worthy of mention to illustrate other findings from the evaluation. The data for the first pair of students, Students A and B, are presented in Table 5.

Table 5: *Descriptive data for Class A including data for Students A and B (ILS – Maths Concepts and Skills)*

	Student A	Student B	Mean	S.D.	Range
CAT-Quantitative	99.00	82.00	85.00	26.00	73:123
Spooncer Test	122.00	101.00	110.00	7.00	95:124
IPML	4.59	4.08	4.03	0.66	1.88:5.33
Gain since IPML	0.51	0.35	0.41	0.20	0.08:1.13
Time since IPML	381.00	384.00	335.00	76.00	124:466

The two students, A and B, were noted for their high motivation in working with the ILS. Inspection of Table 5 shows that they are differentiated quite markedly in ability, as indicated by the various test scores, including IPML. Their motivation perhaps springs from different sources (the parents of A attested to their daughter's love of computers while B was anxious to improve her multiplication tables) but was nonetheless clear to their teacher. Yet try as she undoubtedly did, Student B's Rate of Gain remains below the mean while Student A's rate follows the pattern of her IPML and comes in above it. It is perhaps a slender argument, but motivation and time-on-task are controlled for these two students as is teaching, that is they have the same teacher. The main difference between them is their ability and the more able student progresses at a higher rate with the ILS. This fits the pattern observed for the whole year group above (Figures 1 and 2). The majority of mid-range ability students, like Student B, do not progress as well in the ILS as the majority of the very able (like Student A) or the very weak.

For the very able the ILS system seems not to attenuate the opportunity for success, enabling them to continue to progress rapidly. The very able students, 11 and 15 in Figure 4, provide clear evidence of the exceptional Rate of Gain such able students can achieve. On the other hand, for a substantial number of those who are measured as being very weak (for example the bottom 20 or so students in Figure 2), some level of latent achievement is clearly realised. Students 27 and 28 in Figure 4 also follow this trend to some extent. These students fell more than two and a half standard deviations from the mean on the group IPML scores yet their progress is sufficient to bring them up close to par on the Rate of Gain. It is not unreasonable to assume that without the ILS intervention these students and those in the lower end of Figure 2 would not have experienced this level of success in their learning. (Students A and B are numbers 2 and 4 respectively in Figure 4.)

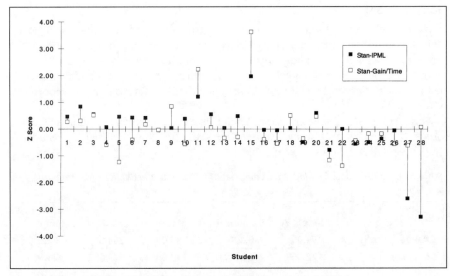

Figure 4: *Rate of Gain vs IPML for Class A - Maths Concepts and Skills*
(Plots of Standardised Z Scores for IPML and Gain/Time)

Two more students illustrate another aspect of the study's findings. The data for Students C and D, members of Class B, are presented in Table 6.

Table 6: *Descriptive data for Class B including data for Students C and D (ILS – Maths Concepts and Skills)*

	Student C	Student D	Mean	S.D.	Range
CAT-Quantitative	109.00	119.00	101.00	10.00	87:119
NFER	41.00	36.00	34.00	6.00	20:45
Spooncer Test	121.00	116.00	111.00	11.00	89:129
IPML	4.74	4.52	4.44	0.35	4.01:5.15
Time since IPML for C	1835.00	–	1507.00	225.00	1090:1835
Gain since IPML for C	3.11	–	1.94	0.46	1.35:3.11
Z-Rate of Gain for C	1.52	–	0.00	1.00	1.22:1.89
Time since IPML for D	–	265.00	236.00	66.00	166:391
Gain since IPML for D	–	0.38	0.29	0.10	0.16:0.50
Z-Rate of Gain for D	–	1.15	0.00	1.00	1.63:1.31

The class is made up of two groups; those who had been using the ILS for two years (for example C) and those who had been using it for one year (for example D); the latter having been part of the control group during the previous year.

Looking down the table, the data suggest that the two girls are quite able, with both of them above the mean on the four measures. Aside from the CAT (Quantitative) score, Student C performs marginally better on these scores. Time spent on the system is, however, a major difference with Student C having completed more than 1,800 minutes on the system while Student D has completed 265. Student C had used the ILS more than anyone else in the class and was known to use it at lunch-times, after school and so on. Their Rate of Gain scores for mathematics also put C in front.

The reason the two students were brought to the attention of the researcher is that they illustrate how prolonged ILS usage does not necessarily impact on the student's performance in normal class. In this case Student D performed much better in class tests than Student C. Examination of the two students' most recent class test scripts confirmed the difference in performance. The exercises were also confirmed as comprising questions very similar to the ILS format (short, drill type or structured questions). It would be reasonable to expect student C to out perform Student D but she did not. Student C made many more simple mistakes and was inclined to explain her solutions much more than D. For example, C would write:

$$3y + 7 = 25, y = 6 \text{ and then include the explanation: } (25 - 7 = 18/3 = 6)$$

$$\text{while D would write simply } 3y + 7 = 25 = y = 6$$

Most of C's solutions had explanations attached in a manner similar to the way the ILS would take a student through a solution. The teacher was worried that while the intense level of ILS work brought its own rewards within the system, it did not seem to bring benefits in terms of the student's wider learning outcomes. The suggestion was made that Student D had benefited as much if not more from being a control student the previous year (that is not having had access to the ILS). The question arises, is it possible that two years of ILS work may boil down to excessive practice on already acquired skills without transfer to higher order learning?

Summary of findings

In the context of the ILS classroom:

- The findings from this study did confirm a positive impact on the academic performance and behaviour patterns of most of the under-achievers examined.
- All students in the study showed some degree of progress on ILS scores (a design feature of the ILS) and this was often accompanied by an increased attention span and focusing on task.
- Many of the very able students in the study sustained high levels of progress through the system.
- Many of the very weak students in the study recorded rates of progress that were on a par for average students. This implies that the ILS is enabling latent potential to be realised.
- Most average students progress relatively slowly in comparison with the very able and the very weak.
- In some cases, where it was a previously acknowledged problem, disruptive behaviour was also reduced.
- Teachers in the study, while stressing the possibility of significant, alternative influences, pointed to the benefits of repetitive practice of basic skills, improved motivation, a better self-image and increased confidence as tangible ILS impacts on the students.
- In some of the cases examined, where the students were assessed to be likely to under-achieve through demotivation or boredom, the teachers were emphatic that the ILS usage was sustaining improvement by challenging the students.
- Some students, who under-achieve in their normal classwork, achieve well on the ILS system. They confirm that they appreciate the structured practice, the non-judgmental

and rapid feedback, the autonomy of learning, the audio guidance, privacy in failing (and in achieving) and a relatively quiet environment free from the distractions of normal classrooms.

- Some students are not attracted to an ILS environment and develop a pattern of under-achievement on the system. These students state that they prefer writing and drawing (graphs and diagrams for example) in their books and the interaction of the classroom. They criticise the repetitiveness of some of the exercises, having to leave enjoyable classes, the US emphasis and various technical irritations relating to earphones, timed exercises and so on.

In the students' normal schooling:

- The teachers reported the improved behaviour and/or participation of particular students including a greater capacity for concentrating on tasks.
- Some students were beginning to display more interest in learning and more confidence and willingness to tackle problems, tasks or questions.
- There was no reported impact on attendance.
- Impact on learning outcomes, that is arriving at acceptable solutions to problems, approaches to tasks or answers to questions, did not necessarily follow from successful ILS experience. There was some indication that the ILS impact is not automatically transferred to success in the more widely based learning of the classroom.

Concluding remarks

Both the teachers and students in this study have high expectations of the ILS they use and for the most part their expectations are warranted. Within the context of the ILS itself, success is generated and there are a variety of knock-on effects such as those discussed in the last section. The very able and the very weak appear to benefit most from the system; the former being challenged and the latter being helped up the learning ladder. However, some low and under-achievers do not respond, due perhaps to a deep-seated disaffection with schooling or to a disaffection with computers. This study has begun to shed light on the benefits that ILS can offer under-achievers and their teachers but much work remains and indeed requires to be carried out to find out if the impact can be more than the simple acquisition of basic skills.

ILS and pupils with special educational needs

Ann Lewis

It has been claimed that a major strength of an ILS is the way in which it can be used to tailor work to individual learning needs (McFarlane 1995). At face value then, an ILS ought to be of particular benefit to pupils with a variety of special educational needs as they, by definition, need atypical routes to learning, possibly just slower paced, possibly qualitatively different (Lewis 1995). Given this it is interesting that research into the use of ILS has produced equivocal results concerning their value for pupils with special educational needs (SEN). What accounts for these contrasting results? Particular benefits for children with SEN of much computer-based learning, including ILS, include the fine slicing of tasks, privacy and potential independence (Neuman 1991) as well as more general enhancing of access to the curriculum (Day 1995). In addition, gains from ILS for pupils with SEN may reflect links with learning style.

There is research as well as anecdotal evidence that many pupils with emotional and/or learning difficulties have an impulsive learning style and so gain particularly from computer-based learning (Hopkins 1991). Alongside this there is research evidence that ILS seem to help, in particular, pupils with aggressive or hurried learning styles (McFarlane 1995). Taken together, these points suggest that children with learning or emotional difficulties will gain from an ILS. However, against the strengths described above there are negative findings. In a review of the effectiveness of ILS learning effects related to pupils' achievement levels Hativa (1994) concluded that in using ILS the gap between high and low achievers widened. Several explanations for this were put forward. Low achievers used the computer-based drill and practice much less effectively than did high achievers. The low achievers were also less flexible in adapting to the computer-based learning environment. Further, several features caused the machine to under-evaluate these pupils and so inhibited pupils' learning. McFarlane (1995) noted that features of ILS design frequently identified as undesirable included time limits for a response when responding to each digit when typed, no means of correcting an erroneous digit once typed, and the lack of adequate explanations when a pupil is unsure about how to solve an exercise. Imposing a time limit was associated, particularly for lower ability pupils, with irritation, decreased self-confidence and an increase in the number of incorrect responses. Pupils with learning or emotional difficulties are often described as highly teacher-dependent. Consequently a lack of personal support and intervention, as when using an ILS, may also limit learning. Given this set of mixed messages, how effective have ILS been found to be for pupils with SEN in the UK evaluations?

The conclusion of evaluators in Phase 1 of the ILS evaluation reflects conflicting perceptions concerning the value of ILS for pupils with SEN. The hypothesis that pupils with SEN would gain particularly from ILS was not supported: 'lower ability students made the smallest gains' (relative to other attainment groups) (NCET 1994:20–21). However, teachers' initial expectations had been that these pupils would be among those to benefit most from an ILS. The apparently conflicting results from a range of previous ILS research plus this anomalous finding prompted the setting up of the small scale SEN-focused evaluation in Phase 2, described in this chapter.

Background to data collection

It was decided to focus on children from mainstream and from special schools with learning and/or emotional difficulties including those children who were new to the ILS system as well as pupils who had already had extensive experience of an ILS. The research questions included:

- Would the reported value of an ILS for some children with SEN (Phase 1) disappear once the novelty value had passed?
- What impact would an ILS have on attitudes and motivation?
- What impact would an ILS have on cognitive strategies applied to English and mathematics tasks?

The short-term nature of the evaluation suggested that a case study approach focusing on individual children would provide the most effective and realistic means of addressing these questions. Findings relate primarily to two subjects (English and mathematics) in version (15) of one program (SuccessMaker) from one manufacturer. Therefore one must be cautious about generalising findings to other versions, programs or manufacturers.

Data collection sample

The following findings concerning the impact of ILS with pupils with SEN are based on research in two schools (one special and one mainstream primary) focusing on ten case study children. The mainstream school operated a suite of eight computers which was co-ordinated by a teacher with particular interest in ILS. She collaborated with class teachers concerning the work of individual children. The special school had networked computers in seven classrooms plus some additional machines in the library and resource room. Data from these case studies are supplemented by reports from other ILS research consultants and from NCET staff working with ILS programs across a range of schools.

In the special school the six case study pupils (two girls, four boys) were selected to represent typical special needs sub-groups – emotional and behavioural difficulties, moderate learning difficulties and autistic. The four case study pupils in the mainstream school (two girls, two boys) were chosen to represent mainstream children with mild or moderate learning difficulties in two age ranges (six to seven and nine to ten years). Work with the case study children took place through a total of nine one-day visits to the schools over three months (March to June 1995) and longer term documentary evidence was also provided by the schools. Each of the one-day visits included:

- Observation of each of the case study pupils using SuccessMaker (English, mathematics and, with upper primary school pupils only, spelling programs). Individual children were observed, using a semi-structured observation schedule, for eight to 30 minutes while using ILS programs.
- Pupil interviews (including post-session evaluation using a semi-structured schedule), informal assessments of learning style.

- Formal self-esteem and locus of control measures using the B/G scales (Maines and Robinson 1993).
- Collation/scrutiny of documents (SuccessMaker reports and classroom records of learning).
- Teacher interviews (using a semi-structured schedule).

School visits were organised to provide at least two observation records (video-recorded at the special school) with an approximately three month interval between the two sets of recordings for individual pupils. Results are reported for the group of ten children except where there were marked differences between the special and mainstream school samples.

On average each case study pupil completed around 30 to 40 sessions on reading and around 40 sessions on mathematics in the monitored period (March to May 1995). The time taken to complete these sessions was between four and ten hours for reading and between six and ten hours for mathematics. Individual sessions were set for four to 16 minutes according to the child's concentration span. Two of the mainstream children also completed 38 sessions each on spelling.

Key findings

Results are reported in three broad sections alongside discussion of some of the ensuing implications for pupils and teachers. First, evidence concerning access to the ILS is examined. This is related to the baseline skills that may be needed before a pupil can gain from an ILS program. The place of an ILS in relation to teachers' diagnostic assessments of children is also discussed here. Second, aspects related to the language of instruction are reported. Third, results of working on the ILS are reported in terms of:

- pupil gains on the grading system internal to the program,
- cognitive strategies being employed by pupils,
- transfer of learning,
- motivation and self-esteem,
- autonomy and self-regulation.

Access

Access to SuccessMaker was not an issue for mainstream pupils with SEN. The management system was used to modify curriculum strands, particularly when children were moving from one module to a new one, but there was reportedly no need to adjust for individual children the time on session, the wait time between questions, or the reflection time between a question and provision of answer or prompt.

Access was a major concern at the special school. Staff there introduced and adapted a wide range of peripherals and software to enable a diverse range of special needs to be accommodated within SuccessMaker. These adaptations included the use of a glidepoint (integral mouse/mat device), trackerballs, voice activated software (not fully developed), a big keys keyboard, various keyboard overlays, a touch window, and the variation of cursor size and maximising of cursor background contrast. Other modifications included physical re-arrangements so that children were seated appropriately at the computer.

There are many obvious benefits in such modification of access but there were also some problems:

- Some children seemed to have difficulties switching between different keyboard layouts (alphabetic to numeric and QWERTY to alphabetical order).
- The big keys and normal keyboards were needed concurrently as the big keys keyboard did not have some keys including < >, minus or escape keys (the latter was needed when staff had to take the child off the program prematurely). Consequently co-pilot leads had to be installed to allow dual keyboard use.
- Headsets needed variable sound controls for each ear. This then required the teacher to check that when a child went on the machine the headset was adjusted appropriately for each ear. The headset adaptor pin projected over the keyboard so a dual socket was needed for headsets to allow adult and child to hear instructions simultaneously.

In addition to physical and hardware modifications, the special-school staff used the SuccessMaker management system to modify session, wait and/or reflection times so that highly impulsive, distractible or anxious children, pupils with motor difficulties, and erratic children had a better chance of responding successfully to the SuccessMaker program.

There were some aspects of access to the ILS that it was not possible for schools to adapt. For example clumsy or motor-impaired children found that an accidental nudge on a neighbouring key meant that a key was wrongly entered. If the child did not position a cursor in exactly the correct position the response was interpreted by the machine as incorrect. Thus the machine appeared not to distinguish slightly inaccurate positioning from an incorrect response. Some children also had problems with the motor-eye co-ordination required and consequently found it difficult, for example, to count up an axis using the mouse.

In both schools the management system was used to switch off particular areas of work or the initial placement module. Issues about access raised questions about minimal competence levels required in terms of, for example comprehension, visual discrimination, attention and co-ordination before a child was likely to benefit from work on SuccessMaker.

Baseline skills

A checklist of baseline skills was devised which might be regarded as representing capabilities needed by a child before he or she could engage with the ILS programme. Special-school staff, particularly those working with younger children, found this to be useful in identifying which children were likely to benefit from SuccessMaker. The checklist comprised ten sections including sensitivity to sensory input, mechanical skills, visual perception, auditory perception, attention, ability to follow instructions, keyboard skills, understanding of the language of instruction and attitude to computer-based work. This list assumes that SuccessMaker is used primarily with cognitive aims in mind:

Provisional 'baseline' checklist concerning attitudes and understanding for pupils being considered for placement on SuccessMaker [* regarded as central or 'must haves' by school staff]

Sensory input
- Past getting sufficient reward from sensory aspects alone e.g. highlighting box/ playing with keys on keyboard.
- Recognises that lighted box does not necessarily signify the correct answer (because an area tends to light up automatically as the cursor crosses it).

Mechanics
- Able to place headset on correctly with ear pieces facing in.
- Able to check/plug in headset.
- Able to recognise if/when volume is appropriate.
- Able to position trackerball/mouse appropriately.
- Able to position self appropriately.

Visual perception
- Able to transfer visual attention from keyboard to screen and back frequently.
- Accurate visual perception of screen image e.g. seeing detail within a picture.

Auditory perception
- Able to interpret US accent at normal voice speed.

Attention
- Able to integrate visual and aural input (even if slightly mismatched/unconventional).

Concentration for 4 mins plus instruction.
- Able to attend to 1 part instruction.
- Able to recall 1 part instruction.
- Able to carry out 1 part instruction.
- Able to listen, wait, then act (inhibition).
- Recognises end of session and responds appropriately.

Keyboard skills
- Able to log on e.g. to type own 3 digit number and own first name.
- Knows how to use delete and/or backspace keys to 'rub out'.
- Able to use mouse/trackerball + switch or touchscreen.
- Understands link between screen image and trackerball/mouse movement.
- Can check/turn capital lock off (or this has been disabled by teacher/management system).

Task-specific skills
- Understands that whole prose passage must be read before questions are attempted.

Language of instruction
- Understands language of instruction e.g. 'mouse' (which may mean trackerball) 'click'.

Attitude
- Understands that computer game skills are not appropriate re ILS e.g. it is accuracy not speed of response which is crucial.

Able to work independently for 4 minutes
- Flexible approach to computer instructions, treated as problem-solving not dictates

Diagnostic use of SuccessMaker

SuccessMaker reportedly aided diagnosis of particular problems for individual children (notably mild visual or hearing impairments).Teachers were alerted to these when children reported being unable to hear headset sound or peered very closely at the monitor screen. It was noted that children known to have language processing problems had particular difficulties following aural instructions on SuccessMaker.

SuccessMaker reports were used to identify gaps in pupils' understanding and changes were made to classroom-based work on that basis. The following comments from teachers were typical and illustrate this point:

> 'It wasn't apparent to me that Emily had a significant difficulty with the concept of tens and units until this was highlighted by her low achievement on this area on the ILS. I am considering having a session a week where specific weaknesses highlighted by ILS can be addressed as I have seen how effective a tool it can be in this area.'

> '[ILS] highlighted visual and auditory discrimination skills as needing development. This information was passed to relevant teachers for appropriate help.'

> 'Michael came to this school only last year so as he spends more time with us we are finding out the problem areas in his learning.The ILS reports act as a quick, sure way to pinpointing an individual's problems unlike any general scheme of work would.'

The use made of such diagnostic information clearly depended in part on communication between staff with specialist expertise in using SuccessMaker who could decode reports and teachers who may have lacked such expertise, particularly in the early stages of using SuccessMaker. Capitalising on the diagnostic potential in SuccessMaker thus required relevant expertise among key staff as well as time for them to work with colleagues in decoding results.

It should be noted that there is a danger here of what Campione (1989) has referred to as the 'leap to instruction'. An apparent lack of attainment in a particular area may be indicative of a lack of ability to apply ideas not a lack of knowledge.

The SuccessMaker reports have the potential to be used to identify strengths but very few staff commented on using them in this way.

Language of instruction

The language of instruction, although potentially confusing on occasion, did not seem to present major difficulties for mainstream pupils with SEN with the exception of spelling, discussed below. However, it was sometimes inappropriate for special school pupils. Problems were encountered by some of these children, especially when new to the system, as a result of several factors:

Cultural factors

Pronunciation affected phonological tasks in which, for example, a rhyming sound in an US accent was not a rhyme in UK received pronunciation.

Nouns Differences between UK and US affected various tasks, especially phonological activities. For example, when instructed to: 'Mark the one beginning with C' the pupil might be shown a bed, a sweet (= candy) and a dog. Unless the pupil recognised that the sweet was a candy the task would be impossible. Similar problems arose with yarn, pitcher, and ladybugs. Several teachers drew attention to this but many of them also noted that these were not long term problems as the children began to recognise and use the US nouns:

'Imogen seems to have got used to the accent and words such as candy so [this] may have initially affected progress but she has overcome this and is now progressing well'

Phrasing of instructions sometimes caused difficulties, for example 'Make the small car be fourth' not 'Put it in fourth place':

Complexity and length of instructions
For example 'Match the ones with the lines touching the shape, not touching the shape, or passing through the shape'. This instruction contains 24 morphemes, and there are also six diagrams to scan.

Mismatch between instruction level and task level
Sometimes high instruction levels were paired with low task levels, for example, when a pupil was asked to 'add up the digits' and could do the task but did not understand the instruction. Conversely, sometimes low instruction levels were paired with high task levels, for example, 'put one more sock than shoes' which required a succession of comparative judgements.

Vocabulary
Use of formal terms for example, digit, plus, minus, capital, vowel', pupils with SEN may confuse more familiar with colloquial terms such as add, take away, big letters. There are arguments on both sides: for retaining simpler, but inaccurate terms, and for introducing more complex but accurate terms. Several teachers reported that the Americanisms and the formal language of ILS had compounded problems for children known to have language processing difficulties.

Pedagogical differences

For example, using letter names in early phonological exercises when the usual practice in the UK is to emphasise phonetic sounds.

Ambiguity in instructions

For example:

- 'Match the ones that are the same' when an array of two sets of three diagrams is shown. This was ambiguous as 'same' might have referred to various criteria (shape, size, position and so on). It was only when the wrong answer had been given that the instruction was clarified to 'Match the ones that look the same but are in different positions'.
- 'Write 1 and 2'. The ambiguity here was in whether the intention was for the child to complete an addition (add 1 + 2 = 3) or writing (write 1 then 2 giving 12) task. Several children were seen to respond to addition tasks as if they were writing tasks.

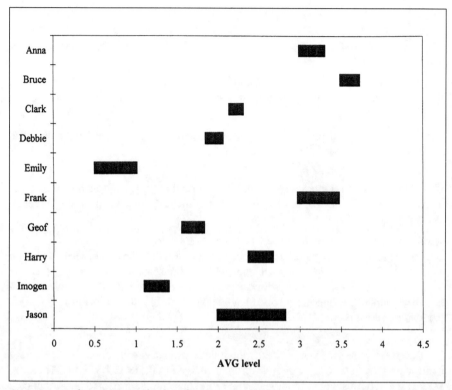

Figure 1: *Reading – AVG start levels and gains*

Results: Learning gains within SuccessMaker

AVG scores

SuccessMaker provides placement information and on-going assessments in terms of AVG levels. These represent US grade equivalents. For example, a grade level of 1.0 is supposed to correspond roughly to the level expected of an average six year old.

AVG data need to be treated cautiously as they *do not seem to be referenced to anything outside SuccessMaker* and it is not clear what the figures represent or whether they constitute a valid interval scale.

Gains within SuccessMaker cannot, from this study, be equated with gains outside the ILS. External standardised measures of reading and mathematics were not made because gains on such tests may not have been apparent in the comparatively short three month monitoring period and would have had a high margin of error. Virtually all the children made AVG gains equal to, or greater than, the three months, that is 0.25 of a year, spent on working on the ILS in the monitoring period.

Gains over three months ranged from 0.18 to 0.52 in reading (Figure 1) and from 0.25 to 0.71 in mathematics (Figure 2). Taken at face value these gains indicate good progress given that all the children had learning difficulties. Some children were making accelerated progress which, if generalisable, would diminish the gap between their levels and those of normal peers.

There was no relationship between start level and gains. In other words it was not the case that children who began with comparatively low levels (as measured in AVG terms)

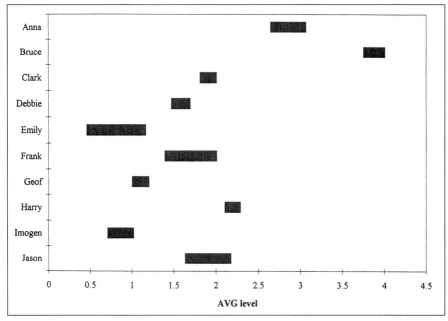

Figure 2: *Maths – AVG start levels and gains*

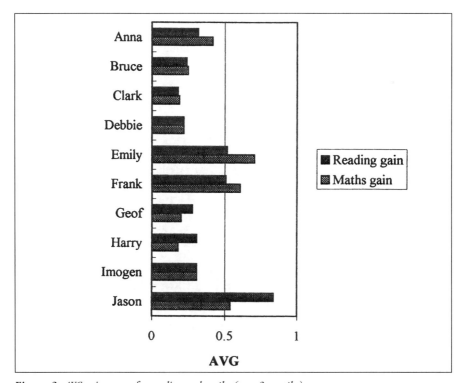

Figure 3: *AVG gain scores for reading and maths (over 3 months)*

made much greater progress than children beginning at a higher level. Interestingly, there was a strong relationship between reading gains and mathematics gains (Figure 3). This may indicate that some children were well-suited to this type of instructional style and so responded well across the subjects.

For special school pupils time on program was related to gains. This relationship did not hold for mainstream pupils with SEN; most of whom, having been on the system for two years, may have found the program more demanding or had been able to move ahead by building levels on some areas and scraping through on others. Over time, unless strands were switched off, such a strategy would become less workable and children would no longer be able to pull themselves ahead in this way.

Spelling was by far the least successful program. Both the older mainstream children were on a spelling program and both made minimal gains (+0.07) in spelling over the three month monitoring period. For whatever reason, this appeared to be the least successful of the SuccessMaker programs as assessed by the internal AVG outcomes.

Comparing AVG gains from all ten case study pupils, older pupils with moderate learning difficulties tended to gain most from the system. The younger pupils (mainstream and special school) tended to gain the least, in terms of AVG gains. Overall in the special school (using whole school data collected by the school) children with speech difficulties made the highest gains in mathematics. Intuitively, this makes sense in that the machine does not, unlike most classwork, require a spoken response and so may be particularly motivating for children with speech difficulties.

The second category of comparatively high gainers were children described as having a poor self-image, probably overlapping with the group with emotional and behavioural difficulties. The impersonal nature of learning through a computer-based package and the sense of starting with a clean sheet may be key factors in the comparative success of the ILS for these children. These points are discussed further below.

Cognitive strategies being employed by pupils

SuccessMaker did not distinguish between different types of errors made by children, and it is probably not feasible for such a system to do so. For example, one child made repeated errors counting nickels. He counted five individual nickel coins (totalling 25 cents) as five pennies/cents. To the system this answer was as wrong as a multiplication error, for example giving 24 as the answer. However, to the child this was a reasonable error but he appeared to gain no more credit for a reasonable error than for an unreasonable error such as a random guess. Thus the program appeared to encourage correct answers but not reasonable near-misses. In contrast, a human teacher would respond very differently to these two sorts of wrong responses. A related point was made by one teacher who was concerned about feedback concerning errors:

'Programs do not make it clear when a child is wrong. Raj thought that the correction was a different sum and continued to make the same mistakes until I intervened'.

Similarly, the program rewarded correct responses although these may have been inefficiently obtained. For example, a child could obtain a correct spelling through letter by letter copying. A more appropriate strategy would be grouping of word parts. So a child was inadvertently encouraged to take a safe but limited strategy, for example letter-by-letter copying of s-h-o-p, rather than approaches that were more strategic and hence more useful in the longer term although possibly incorrect, for example writing sh-u-p. A sense that children were learning procedures rather than strategies was reinforced in what they said about their errors. These were described in procedural terms for example, 'I clicked on the wrong box', rather than being task-related. Similarly one child, when asked about what he did in a session, said 'You push one of them things in the corner, one of them things what go on your belly (pointing to navel) and you get a white or a yellow or a nothing (referring to coloured ribbon shown on-screen when the correct answer is given)'.

Transfer of learning

There was anecdotal evidence for transfer of learning from SuccessMaker to classroom-based work. One teacher reported:

'Bruce's success, progress and confidence using the ILS have highlighted his increasing skills as an independent learner. I believe that experiences on the ILS have especially developed his reference skills so I have been giving him tasks to complete using the CD ROM – something I probably wouldn't have otherwise done'.

Conversely, some teachers were disappointed at the lack of transfer of skills from ILS to class-based work:

'The level of maths that ILS is giving Debbie she is able to do but she is performing the activities by rote. She still needs to use mechanical aids. It is not transferring skills learnt to classroom lessons'.

Awareness of transfer of skills between SuccessMaker and classroom based tasks will depend on how much communication there is between teachers. It is difficult in primary schools to make time for such work, but there were benefits when this was done because class teachers were able to utilise skills introduced in SuccessMaker.

There were concerns about transfer into classwork of inefficient or inappropriate learning strategies believed to have been learned, or reinforced, through SuccessMaker (such as routine carrying in tens and units, letter by letter copying in spelling tasks, and right to left eye movement in scanning tasks).

Some children were apparently able to do tasks on SuccessMaker which they were unable to do when presented as pencil and paper tasks after the session. An example was a child who correctly clicked on one fourth in mathematics exercises in Success-Maker but was confused about halves and quarters in subsequent pencil and paper tasks.

Some SuccessMaker activities were thought by teachers to be of questionable value in relation to the target skill (such as scrambled words in developing reading/spelling).

SuccessMaker worksheets were used in class or for homework to reinforce Success-Maker sessions. However, worksheet print size was too small for many pupils, especially in the special school. There were also difficulties with school printers coping with the demand (of time and resources) for large numbers of daily worksheets.

SuccessMaker sometimes influenced classroom practice directly. For example, one teacher's decision to change the curriculum to reflect SuccessMaker's earlier in-class introduction of phonological awareness. There are some interesting issues emerging concerning transfer of pedagogical style from SuccessMaker to general classroom work (for example use of praise as teachers began to use more positive feedback in class).

Motivation

Pupils were generally enthusiastic about SuccessMaker. Seven children who started at high levels sustained or increased enthusiasm for the ILS after three months. These children, showing impressive maturity, particularly liked the mixture of easy and hard work embodied in a session. Many teachers reported strong pupil enthusiasm for ILS:

'The ILS has been a great success for this child. Being able to put the headphones on and shut himself out of the classroom environment is very important to Richard. He needs the non-contact way of learning as he finds it difficult to relate to many adults'.

'Mandy really enjoys working on the ILS, it gives her quality individual learning time, and praise is given for each correct answer – this is very important for this child.'

Three children from the special school became less enthusiastic. Their reasons reflected a belief that their work was not improving. Several pupils with emotional and behavioural difficulties reported frustration at being given the same questions or questions regarded as too easy. Some teachers' reports reinforced these points:

'After initial interest in ILS Jason resented his classroom work being interrupted when it was his turn to use the program.'

'Geoff's motivation (for ILS) has decreased slightly. He is often distracted by other things going on in the classroom ... It very much depends on his mood.'

Sources of motivation

Learning style.

Seven of the ten case study pupils were described by their teachers as preferring a step-by-step, rather than holistic approach to learning. All six special-school pupils and one mainstream pupil were also described as impulsive in their learning style. These characteristics may make an ILS particularly suitable as it is likely to fit with step-by-step thinking and to curb impulsiveness.

Avoidance of writing

Children were not barred from a task through their inability to use writing as the vehicle to demonstrate learning. Four of the children spontaneously mentioned this as one reason for enjoying ILS.

Session variation

The curricular smorgasbord offered by SuccessMaker was popular with the children and regarded as motivating for them by their teachers. Children had little time to get bored with a particular type of task as the ILS usually dipped into a wide variety of tasks in a session. Several children, with impressive maturity, commented favourably on the mix of easy and hard work.

Game-style

The fun approach and silly reinforcement were liked by all the children. All gave the ILS the top rating for fun on a four point scale at both the start and the end of the monitoring period.

Privacy

Attitude scale results showed that all the children particularly liked the fact that (as they believed) other children did not know how well or otherwise they were doing on the program. In the mainstream school, children thought of as being good at SuccessMaker by classmates were often judged to be so on the basis of time on the machine. Little time on SuccessMaker was equated with cleverness. 'I'm not so good as Peter. He only has to do one piece of work on it and I have to do two'. Mainstream children latched on to this in the absence of other obvious cues (other than topping out on successfully completing a module) to show comparisons with peers. 'Topping out' may have acquired particular salience because it was one of the few cues available to show where classmates were on the program.

The use of a server system in a central resource room curtailed children's ability to see what other children were doing on SuccessMaker. Older special-school children who used a classroom-based machine for their ILS work gave detailed accounts of the types of tasks carried out by classmates on SuccessMaker and, despite the use of headsets in the classroom, were aware of perceived relative positions.

Demotivating aspects

Repetition

While repetition of material was consistently liked by some children – notably those with mild or moderate learning difficulties – it was seen as an irritation by others. Several reported this in interviews; in observations they were noted frequently complaining to the machine saying, for example, 'I know I know you just told me that'.

One child, working through a problem was told by the system: 'Type a number to make the sentence true. 5 is less than what?' (child types correct answer input) '5 is less than 6. Let's check the number line. You were right 5 is less than 6'. The child began muttering 'I know that, I just done that'. This is problematic because such reinforcement cannot be done in a formulaic way. What works for one child may not work for another; what works one day is too slow on another day. For special school pupils such irritation may go alongside dyspraxic or co-ordination problems which require the child to have comparatively long response times. For pupils with emotional and behavioural difficulty, reiteration of correct responses sometimes triggered distractibility.

Errors, especially apparently random/unexplained/unexpected errors

Several children were confused about the source of errors. This led them to try randomly for correct answers and then to be frustrated by repeated errors: 'I don't want to get it wrong that many times' (Harry, second observation). The fact that sometimes a child could only work out what answer was intended by guessing and making errors first, reinforced a sense that guessing was an appropriate strategy and correct answers were indeed attributable to luck. Several children explicitly stated that correct answers on SuccessMaker were the result of a lucky guess.

Enforced slow pace while responding

Being forced to slow down, for example, having to read through a passage of text before responding to comprehension questions was found to be frustrating. One child from the mainstream school said that she had problems reading a passage because reading the passage took too long. Four of the children reported disliking the slow pace at times.

Knowledge of results

The children, particularly those with emotional and behavioural difficulties, were very conscious of their results on SuccessMaker, especially wrong responses. They called up the report screen significantly more often after making an error than after correct responses. In post-session interviews these children were also very accurate in their recall of numbers but not types of errors made. They were vociferous in expressing irritation at being told how many errors they had made.

Cultural mismatch

For several children the error analysis suggested that problems with US pronunciation and terms seemed to be a factor in atypical low scores in some skills (for example auditory discrimination) and so distorted pupil scores. One child had increasing difficulties with spelling and, unusually, began using the audio repeat extensively (more than 50 per cent of the time). Her spelling difficulties may have been compounded by the US pronunciation. Her error analysis over three months showed increasingly erratic spelling errors and a move away from phonetically regular attempts towards nonphonetic, or single letter only, attempts.

Similarly, for several children the error analysis showed that US money was a consistent and atypical source of error. This was an area of concern for some of the class teachers who felt that it was inappropriate that a child having difficulty grasping the English money system should have to work with US currency. The next version of SuccessMaker in which the US money elements can be turned off will avoid this problem.

Self esteem

The case study children ranged, on a standardised self-esteem scale (Maines and Robinson 1993) from very low (one child) to high (three children) with the rest being low (two children) or normal (four children). The extremes were found among the special-school group. Predictably there was little change in self-esteem levels in the short monitoring period. There was no association between level of self-esteem and progress on SuccessMaker.

The children were extremely accurate in their recall of correct and incorrect responses in sessions as well as in recalling broad areas of difficulty such as finding the comprehension strand difficult.

Self regulation

On the standardised measure of independence in learning there was a slight shift towards children moving from normal to internal locus of control for both school groups. This finding supports the teachers' views that SuccessMaker encouraged children to be more independent and self-regulated in their learning. SuccessMaker was seen by many staff as fostering autonomy and independence in learning. These were regarded as particularly important benefits for pupils with emotional and behavioural difficulties and for mainstream children with impulsive behaviours.

Children's attitudes to work on SuccessMaker had made many staff reconsider the extent to which children might be given more autonomy in managing their learning. Special-school children seemed to perceive their work on SuccessMaker to be technology-bound; that is they did not use external resources such as pencil and paper for rough working out, to help them with a task. Many of these children either did not reorganise peripherals to allow them to work comfortably or were slow to do so. For example, some children did not move the trackerball/mouse to their preferred side; or they wore headphones without connecting these to the machine.

At the most basic level, each child had some autonomy on the ILS as soon as he/she could log on independently. This was not a problem for mainstream children. Most of the special-school children were able to do this using a three letter number code plus first name. An overlay with a sequence of coloured blobs to push was planned as an alternative for children who had difficulty logging on. The system needed to be simple enough for these children to manage it successfully but sufficiently tamper-proof to prevent children deliberately or otherwise logging on in another child's name. Autonomy on the system may encourage children to play around, for example playing with the on-screen protractor and ruler.

Some children with emotional and behavioural difficulties were found to be so adult-dependent that it was not sufficient for the system to move them on. They still needed a nod of approval from the teacher at frequent intervals to sustain work on SuccessMaker. Teachers felt that SuccessMaker was a valuable tool in weaning children off dependency on teacher feedback. This applied to special school and younger mainstream children.

Conclusions and some wider issues

Overall, SuccessMaker's approach was liked by pupils with special educational needs and by their teachers; the reservations were about content. The enthusiasm it generated is a major asset for pupils who have had sometimes prolonged experience of school failure.

All children made good gains in learning in terms defined within the program (AVG gains). It is not possible in this small scale and short-term study to establish whether these were generalised outside the program or sustained over time.

There was some evidence that children were learning procedural rather than strategic rules and this warrants more examination.

Behavioural and attitudinal changes, towards greater autonomy and self-confidence in learning, may be particularly important benefits of an ILS for this target group. It would be valuable to ascertain how various ILS and other approaches compare in this respect.

The system required considerable skill and expertise (plus the time and training to acquire these) from specialist staff within the schools. Judgements about whether the use of an ILS program is the best use of such scarce resources is beyond the scope of this study.

There are complex issues concerning expertise in using and controlling Success-Maker. The system needs at least one or two well trained managers in a school who have a good understanding of how it works and can use the management system appropriately. However, if such individuals are seen as the sole recipients of this knowledge then it disempowers other staff. When expertise is gradually devolved to other staff, made easier through in-class use of SuccessMaker, then there are considerable benefits. Success-Maker can be used as a vehicle for more generalised IT training and to overcome teacher apprehension about IT.

<table>
<tr><td>CHAPTER
11</td><td># *Able students working in ILS environments*</td></tr>
</table>

Susan Rodrigues

This chapter is about thirteen able secondary students working with ILS. Seven students attended a school where SuccessMaker was used for mathematics and English, and six students attended a school where the Global Maths system was used for mathematics. The chapter shows how students' attitudes towards, and their perceptions of, ILS developed. It presents excerpts of tasks and interactions in which these students were engaged while working within ILS environments. The students' interactions and perceptions are considered and the models of learning implied by each ILS were studied.

The ILS project adopted teachers' conceptions of ability which varied between the two schools. In the school using SuccessMaker the students had been successful in a verbal reasoning test and were set according to their scores on the 12-plus selection test. The cohort of seven able students had verbal reasoning scores in the range of 225-250; in addition to using the verbal reasoning test, teachers at the school using SuccessMaker also tested some students' imaginative and creative abilities.

The Global system was used in a boys' school where, for mathematics, students were grouped by mathematical ability. Six of the Year 10 students from the highest set were selected by their teacher as able, based on their mathematical ability and, in some cases, their IT expertise.

Students' attitudes toward the ILS

Students had been using SuccessMaker for longer than two months and in general they had positive attitudes toward ILS. They perceived the system to be enjoyable and fun because they were using computers, although for some able students the novelty was beginning to diminish. Though the students were still keen to work with ILS, none of them said they would extend the time they spent on the ILS system.

In contrast, able students using the Global system were vociferous about their dissatisfaction with ILS, and very critical of the Global system's ability to meet their needs. Richard, a student, summed up the views of his peers:

> 'I think it's very good for people who need confidence in maths and people who go at a slower rate but for our level I don't really think it's that suitable. It doesn't stretch you. It is not challenging enough. Good for people who need that sort of pace, but for us, who know most of the stuff already, it gets a bit exasperating at times. ... I am not sure on an academic level whether I would stick it out! I'm not sure whether I would actually use this for revision at all. Because I think it would take too long.'

The students using SuccessMaker were more positive about the system. Some believed it provided them with opportunities to work privately and helped them learn. For example Suni said:

'You learn more things.... more spellings, more maths, more English and everything.'

However, some of the students using SuccessMaker were concerned about certain aspects of ILS:

'You can make very simple mistakes and it will take it as wrong. Because the computer doesn't think.' (Jon)

'...like with the division in maths, I know how to do it a different way, but it is like it sort of teaches you how to do it a completely different way.'(Sally)

'We keep on getting the same questions over and over again. ...it is boring.' (Zina)

In general, students using SuccessMaker were more motivated toward ILS than those using the Global system. However, there was one aspect common to both cohorts of students. If the ILS problem was seen to be less polished than the students' own level of understanding or the context was inappropriate or more confusing, the able student was more likely to have negative attitudes toward ILS, was unlikely to be motivated to use the ILS, and had even less chance of learning.

The learning process requires students to reflect on past experiences and their prior knowledge, to help them make sense of current stimuli. When working on the ILS systems, students used existing knowledge to help them make sense of problems posed by the system, but the ILS worked on an assumption that there was only one approach to problem solving and that appropriate contexts were not an issue.

For students working with the SuccessMaker system this was not overly problematic, for the system would accept the students' answers. Although it might take them through a different methodology it did not penalise them for using their experiences. However, the students using Global were penalised: if their prior experiences did not match those expected by the computer and consequently they were denied success. Able students were likely to contest the computer response, especially when the problems posed were arithmetically simple and when the context cued them into believing the conceptual demand was low level. Consequently, able students working with the Global system developed less positive attitudes than students working with the SuccessMaker system. As a result students' existing problem solving strategies were insufficiently influenced by the ILS systems.

As Carey (1986) has stated, influencing student concepts sufficiently to promote conceptual change has proved to be rather difficult. In the case of ILS, the conceptual change may have failed for two main reasons: the student's ideas were not considered or challenged and/or the student had their own successful methods of problem solving and their own valued explanations. If learning is viewed as conceptual change, then ILS has to encourage students to review their existing ideas. Posner, Strike, Hewson and Gertzog (1982) have suggested that four key factors are necessary if new concepts are to be assimilated or accommodated into a student's existing schema. These factors are: dissatisfaction, intelligibility, plausibility and fruitfulness.

Dissatisfaction occurs when students are unhappy with their existing ideas because they present insurmountable barriers and difficulties. Students have unsolved problems and they have lost some degree of faith in the ability of their current concepts to deal with the problem satisfactorily. The second factor, intelligibility, requires students to be able to understand the new concept. The concept has to be easy to follow, to enable students to understand it and to reformulate an internal representation to depict this new understanding. The third factor, plausibility, requires students to believe in the new concept or the new concept must appear reasonable. It has to make sense. Plausibility is a result of the perceived consistency with other concepts held by the student. Finally, if the concept is to be used it has to be fruitful, that is students have to be able to use these new concepts to explain ideas that the old concepts could not address. A new concept has to offer something new that is of value.

> 'The authority of the teacher and the credibility arising from use of the computer and text books, are all conducive to promoting plausibility, whereas dissatisfaction and fruitfulness are harder to achieve' (White and Gunstone 1989).

However, the ILS used by the able students struggled to meet some or all of the four criteria described. The majority of the students had existing ideas that were not challenged by the ILS, so many of them experienced no dissatisfaction with their own ideas. Also the mathematics concept on Global gave an impression of being simple, and in some cases was simple, so students were even less inclined to alter their existing successful, in-class, strategies. Sometimes the contexts provided did not make the concepts seem plausible or intelligible. In these circumstances, there was no basis on which new concepts could appear fruitful.

To illustrate this dilemma more clearly here is an example of one student's progression through one session on the ILS. Brian was working on the Global system at level 8. According to his teacher, he was expected to get an A in his forthcoming GCSE, and was considered to have good problem solving skills and to be generally intelligent. While Brian was working on the system, I sat alongside him and noted and taped his interactions as he worked. Occasionally he was asked to explain what he was doing. The transcripts provided are presented with a commentary to provide the context:

Transcript	Commentary
R *What is this one about?*	Brian was asked about the specific question he was working on.
B *I'm not sure at the moment. ...Use all the items to design your garden.*	
R *What items?*	He read aloud.
B *I don't know.*	
R *So why did you click OK then if you didn't know?*	The screen is divided with a vertical line. In one half is a green patch, in the other are paving stones, fences etc.
B *5 panels at.... (stopped reading aloud)*	Brian clicked the OK button and concentrated on the next question that appeared on the screen. He muttered and keyed in an answer. The computer said try again.

Brian had ignored the context of the question and rushed into what he perceived was the real mathematics. In the process he missed information that might have been of some use to him but, more importantly, the context did not make the question intelligible. The following transcript is from the same ILS session and still involves Brian.

Transcript	Commentary
R *Now I don't understand what you are doing.*	The next question on the screen was a simple arithmetic calculation which Brian started to read aloud. Then he keyed in a figure, and as he did so, he explained what he was doing. The figure on screen was £5.69 and the screen instructions were to use rough estimates.
B *Suppose your garden uses two panels, each one costs, 'cause you need to use two panels. Each one costs £5. If you say roughly £5.70 and if you want to use two of them, so it is two of £5.70, £11.40. Is it? Yeah? No! That is wrong, cause it just said it is!*	
R *I know. Why, why do you think it is wrong though?*	Having calculated his rough estimate he keyed in £11.40 and was astounded when the computer told him to try again.
B *'Cause it, too close, probably. Because they probably want you to use £6 or something.*	He decided he must have been too accurate.
R *Oh right, right. Because it said a rough estimate.*	Meanwhile he was already keying in a new response.
B *Hmm! Different. I'll just try again and see what happens. See what it wants me to do. ....*	He laughed when the computer told him to try again. In frustration he escaped to the beginning of the programme. He read the screen aloud. It told him to use one significant figure.
R *So why didn't it take it the first time you put it in?*	
B *Because it was too close. Because I put 5, so it must have been to £6 but when I put that. Round off to one significant figure.*	Once again he keyed in the information, once again he was unsuccessful and once again he laughed, although this time it was in disgust.

The question was not intelligible and caused immense frustration because of the simplicity of the arithmetic. Brian's own problem solving skills and his own answers, which seemed perfectly plausible, were not being accepted. This was a common problem for all six able students working with the Global system. Their answers were often more detailed or accurate than required by the system. Consequently the system rejected their responses and did not make explicit how these students could have their response validated. Asking these students to discard their sophisticated mental models was resulting in frustration.

Also asking for rough estimates did not allow for a range of correct responses. The help provided, suggesting the use of one significant figure, did not specify whether the initial figures, or the answer, or both, were to be rounded to one significant figure. Consequently, students were not only dissatisfied with the new problem solving experience, but felt the system was incoherent and implausible. From a research point of view it was difficult to determine whether the system was assessing students' mathematical ability or their ability to interpret the question.

Brian had finally escaped from the task, gone back to the main screen to seek help and then returned to the same level. The computer provided a similar question to the one he had been set earlier. This one was about five panels costing £11.25 each. The computer asked what was the cost of five panels and once again the screen said to use rough estimates. After no success Brian sought help and clicked on to the first aid symbol. The help again suggested using one significant figure and once more Brian tried to key in an answer. Once again it was not accepted and he made another attempt:

Transcript	Commentary
R *It is just not very keen on accepting your answers. Is it?*	Talks aloud as he keys in.
B *No. Try 50. Try 50 Oh! Wow!*	The computer accepts his answer much to his surprise.
R *Now why do you think it did that?*	He has finally deduced that the computer wants the rough estimate to start with one significant figure. He thought he had finally interpreted the computer's problem solving model.
B *Cause they wanted the, basically not even to one significant figure!*	
R *But then why didn't it take ...*	
B *It's wrong. Cause they wanted the estimate to begin with for the original so it couldn't be 11 or 12. It would have had to have been 10.*	

Brian moved on to the next question which was very similar in concept. Unfortunately, once again Brian had little success and his newly-found insight, that the system wanted one significant figure, was not fruitful:

Transcript	Commentary
B *Suppose you had to lay 39 paving stones. Paving stones using the 7.28 is closer to 10 so 400. No! 390. Oh no, that has to be to, umm, basically because this, it was a bit weird before. You know, I'll round that down to 5, it is closer, so, 40 times 5, try. No!*	He read the question aloud and keyed in 400. His reasoning was that 39 was closer to 40 and 7.28 was closer to 10. He tried again. Once again an incorrect message and a request to try again. So he rounded up 39 to 40 and decided that 7.28 was closer to 5.
R *OK, why did you round it up to 40 and why did you round the other number down to 5?*	With persuasion he decided to try 7 and 40 and keyed in 280. Once again he was judged incorrect and the computer provided the expected response: 300. It required one significant figure at the end of the problem as well. Brian was still bemused.
B *Because £7.28 is closer to 5 then it is to 10*	
R *Why not just closer to 7?*	
B *Because, yeah, I suppose so, but it says rough estimate. Estimate. So, and they haven't really accepted it so close in the other two. I'll do 7! 300? Hmm?*	

Brian was not receiving any credit for his responses, which he knew were plausible. However, what he had noted was a pattern in the question pairs, and this deduction became apparent when he instantly resolved the next problem in the question pair. Two questions had been presented for every level he had tried so far. When the next question in his current pair appeared, instead of calculating the answer, Brian resorted to a process of elimination. He had keyed in the answer before I was even able to read the first line of the problem and he had got it right!

Brian explained that the two previous questions had exactly the same numerical answer and he then theorised that each pair of questions on any one screen had the same numerical answer. He had got the answer for the first question wrong several times but the computer had finally provided the correct response, so he simply keyed the computer provided answer from the first question as the answer for the second. It was correct. He was jubilant.

Brian had persevered, although whether this was due to the fact that an observer was present cannot be determined, for many of the other students did opt out. As Brian explained:

> 'You think, oh, how am I going to do this and then you just think, oh, I'll go out of it and you just go onto another one, like another level.'

Brian's view of the Global system was supported by his peers, for example Sukhpal said:

> '...it is a bit weird, because it told me to give it the answer, and I gave the answer about three times and then it gave the answer but it was to two decimal places. But it didn't tell you anything about that. ... [There were] not many questions. There was only about one or two questions in this thing and they were quite easy. ... You need more questions really. A few hard questions to do... It is not exciting, but, sometimes it is frustrating.... like it is not even interesting.'

Sukhpal did not think the questions themselves were difficult. The difficulty lay with interpreting the question, because the contexts were causing problems as they provided insufficient information about the degree of accuracy required. Furthermore, the mathematical concepts within the questions were lacking challenge, as Matthew commented:

> 'And it's sometimes too easy. ...some of the questions are really stupid like, what's the area of a square where the sides are four by four. ...It is not actually continuing with what we are doing, (in class) you know. (It is) more of a 'mucking about on the computer' lesson.'

In line with this theme of poor explanations and few examples, there was also an issue of expectation and alignment with the standards/levels of classroom mathematics. The students perceived some discrepancy in the levels on the ILS, as Stephen said:

> 'Most of it is quite easy.... some of the higher levels are easier than you expect them to be. ...They could have a lot more examples. In some cases there is no explanation at all on what to do.'

As a consequence of all these issues, the Global system appeared to be erratic and incoherent. Although the questions were simple enough the guidelines provided were insufficient. Thus the degree of difficulty was not due to the conceptual understanding required, but due to the presentation of the problem itself. Whereas a less able student might have chalked this up to experience, and/or accepted it as a failing on their part, the more able student was likely to question the response and to become disenchanted with the system and consequently less motivated to use it.

For many academically able students their existing experiences and beliefs have enabled them to make sense of new information and rapidly make progress through the schooling process. Often this progress is commended, the success acclaimed, and the expertise noted. For these students the expectation is one of success. Hence to be faced with simple arithmetic, and to be told that their answers were wrong, did not endear the ILS to these students. Neither did the system disqualify their original strategy or challenge it sufficiently to extend their existing problem-solving repertoire. As White and Gunstone (1989) have suggested, if the students' original problem-solving methods were shown to have flaws or could be further developed, then they might be disillusioned with their existing strategies. This changing of the status of the concepts held, lowering or raising them, would be crucial. The more often the students strategies are successful the greater the confidence they have in them.

For the students using the Global systems the status of their existing concepts increased and the ILS was found wanting as it failed to meet some problems or present successful new strategies. Furthermore, the system was seen to be too extreme, as Brian explained:

'it's either really impossible and doesn't show you ...how you actually work it out or it's just completely easy'.

Some of the students using the SuccessMaker system also thought the US approach was problematic, even though the mathematics concepts being promoted were easy. For example Helen said;

'because the Americans they do different sums, they work it out different to us,'

All the able students using the SuccessMaker system recognised this difference in approach. For example Suni stated:

'I find some of it frustrating, 'cause it is like easy, but it just takes ages to do something about it. Just the way they do their sums, like they make it longer, harder. It is not harder because it is difficult, just hard because they take the long way round and I don't understand how they do it and I know the answer'.

A view endorsed by Sally who said:

'like with the division in maths, I know how to do it a different way, but it is like it sort of teaches you how to do it a completely different way'.

However, unlike the older able students using the Global system, the SuccessMaker students adopted the US system for ILS use and used their own models during their classroom lessons. Consequently they operated under two different schemes.

The contexts in which concepts were embedded were seen to be instrumental in influencing the students' perceived value of the ILS. All the Global users commented on inappropriate contexts and intimated that the software would be more suitable to lower ability students and younger children. For example, Stephen said:

'The graphics are a bit childish... you could probably learn a lot more from a text book. This is childish. Well like elephants go to estate agents, it is not really realistic'.

The reward system and the demonstrations were often ignored as the students sought the real mathematics. In contrast the only contextual concern on the SuccessMaker system was the US jargon used.

'It is American and you have to get into the like their way, the American style and their way of doing everything. There is a certain way in the spelling that you have to know...and then they use cents and dimes and all that'.

Overall the US context did not appear to affect the students to such a detrimental extent as the Global system.

Implications for able students

ILS use a mastery approach to learning, in which each student is provided with a series of tasks to master to make progress to the next series of tasks. The tasks are normally sequenced according to an expert's notion of hierarchical difficulty and the assumption is that with correct teaching and sequencing the student will be able to master the concepts and hence make progress. Progress is ascertained through criterion-referenced assessment. Consequently, learning should occur through well-designed teaching based on learning hierarchies (White 1973). Most ILS are underpinned by this reasoning.

There is a conflict between this and current cognitive theories of learning. Current theory expects students to construct their knowledge. Students are thought to achieve conceptual development through social interactions with their environment and through reflecting on personal experiences. Therefore it is not so much the teacher or computer who has the ultimate responsibility for conceptual development but the student who has to develop and employ higher order learning skills.

Cognitive theory contends that students need to construct and reflect on their learning, in effect to take control of their learning. The ILS provided algorithms which the student needed to understand and repeat in order to progress. The intention was to maximise performance by striving for a predetermined end. This in effect meant that the student had to understand the computer's algorithm and then match it in order for them to be deemed successful. For an able student, especially a secondary age student, this is problematic as the students have been acclaimed for the outcomes of their own mental models. Instead of having these outcomes validated, the student is forced into a situation that requires them to represent differently that which is already known to them.

To a certain extent this could be useful in promoting higher order learning but in practice it tended to be perceived by the students as a fruitless exercise. A couple of students using SuccessMaker said the system taught them to do mathematics the US way and as a consequence encouraged them to rethink, although they knew the answer. They couldn't use their own strategy on the computer because it would not accept it and marked it wrong.

Students working on SuccessMaker had developed strategies which helped them cope with the US nature of the system. Even so, they were frustrated by the different approaches of the ILS system, especially as it did not match their own, and in their everyday school life they were used to being successful. Consequently, some students were observed having deduced the answer to a question almost instantly, but working in reverse to sort out a methodology that matched what was expected by the ILS.

Conclusions

This small scale research study details some of the strengths and constraints of current integrated learning systems, especially when working with able students to support conceptual development. The study suggests that:

- ILS need to challenge students' concepts more effectively and present new learning in a manner which is intelligible, plausible and fruitful for the student.
- It is difficult to provide contexts which are appropriate to able students which they will consider relevant to their age and maturity.
- The steps within ILS need to be carefully determined and test questions need to be carefully worded because (a) able students are very perceptive regarding the

appropriateness of the level of work they, and others, are being asked to complete, and (b) able students are also very astute at determining patterns; and if there are simple patterns to the test questions to be discovered, they will more than likely discover and exploit them.

- The number of questions relating to each concept needs to be increased to provide students with opportunities to demonstrate newly gained insights and problem-solving strategies.
- ILS which allow students to opt out easily result in incomplete assessment records. When students find the ILS to be incoherent, ambiguous and of little further use to their academic study, they opt out.
- ILS models need to take into account a range of possible mental models or problem-solving strategies, in order to validate the able child's response, rather than expect the able child to validate the computer's model through exact matching.

Effective teaching is assumed to mean employing strategies which meet the needs of the student and enable students to develop transferable intellectual concepts and skills as well as social skills. If ILS is to be effective, it too must employ strategies which meet the needs of the student, rather than the student having to meet the strategies of the machine. This includes meeting the needs of the able student.

The use of ILS by pupils for whom English is a second language

Colin Harrison

Bilingual learners and ILS: what are the issues?

Colleagues who do not work closely with pupils for whom English is a second or additional language (E2L) sometimes make the understandable assumption that these pupils form if not a homogeneous group at least a group about which broad generalisations might be made concerning likely educational needs. Such an assumption might spring from a sympathetic awareness of the need to take account of cultural and linguistic diversity, and a recognition that it is essential to plan and resource the needs of E2L pupils so as to offer appropriate differentiation in areas such as subject knowledge, language knowledge and motivation.

This chapter outlines educational theory and reports research findings on the use of ILS by pupils for whom English is a second or additional language. First, it is important to emphasise that making generalisations about the needs of E2L pupils is extraordinarily difficult. The most important reason for this is the diversity of the group. One London school which I visited reported that in a single year group there were children who between them had the following home languages: Amharic, Arabic, Bengali, Creole, Egalu, English, Eritrean, Farsi, French, Greek, Gujerati, Hausa, Hindi, Kutchi, Persian, Portuguese, Punjabi, Pushto, Somali, Swahili, Tamil, Twi, Turkish, Urdu and Yoruba. Eighty per cent of the school population was bilingual. Within this language community were pupils who had been in England since birth and who were fluently bilingual or trilingual; other pupils had been in England just a few weeks. Of those who had been born outside the UK, some had attended school for as many years as their English counterparts before coming to England, and had been doing more homework than their English counterparts during that period; others had come from areas in which formal schooling was not available at all. Some children had come to the school from a stable political situation, but others had arrived in England after having suffered years of trauma as a result of civil unrest or war.

In considering the need for a teacher to take account of individual differences, there is the delicate matter of the interaction between learners' intelligence and their language knowledge. Of course, a teacher needs to take account of previous learning and background knowledge, but to even use the term intelligence is to invite a challenge from some groups, who too often see it as a crude attempt to stereotype, often with a perspective which is at best negative towards minority groups or at worst racist.

In short, therefore, it is very difficult to make generalisations about the learning and learning needs of E2L pupils. I shall attempt some generalisations - this, after all, is one reason for carrying out research - but they will be guarded ones.

A further reason for being cautious about making generalisations about E2L pupils relates to how teachers approach the issue of meeting such pupils' needs. In talking with teachers about E2L pupils and ILS my experience has been that the more experienced they are in dealing with the needs of E2L pupils, the more likely they are to conceptualise the pupils' learning needs in a manner which does not highlight E2L as an issue, at least for the majority of pupils. The more experienced the teacher, the less likely they are to see the second language issue as a problem, it is simply one part of the make-up of a child, whose needs have to be met taking account of dozens of factors. This is not to say that experienced teachers were unaware of the issue, but rather that they tended to see it in individual rather than in general terms.

In one school I visited, I asked the head of mathematics whether E2L was an issue in a Year 10 class which had a population of 70 per cent south Asian language speakers. She replied, 'I can't really say. I've only really got one E2L pupil, a Japanese pupil, and it's not a problem for her'. The language needs of the other bilingual pupils in the class were part of that teacher's everyday planning, but she did not perceive meeting those needs as a problem.

Having indicated the need for caution, however, it clearly is the case that pupils who come to a classroom with less English than their classmates need learning support of various kinds, and one question this chapter addresses is whether ILS can provide some of that support.

In the primary schools I visited, where a significant proportion of the pupils were bilingual, it was not felt that bilingual pupils coped less well than their monolingual peers with ILS. One teacher, commenting on the SuccessMaker program, which had been used in his school with Year 6 and Year 7 pupils, said that ILS was 'a big benefit' and that 'the biggest gain in ILS was in self-organisation'. In his view, it helped the children to become well organised and they were highly motivated to use the system, because it enabled them to be 'on task at their own level'. I asked this teacher whether Success-Maker was reliable at pitching work at the appropriate level for children for whom English was a second language. He replied that this had not shown itself to be a problem.

Not every primary school has found that ILS increases pupil autonomy, however. In another primary school I visited, where Global English and mathematics were in use, the teachers felt that the E2L issue was not a separate factor in evaluating ILS, but they were somewhat indifferent towards the system. This was for two reasons: first, they felt that the children were not able to work independently because when they encountered a new topic they needed too much help from the teacher; second, the content of the Global English did not overlap with the school's own curriculum and values in English teaching, and was perceived as arbitrary and dull.

What both these primary schools had in common was that the teachers' evaluation of the systems did not identify E2L as a separate issue. However, the schools did not share a common view of the potential of ILS for those children. In one school ILS was seen as beneficial for all pupils; in the other, one teacher said of ILS, 'Why are we using this incredibly expensive technology to be so boring?'

In the secondary schools I visited there were similarly polarised views, but at secondary level teachers felt that E2L threw up a range of issues and challenges which were different from those related to other types of need. In the London school mentioned earlier, there were a number of pupils whose English had been classified by the local authority as being at beginner level, and this had major implications for their autonomy of learning as well as for the content of what was taught. The teacher with responsibility for special needs in this school put a great deal of time into organising the administration, record keeping and maintenance of the SuccessMaker system, and was confident that even though the learning gains recorded were sometimes limited the ILS system was of great value as a survival package which could be used with pupils with very different levels of subject knowledge and knowledge of English.

Bilingual pupils' progress on ILS

Consider the following notes on Waseem (all names have been changed to protect anonymity), a Year 9 pupil, who had been assessed at beginner level in English by the local authority, and who had only been in England a few weeks when this record was compiled:

> Initial Placement Level in Maths 5.2; now 5.25 after 3:08 hours (41 sessions). A frequent crasher of the system. Needs close supervision. Just begun to get into the work recently, and is settling down to the work. Is getting the hang of the money questions, using the card with US money on it. He has not used the help facility, but the timed-out switch has been activated by the system to help him with calculating means and averages. He has now recognised and can use the word average. There are definite problems here. At level 5.2 the language demands are (understandably) great and progress is likely to be less than dramatic. For instance, using the glossary is difficult if you are unsure of alphabetical order. Working through these things with the pupil is therefore essential, in order to assist in developing independence. There are perhaps other cultural differences in how mathematics is done in other countries. (Another teacher has commented that Waseem seems to use logic in unfamiliar ways.) In reading, his initial placement level was 2.84; after 12 sessions, total length of time 40 mins, he is at 2.85. This suggests that little is being achieved currently.

These notes might suggest that little or no progress was being made, but gains in unit level scores are not the only basis on which a teacher might decide that a pupil is profiting from working on ILS. A 13 year old might have quite an extensive knowledge of mathematics, but would not progress at first because of his lack of English (not to mention an unfamiliarity with the dollars and cents of the SuccessMaker system); level 5.2 represents a mathematics level rather higher than that achieved by most pupils in this special needs class, and it would therefore not be surprising if learning remained on a plateau before it speeded up again.

Another point made by the class teacher was that ILS offered Waseem more regular access to differentiated individual work than was possible in classes of 30 pupils in normal lessons. On the basis of his observations, the head of special needs was confident that Waseem was gaining from the ILS work, although this would not have been the case had individual support from the teacher not been available at the terminal.

Compare the notes on Waseem, who had only recently arrived in England, with those on Neetim, a pupil who arrived in England one year earlier and had also initially been assessed as being at beginner level in English:

> Neetim has spent 18 hours 23 minutes on mathematics over 272 sessions, which is very high, but he has made good progress: 3.73 up to 5.37, a gain of 20 months over 15 months. This is quite good progress. Neetim is quite good at telling the teacher

if he accidentally crashes (which is easily done – a mouse click in the wrong screen zone can bounce you out of the system and into Windows). In reading, Neetim has gone from 2.80 to 4.26 (a gain of 18 months). This again seems to be a reasonable amount of progress, given that Neetim is not a very able pupil.

The teacher who made these notes was well aware that interpreting gain scores on ILS systems was problematic, and that to represent the numerical scores in months or years might not be reliable or valid. Nevertheless, in his experience the scores did have some validity and were very useful in providing both teacher and pupil with some objective evidence of Neetim's progress. In this school, therefore, it was felt that while ILS was not specifically targeted at the needs of bilingual learners, the system offered useful, differentiated opportunities for learning, which added a helpful dimension to the provision available through other parts of the curriculum of the school.

What sort of language development is needed for bilingual learners? A contrasting view

A rather different approach to evaluating ILS at secondary level came from another school. Here a number of teachers began by considering the question of what sort of language experiences should be offered to pupils who were not yet fluently bilingual, and for whom English was a second language. Their conclusion was that ILS did not offer the appropriate experiences. These teachers made the point that evaluating the effectiveness of ILS for E2L pupils was a complex matter.

One of the school's language support specialists talked to me about plans by one company to include digitised speech in Urdu on a CD-ROM to support pupils from minority groups. In her view, while this might be well-intentioned and creative, the problem was that while the school had 70 per cent of pupils whose home language was from the Asian sub-continent, not all pupils from minority groups spoke Urdu, and others would be familiar only with a dialect form.

The head of English was also cautious about the potential of ILS for assisting the language development of E2L pupils. She was enthusiastic about implementing new technology into English lessons, especially in the areas of word processing, drafting and redrafting, publishing, using CD-ROM for research and investigations, and using the Internet. However, while it was clear how all these innovations could be fitted into current planning and National Curriculum targets, it was not yet clear how Global English could be integrated. She also felt that what would enable E2L pupils to improve was not an Urdu version of computer instructions, but rather their being offered good models of spoken English in the classroom, augmented by individual support of two types – that provided by the staff of the school, and that provided by other pupils, particularly through the school's paired reading scheme. While she acknowledged that it was important to remain open to learning about the potential of Global English, her current position was that English time was 'too precious to be lost on Global English', which she saw as based on sets of decontextualised skills exercises which the children found boring.

This negative view of ILS was held by all the teachers in the English, special needs and language support departments, but not by the deputy head or by the head of mathematics, who were much more positive. ILS mathematics units were used to augment learning and were perceived by these teachers as helpful and effective in revision and reinforcement. In their opinion the mathematics units were enjoyed by the pupils for three reasons: first, because the computer offered stepped and graded exercises to reinforce learning; second, because it offered the pupil assistance if too many errors were recorded; and third, because any failures in learning were private, not public.

Bilingual pupils and ILS

I observed no differences between the use of ILS by E2L pupils and non-E2L pupils. It seems likely that the only group for whom special provision is necessary is that of beginners in English who enter the UK school system at secondary level.

In general it is pupils with special learning needs for whom ILS is likely to create difficulties, and contrary to some views the majority of E2L pupils are not in this group. Of the pupils observed, Paul, a Year 3 pupil, told me that he spoke English and Cantonese at home and went to classes on Saturday to learn Mandarin. He told me with precision how he logged on '...I memorise my log-on number...' and about the mathematics activity he liked best, Towers: 'I like Towers. There are two kinds of buttons. If you are correct, you gain. If not, then the rabbit gains.' I asked him whether he could hear the English that comes over the headset clearly enough. He said that he could, but that he did have a problem with the Sentences units (in Global English), 'I didn't know what to do, until everybody helped you'.

As an example of a more challenging case, the co-ordinator in a secondary school using SuccessMaker told me about Ikram, a pupil who had arrived at the school with no English in December 1993. He was from Pakistan and began on the Reading Readiness materials, but has progressed on to the Initial Reading units. The learning gains were not spectacular in Initial Reading, but these gains were important and were made in a context in which it had not been possible to offer much supplementary individual teaching. Ikram had now just begun to make use of the Science units and the teacher explained that this was to connect up with the National Curriculum science work which was occurring in other lessons, on the theme of forces and Newton's laws. Ikram's scores were low but the teacher did not interpret this as implying that there were no learning gains from this experience for him; the language experience, repetition and relevant content all made the SuccessMaker science activity potentially valuable support for his learning.

The school co-ordinator for ILS had no doubt that, provided the teacher is monitoring progress and selecting appropriate modules, learning gains could be made by E2L pupils using ILS for independent study, even with very low proficiency in English.

Are ILS materials appropriate for E2L pupils?

In discussions with sixteen teachers, all of whom were experienced in a bilingual context, I found that views on this question were mixed.

Teachers in one primary school which used the Global materials, and in which the staff were enthusiastic about new technology, did not feel that Global programs fitted in well with their approach to learning, though this problem was not confined to E2L. They talked about the contrast between Global's English materials and the Broderbund *Living Books* programs to which they had access through a CD-ROM player. Teachers commented that the front page of Global (the signpost) was lovely, but that it led to drill and practice. Global programs were described as 'worksheets on a computer', and pupils at their school were not really used to doing this kind of work. The school's philosophy was much more geared towards open learning.

Teachers in this school had tried the English worksheets which accompanied the ILS. They had found that their pupils did the gap-filling tasks readily enough, but balked at the rhyme-producing tasks, which they found arbitrary and difficult. In the teachers' view there was 'no input, no investment and no audience' for the children. There was also a problem in some cases with the difficulty of the prose. For example, it was more demanding to read and comprehend the instruction: 'Fill in the missing letters. Next, write the boxed word under each sentence.' than it was to carry out the task associated with these instructions.

By contrast, in another primary school, the reliable match between pupil and work, which SuccessMaker attempted to make was felt to be offering every pupil, including E2L pupils, an opportunity to succeed at their own level.

At secondary level teachers felt that SuccessMaker was not wholly appropriate. Clearly it was not designed for E2L pupils and the package was written for a US classroom. However, the point was made in one school that SuccessMaker work was preferable to sitting in a classroom with a worksheet and being unable to cope with it, or copying from a book. In their other lessons, new arrivals to the UK had to do geography, history, French and so on in a class of 30. The ILS co-ordinator suggested that, ideally, an E2L-focused course would retain the high (and effective) emphasis on the visual, using colour, animation, diagrams, and the breaking down of problems into small steps. However, for beginners in English, even teenagers, the language was the problem. For example, the help system could be too difficult and could only be used with teacher intervention. What was important was moving children on, and here it was felt that ILS had potential – worksheets tended to cover work which was already understood, so there was little language-differentiated work done in the normal curriculum of many E2L children which would lead to new or accelerated learning.

The ILS co-ordinator felt that nearly all beginner level pupils who were in Year 7 were able to get into the SuccessMaker system and make some progress. Perhaps surprisingly it was a small number of the Year 9 beginner-level pupils who became frustrated and who found it difficult to settle into the work. This may be because older pupils perceived the simple work in English to be beneath them.

In another secondary school using the Global ILS, bilingual pupils worked just as effectively as monolingual pupils, particularly on the mathematics units. Students were using the computers in the mathematics department practically every lesson, and the placing of the workstations around three sides of a regular classroom meant that pupils could support each other and have a teacher close by if a serious problem occurred.

Do E2L pupils learn more effectively in some subjects than others?

Overall the feeling of the teachers whom I interviewed was that in learning from ILS English was less satisfactory than mathematics. In the Global ILS, the teachers and older pupils felt that the English units were more boring and also less varied than the mathematics units. The only unit in Global English which pupils felt was 'good' was the Parrot mode work, in which they could record a word or phrase digitally, and then play it back, but the educational purpose for this was not clear to the pupils. On the three separate occasions when I observed pupils using Parrot mode, they subverted the educational goals and recorded phrases for their friends to listen to.

At secondary level, two bilingual Year 10 (age 16), pupils whom I interviewed were polite about the Global English software, though they did have some negative comments to make. Usha said, 'It needs to be adapted for people with a much better vocabulary'. She regretted that it was not possible to choose a harder ILS module, as in mathematics. The girls encountered nothing in the hour they spent with me which seemed any more difficult than Year 7 work, in their opinion. Jabeena felt that the generous spoken praise which Global English gave its users was helpful. She did not have anything more positive to say about English, but was positive about the Global French program, which she and her friends enjoyed. She liked the speed tests, which permitted competition against friends who were at the same stage. Jabeena also stressed that she felt that she learned new things in French; she did not feel that she had learned anything new from the time she had spent on Global English.

The teachers recognised that a great deal of work from psychologists had gone into the production of Global English, but questioned whether there had been any significant input from English teachers into the planning of the units, as their content was so remote from the kinds of activities carried out in comprehensive school English departments.

Students' evaluations do not always prove a reliable guide to learning potential, though they can be very revealing. At a primary school I visited using the SuccessMaker, one bilingual pupil volunteered a spontaneous summative evaluation for me to write down: 'Computers – I love them!' he said. He was charmingly positive about the work, and very frank about how he tackled it: 'I'm doing really well on reading – I don't even need to read the story, I can just answer the questions!' When asked whether he needed to read the story sometimes, he said, 'Yes. Today there were some really long words – I had to look at the story'.

The problem of pupils playing the system to manipulate scores was encountered quite often in all the English units. Some E2L pupils concentrated on speed in the SuccessMaker reading modules. This was not too much of a problem in the case of questions which had only one sentence on the screen and required one-word answers, either multiple-choice or cloze, but it did become a problem with the short-passage items. One bilingual primary pupil, Shahid, began clicking answers before I had read two lines of the eight-line passage on the screen. Shahid had not had time to even read all four multiple-choice answers. His strategy seemed to be to look for an acceptable sentence in the answers and to highlight and select this, then to go for another if this was wrong. If he was wrong, the correct answer was offered and this gave in one line a clue to what was happening in the passage in a much more convenient form than having to read the whole thing.

Shahid worked much more carefully on the mathematics unit, however, which seemed to be more difficult to tackle by intelligent guesswork. He made regular use of the glossary feature, handling difficult phrases such as 'regular polygon' or 'parallelogram' by looking the words up on-screen. Shahid had an intelligent short-cut for accessing the needed item. He knew that if you wanted to find the glossary information on a parallelogram it was not necessary to type in the whole word. Requesting a gloss of the first two letters 'pa' would produce a failure message, but would put up that section of the list of words in the glossary from which he could click to select the full word.

In one secondary school it was clear that many bilingual pupils were using or had worked with four, five or even six SuccessMaker units, and the ILS co-ordinator himself selected from a wide range, including Reading Readiness, Initial Reading, Reading Workshop, Reading Investigations, Spelling, Discover English, Science Discovery, Initial Maths, and Algebra.

Conclusions

Overall, opinions on the potential of ILS for bilingual children are varied. ILS has mixed reviews even from the experts – the children, and those teachers who are closest to them. However, there seems to be some potential for ILS across the curriculum for bilingual children, provided that the program is the right one, it has the teacher's confidence, and some teacher support is available.

Not surprisingly, teachers reported that setting up ILS and managing the information generated by the system was not a trivial matter. They felt that their biggest problem in using ILS was that there was just not enough time in the day for a teacher to make all the interventions which would be helpful, or to make full use of the records generated by the ILS system.

Teachers were cautions about reports generated by the Global program; they said that these were 'not hugely helpful', although it was felt that the information about how much time pupils spent on different activities was perhaps more useful than data on unit scores, which could be misleading. Some teachers regretted that pupil histories were not yet available through the management system. One teacher was in favour of individual workplans, but added that it was time-consuming to produce them, partly because the teacher did not have immediate access to information concerning the levels of each module in mathematics.

In a primary school using SuccessMaker, the co-ordinator reported that he would like more time to make use of the computer-generated reports. For example, reports gave evidence of skills needing more attention, but they need to be differentiated into those which are 'in review' because a child had just begun a unit or because learning was progressing slowly. With more time he could integrate this information into computer- and non-computer-based learning more effectively.

The co-ordinator in the London secondary school I visited was exceptional in the full use he made of SuccessMaker records. He also made them available to other teachers and had given in service training to other staff. The mathematics department seemed the one most likely to move towards being able to make independent use of these records. It was felt that Grouping Reports, which highlight individuals and groups performing above or below expectations in specific areas, could be useful for teachers other than the co-ordinator. Clearly there would be curricular implications from this, but there would seem to be even greater potential for monitoring and extending the learning of bilingual pupils if the data generated by the system were used more fully.

It seems appropriate to end this chapter with a list of plus and minus points for ILS in relation to bilingual learners made by a teacher in a primary school in Lancashire:

Plus points:

- Children do improve their knowledge of mathematics and English.
- It's very good for slow learners because they fail privately and can go over work again.
- It can be excellent for developing confidence.
- It develops concentration span (for most children).
- It increases IT skills and confidence with new technology.
- It develops personal organisational skills and independence in learning.

Minus points:

- It disrupts other activities.
- It is very expensive.
- It is difficult to assess the true learning gains.
- It reduces teacher control over the curriculum.

I asked this teacher whether ILS could replace a teacher. She replied: 'If the children do gain from ILS, it's because the teacher's made sure they do!'

SECTION 3

Focus on teachers

This section explores the relationship between teachers and ILS, looking at attitudes to the system, at the use of diagnostic information they provide, and at opportunities for professional development.

CHAPTER
13

Teacher responses to ILS

Tony Lawson, Jean Underwood, Susan Cavendish

and Sheila Dowling

'It's like being given a huge box of chocolates, but only taking a bite out of the strawberry cream', Julia Morris, Co-ordinator of ILS at Ashlawn School, Rugby.

Julia's comment about her school's experience of the SuccessMaker ILS encapsulates the attitudes of a large proportion of the teachers caught up in the evaluation of ILS systems during 1993 to 1995. Whether they were willing volunteers or drafted conscripts, the majority of the teachers involved expressed a sense of excitement that they were engaged in something which was of great benefit to their pupils, but also felt that they had merely begun to scratch at the surface of a development with enormous potential. We intend therefore in this chapter to document the features which led to the over-whelming level of enthusiasm for ILS by teachers and to lay out their concerns and hopes for the future of ILS.

The importance of teachers?

The reactions of teachers to innovations in information technology are important because hardware and software operate within a 'sociotechnology'. That is:

'an institutional arrangement where technical and social factors are mixed to form a purposive ensemble focused on some objective specific to that kind of institution.' (Ryan 1987, p 13).

Ryan argues that the introduction of new technology into classrooms cannot, of itself, transform education. There is a massive inertia in the socio part of the sociotechnology, of which teacher's attitudes, prior experiences and traditional expectations of what constitutes education are a part. Mellar *et al* (1994) employ the concept of teacher ideology to describe beliefs about the essential features of teaching, such as how teaching should be performed and how performance should be evaluated. This ideology is acquired through a process of socialisation involving training and personal experience, as well as wider socio-cultural ideas about the role of the teacher. Teacher ideology impacts on teaching style, which therefore tends to be very stable. Any innovation, especially one which employs unfamiliar resources such as computers, can be seen as a challenge to previously cherished beliefs and practices.

The stereotypical view of teachers' attitudes towards computers and their application in the classroom is one of indifference at best, and hostility at worst. Collins (1994) argues that traditional teacher attitudes towards computers were that they were an add-on to the teacher - another resource - not an integral part of the education process itself. However, she also argues that there is some evidence that teachers are 'rapidly breaking free of the stereotypes held about them,' (Collins 1994 p32). If this is so then we should expect the group of teachers typified as early adopters of innovations (Hoyle 1976, p32) to be foremost in this change.

The importance of the teachers in the ILS project is that they therefore represent a group of early adopters of innovation. They are at the cutting edge of educational innovation in the UK and an important case study of teacher attitudes towards information technology which delivers to students in the classroom, rather than just being a resource for teachers. They find themselves in the same position as the teachers described by Dwyer in the Apple Classrooms of the Future Project (Dwyer 1990). While committed to the ILS project, they often brought with them a view of schooling based on traditional notions of appropriate instruction. This led to inner conflict as they explored a different method of instruction and adapted their attitudes in the light of their experiences with it.

Data collection

The data were gathered from teachers involved in Phase 1 and Phase 2 of the school's ILS evaluation project, as well as from tutors in a feasibility study of ILS in further education institutions, undertaken for NCET in the 1995 Spring term (Underwood *et al* 1995). Information was gathered about a third ILS – TRO Plato as well as for Success-Maker and Global. TRO Plato is a US system, more open than SuccessMaker, but less developed in its diagnostic and management capabilities. Its advantage in the further education sector was that its focus was on the later stages of secondary and early tertiary education.

Information was gathered using a series of interviews and questionnaires. Those surveyed included very experienced co-ordinators of information technology, classroom teachers who had built up considerable expertise with ILS, and teachers with very limited familiarity with the system they were using. In total, more than 100 tutors were interviewed. Ideally tutors contributed at the start, mid-trial and end of the projects. Some tutors were surveyed only once during the course of their experience. Other tutors were followed through their entire involvement with ILS. The teachers surveyed were from across all age phases of schooling: primary, secondary, and those working with adult learners in FE institutions.

Overall reaction of the teachers

At the beginning of the three projects teacher expectations about the effects of ILS on their students were high. Nearly all of the tutors surveyed at the early stage expressed the hope of positive outcomes for their students. The main focus of these expectations was the increased motivation and confidence which the teachers believed would follow their students' exposure to ILS. They also believed that this engagement by the students was likely in itself to lead to learning gains. Allied to this expectation was the belief that ILS would lead to more independent learning by the students, with beneficial consequences for performance.

This faith in the effectiveness of ILS in fostering learning gains, before any evidence had been collected, suggests that it is powerful as an idea, with teachers anticipating the advantages which should accrue from a mode of learning which is differentiated, individualised, self-pacing, private and reinforcing. As Angela McFarlane (1994) pointed out, the attractiveness of the idea is not without its dangers:

'Teachers want to believe the system print-outs so much so that one comment I received was that the management system was wonderful, customising the work and keeping track of the results, but some of the course content was a bit doubtful. Well, just what is the value of a system which is good at managing poor content?'

However, in the early stages, the teachers involved in the project were, recognising the potential of the system, rather than responding to their experience of it. The idea was powerful to them because they could see that if they could become familiar with the management system they could chart the individual progress of their students and help them learn effectively. This was particularly true of SuccessMaker where the diagnostic and management tools were seen by the teachers as providing an enormous amount of information about the students. Indeed, teachers were concerned that they would not be able to keep on top of the sheer volume of information that could be called upon.

As the tutors watched their students perform on the ILS the majority felt that their expectations were being confirmed. In particular, teachers were impressed with the increased motivation and concentration they observed amongst their students. It was noted that the students came into the ILS setting and quickly started work with a minimum of fuss and disruption. Teachers also commented on the increased time on task exhibited by the students and the concentration they brought to bear when working on the ILS. As John Clare ("Hey! Just look at what I can do" *Daily Telegraph* 21 Sept 1994) reported about the reaction of Martin Davies of Stoke Park:

'It's the way the system engages the students' attention that is so striking.' Mr Davies says. 'One of Her Majesty's Inspectors came to look at it the other day. He said that in a poorly taught class he would expect the students to be on task for 40 per cent of a lesson. With a good teacher that would rise to 60 per cent. Here he judged the figure was 95 per cent. He was astounded.'

Though increased motivation and a lack of disruption were not universal amongst the students, teachers believed that for the large majority, the ILS experience was a positive and enjoyable one. Those students who tended to be disaffected from the ILS experience were identified by their teachers as students who were difficult to motivate in all learning situations. Indeed, the control potential of denying access to the ILS was often recognised and sometimes used by teachers faced with discipline issues in their everyday class work.

Other perceived benefits from ILS use were concerned with a greater readiness to take control of their own learning by the students. This was particularly so for the more able students, who were seen as exhibiting a greater willingness to tackle problem-solving tasks on their own. However, greater self-organisation was also noted throughout the whole of the ability range. Similarly, all students were perceived as improving their keyboard skills through exposure to the ILS. A large number of teachers also detected a greater confidence amongst the ILS pupils as they made progress at their own pace.

The effect of this increase in motivation and focus was firmly believed by the majority of teachers to be an increase in performance. Many looked forward to the results of the evaluation project to confirm what they already thought was happening. Their instincts and experience of individual pupils, as well as groups of ILS students, suggested to them that there were real learning gains being made, as well as the behavioural improvements they could document. Where teachers were adept at using the reports provided by SuccessMaker, they could chart the improvements which the system calculated their students were making and expected those improvements to be reported in the independent evaluation.

There were dissenting voices amongst the teachers. However, there were many different reasons for this negativity. In one case it was clearly a disappointment that the system had not fulfilled the very high expectations which the teacher had in entering the project. In other cases, it was frustration with technical problems, preventing the optimum utilisation of the ILS, which led to negative comments being made. This was particularly true of schools using Global software. In a third concern was expressed by a teacher that ILS could be used as a substitute for teachers, with a consequent loss of employment.

What is remarkable, however, is how few negative attitudes were recorded from such a disparate group of teachers. Whether they were in the primary, secondary or further education sector, were experienced with IT or novices, or using SuccessMaker, Global or Plato, the overwhelming majority of the teachers expressed positive attitudes towards their experience of working with ILS. Even those who were initially suspicious of ILS ended the project with a more positive view:

> 'Even some of the most sceptical teachers have come round to ILS, as they have discovered considerable benefits. By removing a dozen pupils at a time, it has enabled them to concentrate on smaller groups. Marking and recording of achievement has also been done by the computer, which can print out reports for parents. Behaviour has been affected, too, with the system having a calming influence upon pupils.' (Macdonald 1994).

Indeed it is difficult to convey the real excitement with which many teachers talked about ILS. Comments such as 'excellent', 'very pleased' or 'useful teaching resource' cloak rather than illuminate the animation and enthusiasm of many of them when they were talking about ILS. What was even more surprising to the researchers was that even when faced with formidable technical difficulties in the form of system crashes, loss of data, screen freezes and the like, the attitude of the majority of the teachers involved remained very positive.

Positive features identified by teachers

Positive comments from teachers mainly focused on the way in which the ILS allowed students to follow individualised programmes of study. Many teachers felt that the ability of the student to progress at their own pace and at an appropriate level was a crucial feature of the motivational pull of the systems. The instant feedback of SuccessMaker was also strongly approved of. Not only were students praised for correct responses to problems but they could also chart their own progress over each session to see how well they had performed. Moreover, teachers could also call upon the session reports to identify where progress was being made. As teachers became more adept with the diagnostic and report systems, particularly of SuccessMaker, their ability to focus on individual needs was enhanced.

Another strongly favoured feature of ILS was its privacy. Teachers felt that students were motivated because any failure was for their eyes only. The relationship between the individual student and the system was a personal one, in which the ILS took the role of confidante as well as teacher. The chances of public humiliation after giving a wrong answer were minimised by this confessional-type relationship. But the privacy of the system was argued to have another advantageous effect. The ILS did not allow those bright students who wanted to be seen as average to hide their ability. Whereas in a normal classroom such students might disappear through non-involvement, the recording system of the ILS allowed both the student and the teacher to see where success was being achieved, while retaining a public face of averageness.

While most teachers were reluctant to put forward any evidence of transference of skills and knowledge into normal lessons, several did note that there had been an attitude change towards the subject by some students through the use of ILS. This mainly took the form of students being more willing to settle down quickly to work in the normal classroom. One further education college reported increased attendance at normal lessons as a result of the introduction of the ILS. Any further transference was argued to be likely to occur after more exposure to the system than the duration of the project had allowed.

Teachers' critical comments

Overall the reactions of tutors involved in ILS were positive and encouraging, but not uncritical. On the contrary, the teachers surveyed took very seriously their involvement in an enterprise which was innovative and challenging and which they perceived was not without its dangers and disadvantages. They took care to document and report the problems they encountered with the systems and the different effects ILS had had on different types of pupils. The problems experienced with the systems were often of a technological nature, but a number of negative student outcomes was also noted by the reporting teachers. These were summarised by McGill (1994) as:

'demotivation, repetition of favoured programmes, boredom and guessing.'

The most commonly cited problem was demotivation, though this was caused by different things in different institutions. In those institutions where technical problems had been formidable there had been an initial general loss of student motivation, as systems kept crashing or freezing, or modules in the ILS had to be repeated because of data loss. As the technical problems were resolved, student motivation improved, but never reached the same levels as students in those institutions where the system ran well from the start. These technical problems could have produced a negative reaction amongst staff. The researchers were surprised at how indulgent teachers were of these problems, explaining them as teething problems or as something that should be expected as 'it is early days yet'. Part of this retention of interest by staff can be accounted for by the response of the providers, which was generally recognised as fairly prompt and efficient. In only one FE institution did dissatisfaction with the providing company lead to a harsh report by the teacher involved.

Another aspect of demotivation which teachers noted was the reaction of students themselves to the idea of ILS. Across several schools there were individual students who were resistant to the idea of ILS. In one case in particular, two students were reluctant to go on to the computer because, they argued, that it identified them as "thick", that is of low ability. The teachers involved took great pains to persuade them that this was not the case, and, although they continued to be suspicious, the teachers believed that they had benefited from the experience.

Amongst the FE teachers, the inappropriateness of some of the material on Success-Maker was cited as a demotivating factor. The babyish reward mechanism and the use of icons and pictures appropriate to younger children were the main reason that some adult learners were resistant to the systems which had been developed for school children.

A crucial feature of the demotivating process was the occurrence of boredom and loss of interest amongst a number of groups of students when they had been on the system for some time. The repetitive nature of the activities and the lack of variety in some modules was noted by staff to lead to increased disaffection amongst, in particular, the very able and the least able students. Teachers believed that such students were still learning, but that their engagement was diminishing as they were required to carry out similar exercises for long periods of time. It was this factor, combined with timetabling issues, which led to changes in the amount and frequency of ILS use in many of those institutions which were involved in both the first and second phase of the project.

Other criticisms of ILS by teachers focused on the content of the modules which the students experienced. The US systems inevitably came in for some criticism over Americanisms. In SuccessMaker, this was mainly concerned with the use of dollars and cents for mathematics problems, and US spellings in the English modules. There were also some cultural references which misled British students. However, as familiarity with the systems increased, teacher criticisms of this aspect diminished. More seriously, teachers were concerned with SuccessMaker's lack of fit with National Curriculum attainment targets and the limitations which this placed on its suitability. With Global, teachers' main criticism concerned the errors which were found in the relatively new material, both in the mathematics and English modules. The effects of such errors on the students was seen by the teachers to be negative, though most teachers were quite pleased if their students stuck out for their own correct answer against the system's incorrect one. However, this did have an effect on the score which students could achieve in modules which contained errors.

The issue of control

These criticisms did not undermine the general approval which the teachers had of ILS. In the majority of instances the critical comments reflected a process of teachers getting to grips with the potential of ILS and looking at ways in which its deployment in schools and its content could be improved. Teachers were concerned here that they should have control of the system rather than vice versa. This is important because a central tenet of teacher ideology, as traditionally formulated, is that teachers should be in charge of what goes on in the classroom. This perceived need to control strikes at the very heart of the teachers' involvement with ILS. Because information technology has a high potential for going wrong, it represents what Mellar *et al* (1994 p211) call 'an area of anxiety' in which the teacher's confidence in their own ability to control the classroom can be undermined by a lack of technical competence. As Underwood and Underwood (1990) point out, under-users of computers are those who lack confidence in their own technical ability and who are unsure what to do with technology in the classroom. The implication for the ILS teachers is that, as they gain knowledge of and confidence in ILS, their ability to use it in educationally fruitful ways will increase.

As the project evaluation proceeded it became clear that the teachers were beginning to get to grips with ILS and adapting it to their own ends. In interview after interview, the teachers went through a similar sequence. They were firstly enthusiastic about ILS. They then qualified their overall approval with some cautious comments, voicing general and specific concerns about the effects of ILS. But they also usually ended with a strong endorsement of the system and expressed the desire to see it retained within the school. Towards the end of the evaluation period, a common reaction was an expression of frustration by teachers as the potential of the system was recognised, alongside the realisation that individual teachers needed more time to understand and employ the system to its maximum effect.

The issue of control which was the central concern of many of the teachers had several dimensions:

- the constraints imposed by the system providers;
- the perceived threat to jobs;
- unfamiliarity with the system;
- insufficient use of the reporting system;
- the issue of integration.

The lack of flexibility in using the system under the provider's instructions was disliked by many, and teachers in different schools quickly evolved different models of use which better fitted their educational perceptions and needs. This need to control ILS rather than let it control them was visible in Phase 1 and Phase 2 of the project. In Phase 1 schools were constrained to adopt the method of use recommended by the provider. In many cases, teachers decided that this was not the best way to deploy the system, for educational and timetabling reasons. In Phase 2 they therefore adopted a number of different ways of using ILS with their students.

In a number of schools the typical Phase 1 model was retained, half the class on the system for half the lesson, while the other half of the class was taught by the usual classroom teacher. However, in other schools the amount of time students spent on the system was reduced, either because teachers felt they needed to take back to normal teaching some of the time they had given up, or because they felt that relentless everyday use led to student disaffection from the system. In these cases teachers referred to the educational justification for the changes that had been introduced and also kept under review the new modes of working which had been developed. This process of re-establishing control over the student's educational experience was cited as an important event by many of the teachers.

The threat to jobs

ILS was seen by a number of teachers to represent a potential threat to jobs. This was most marked amongst tutors in the FE sector who had the least experience of working with an ILS and who were perhaps working in a different job climate than teachers in schools. In particular, the FE sector is more likely to employ teachers on short-term or temporary contracts. This was sometimes expressed explicitly, but was also present in such comments as 'machines cannot replace the teacher–pupil interaction'.

While in some schools teacher intervention with students while they were on the system was minimal, for others it was important to the teachers that they were seen to be actively involved with the delivery of the material by the machines. There were many thoughtful contributions on the need for students to have social experiences in the classroom as part of a full educational entitlement. So even where the recognition existed that the ILS was an efficient delivery mechanism for basic literacy and numeracy, teachers were careful to identify a proper and essential role for student–teacher interaction.

Unfamiliarity with the system

A common concern in many schools was the lack of knowledge and familiarity with the ILS itself. Especially at the beginning of the project, many teachers felt that they had little conception of what their students were actually doing. This initial ignorance of the content of the ILS made for a great deal of uncertainty amongst teachers. They knew that something exciting was probably happening, but what this consisted of was often a black hole to them. As the project progressed and the teachers became familiar with what was happening to their students, this fear subsided and the teacher began to put forward strategies for change, so that the ILS would be used in different ways, for example targeting students with literacy problems or using it as a revision tool.

Insufficient use of the reporting system

As the project evolved a new concern emerged. Few teachers, beyond the co-ordinators, had much experience of the reporting systems in the ILS, even by the end of the evaluation period. Their awareness of what was available in the reports gradually increased, though there were some critical comments about the complexity and opaqueness of the reports, especially in the Global system. However, as knowledge of the reporting system increased, so did the frustrations expressed by the teachers. They were beginning to recognise the potential of the ILS reports for diagnostic and remedial intervention, but were hampered by a lack of time to get to grips with this power to benefit their students in the way that they began to believe could happen through ILS.

This feeling of frustration was expressed most strongly in virtually universal comments about the need for more time and more training in the use of ILS. Most teachers were happy enough with the initial training provided and with the support offered by co-ordinators and technicians day-to-day. But a constant plea was for ongoing training, so that their ability to utilise ILS to its best advantage would be enhanced. They also expressed the need for some differentiated training to take into account the varied roles of staff involved in ILS, from system managers to tutors. In the end of project interviews, many teachers expressed the view that their next cohort of students would begin to see the real benefit of ILS, because they, the teachers, were more confident in its use, were able to adapt the system to their own purposes, and to deploy the full capacity of the system to improve the attainment of their students.

The issue of integration

A further aspect of this development of teachers' capacities with ILS can be found in the issue of integration. At the beginning of the evaluation projects ILS work tended to be stand-alone, with little connection between the ILS sessions and what went on in the normal classroom. This was not just an issue of familiarity with or unsuitability of the content of the systems. Teachers initially were unsure how to integrate, for example, the mathematics modules with the normal mathematics curriculum. There were three dimensions to the problems they faced in doing this. Students were firstly following individualised programmes at different levels, and though teachers do have some control over content in ILS systems, it would take a brave individual who would intervene in a strong fashion at the onset of an unfamiliar system. Secondly, the frequency and pacing of the ILS experience was initially out of the control of teachers, which made integration difficult. Thirdly, some departments were happier with the ILS content than others. This was particularly so with the Global system.

The solutions to integration therefore took many forms. One institution using SuccessMaker gave over basic numeracy entirely to the ILS. Another mathematics department used Global modules once a week as reinforcement and revision for taught material. A further mathematics department had matched Global modules to National Curriculum attainment targets and had completely integrated them into their schemes of work. Much more common was the recognition by teachers that there was potential for integration and that this was a desirable outcome. However, the teachers felt that they had not been given the time to achieve this in any reasonable way. Therefore any integration was haphazard and related to particular aspects of the ILS content rather than planned.

Primary and secondary teachers' reactions

There were few differences in primary school and secondary school teachers' reactions to these issues. While secondary teachers were more likely to attempt to integrate ILS material into their normal curriculum work, they were also more critical of the details of many of the modules. Primary school teachers were more critical of technical difficulties they experienced. This was particularly true of the primary teachers working with Global. There was also in the primary schools less patience with the problems that Global had in installing the English modules and this often led to negative perceptions of the actual content, which was seen as too difficult for their children.

Conclusion

These criticisms were minor when set against the overall approval of ILS which the large majority of teachers put forward. As in any innovation teachers had worries and concerns with their own performance in a new situation and in the effects that ILS could have on the pupils in their care. This feeling of responsibility towards the students was everywhere expressed in all sorts of ways. But by the end of the project most of the teachers involved were convinced that the ILS had been of benefit. They argued that it was not the answer to every educational problem and that it needed time, thought and training for the full beneficial effects to be seen. But it did work for them and their students, if only in terms of the way it engaged and motivated large numbers of students across the full range of ability.

ILS – A tool for the professional development of teachers

Jane Spilsbury

The impact of ILS on teachers' professional development did not feature in the main evaluation by the Leicester University team. However, during their school visits NCET project staff noticed that ILS did affect the approaches to teaching and learning used by some teachers and that in some cases they were becoming more confident in their use of IT generally as a result of using an ILS. This chapter describes these observations and draws on relevant observations of Underwood *et al* (1995) and other evaluators.

NCET observed in its report on the first phase of the project that:

'there was a close correlation between the involvement and enthusiasm of staff involved in the project and the model of organisation used in the school, (NCET 1994, p35)

Several effects were noted:

- Teachers began to examine their management of resources more closely.
- Classroom management issues were highlighted as vital to the success of ILS.
- Some teachers began to review their approach to teaching and learning styles.
- Teachers realised that in ILS they had a powerful tool for differentiation.
- IT competence and confidence developed, even in previously IT resistant teachers.
- The increased awareness of learning development led some teachers to studying for further degrees, and in other cases to promotion.

These developments surprised many people involved in the project but were welcomed by all as an unexpected side effect of the introduction of ILS. During the second phase of the project NCET staff and evaluators recorded examples of teachers' professional development. We also became aware of research done in the US on stages in the professional development of American teachers as they implemented ILS. In the report writing stage of Phase 2 it became clear that these stages of development mirrored the criteria for effective schools described by the Office for Standards in Education (OFSTED) publication, *Key Characteristics of Effective Schools* (Sammons 1995).

Criteria for effective schools:

Professional leadership	Positive reinforcement
Shared vision and goals	Monitoring progress
Concentration on teaching and learning	Pupil rights and responsibilities
Purposeful teaching	Home–school partnership
High expectations	Learning organisations

This chapter elaborates on these observations in the US research and links them to past research on professional development. Finally, we hope to show how schools might use the professional development side-effects of introducing ILS to meet some of the criteria set out in the effective schools documentation.

Theories of computer-based learning

Much research has been done in the US and in the UK on the impact of computer based learning on pupil achievement. Although this research is not specifically related to ILS it provides an interesting starting point because it focuses our attention on pupils' learning. We must remember why it is important for teachers to improve their practice: to help pupils to achieve their full potential.

In a study by Dalton and Hannafin (1988) four groups of pupils studying concepts and applications of *pi* were exposed to four different teaching approaches representing different combinations of teacher led learning and computer based learning:

- Group one were taught entirely by the teacher TT
- Group two were taught first by the teacher; they then practised on the computer TC
- Group three were introduced to a concept on the computer; they then practised with the teacher CT
- Group four worked entirely on the computer CC

The results of this study showed that the greatest learning gains were achieved by the two groups receiving combined instruction from both the computer and the teacher. Interestingly the TT and CC groups performed equally well, as did the TC and CT groups. Many other studies from around the world draw similar conclusions.

How is this related to the impact of ILS? The research of Schnitz and Azbell (1988) analyses the impact of ILS with different levels of teacher involvement. They took as their starting point the reported different effect sizes produced by the use of ILS. For example, in an analysis of 254 controlled evaluation studies Kulik and Kulik (1991) reported an average effect size of +0.3 in favour of computer assisted learning. However, in 1994 NCET's study of ILS reported an average effect size of +0.4 over six months. Clearly there were issues to be explored about the circumstances of the use of ILS that produced the most substantial gains. As a result of their research Schnitz and Azbell produced a model of the level of teacher involvement in the implementation of integrated learning systems. They identified four levels:

- **Novice** – the teacher is minimally involved; the system runs on autopilot.
- **Practitioner** – uses reports to check skills mastered and will vary the time on system if necessary.
- **Integrator** – the system is used to complement classroom instruction.
- **Extender** – the system is used not only to complement, but to extend curriculum provision and work goes beyond the system's inherent design.

Their study compared the learning gains achieved by different groups of pupils whose teachers fitted each of these categories. They found that a pupil's achievement increased as their teacher became more involved in the implementation of ILS. It is interesting to note that in some cases, where the teacher remained at the novice stage, the results showed that the use of ILS could be negative. That is, that the pupils actually regressed.

Similar findings have been reported in research by Apple Corporation on the *Apple Classrooms of Tomorrow* (nos 8 and 10, 1990; nos 13 and 15 1991).

Is this evidence supported by the use of ILS in the UK?

The Leicester evaluation found that in some cases the size of the learning gains achieved by pupils in UK schools could be linked to the level of involvement of the teacher. In terms of gains in reading, where only two schools on the project using SuccessMaker achieved gains, the teachers' intervention in the management system played a very significant part in bringing about these gains.

Specific features of an ILS which can aid teacher development

Returning to my list of perceived benefits to teacher development, we can match the features of an ILS to the aspect of development each has been seen to help.

Teachers became increasingly aware of the process of pupils' learning

NCET project staff observed that teachers using SuccessMaker became more reflective and analytical as a result of working with the diagnostic feedback on student performance. Some teachers have described SuccessMaker as a critical friend in the classroom, against which they can verify their professional judgements. The headteacher of one school commented that: 'The ILS system has been a unique way of helping teachers to further their understanding of the learning processes in children'.

Where the greatest learning gains have been achieved, teachers are fully involved in the use of SuccessMaker and they have intervened by tackling areas of difficulty they have witnessed pupils experiencing on the system in their classrooms.

Integration of work done on SuccessMaker into classroom work is central to the effective use of this ILS. Teachers have used the diagnostic computer feedback to facilitate this. Of the three systems used on the project, SuccessMaker provided the most detailed reports on pupil achievement, which enabled teachers to identify particular strengths and weaknesses for each pupil and to focus on those in their own teaching.

In one primary school using SuccessMaker the headteacher introduced a system of observation for his teachers to watch pupils using ILS and allowed them time to analyse the reports. He realised that successful implementation of ILS would involve the class teacher as fully as possible so that work done on the system could be integrated into other classwork.

Some teachers using Jostens software reported that ILS helped them to consider and address assessment needs and that it improved their own self esteem and professional updating.

The headteacher of a secondary school using SuccessMaker reported that for the first time ever the mathematics and English departments were collaborating and co-operating.

Teachers realised that in ILS they had a powerful tool for differentiation

The detailed information presented to teachers in reports from some ILS enable them to identify specific skills that they need to concentrate on in their teaching. These may be different for every child in the class. The report information, combined with the flexibility of the management system, enables teachers to differentiate the pupils' work to meet individual needs.

Teachers in a number of schools using the SuccessMaker Language Program had been concerned that children moving from the Initial Reading (IR) module to the Readers' Workshop (RW) module became disaffected and seemed not to be coping.

In one of these schools the teachers examined the reports from IR, which gave feedback over a number of reading skills ranging from letter recognition to paragraph comprehension. They found that pupils had completed IR without having mastered the comprehension strands. In some cases pupils had avoided comprehension completely but were still able to finish the module. Teachers decided to re-enrol pupils on IR, switching on only the comprehension strands and increasing their support of pupils. Pupils then moved on to RW better prepared to cope with the comprehension level demanded of them. This is one of the schools where learning gains in reading have occurred.

The headteacher of a very small primary school using SuccessMaker feels the system has done even more than he had expected of it, particularly in the area of differentiation. This small rural school with just 40 pupils on roll was organised in two 'family' classes covering Key Stage 1 and Key Stage 2. Use of SuccessMaker has gone a long way to allay worries due to the large age range in each class.

Some teachers began to reassess their approach to teaching and learning

SuccessMaker relies on the use of praise to motivate pupils. In schools in the US elaborate wallcharts are used to encourage pupils to achieve high percentages of correct answers in each session. In this way, expectations are raised without pupils being in direct competition with each other.

In Phase 2 teachers noted that enthusiasm was still high among groups who continued with SuccessMaker from Phase 1, although it had levelled off in some cases, so that reinforcement motivators were used. For example, one school employed a gold/silver/bronze medal system for percentage achievements.

One evaluator commented that she had noted an increase in the use of praise by many of the teachers in one school since the introduction of ILS.

There is evidence that teachers' perceptions and expectations of pupils has changed as a result of using SuccessMaker. Many teachers have commented that they have been surprised by the levels some of their pupils have achieved using the system.

Some mathematics teachers reported that they had changed their approach to whole class teaching to accommodate SuccessMaker. They felt they had to use more flexible teaching methods because pupils in the same class were no longer at the same stages in the National Curriculum, so they found small group work more appropriate when introducing new topics.

IT competence and confidence developed, even in previously IT resistant teachers

Evidence shows that the daily use of ILS has built teachers' confidence in using IT and encouraged them to look for IT solutions to other curriculum and pedagogical issues. Teachers who were previously resistant to IT have been able to see the value of computer delivered curriculum materials controlled by a management system and have been keen to use them. Within the project this has been described as The Trojan Horse Syndrome because it is an unforeseen side effect of the introduction of ILS.

'Staff who have managed to be too busy to use IT are now caught and wish to extend their skills and use it. The cheapest and most useful Inset we have had!' (Headteacher of a special school.)

'This is the first time in eight years' experience of IT networks in school that a system has been so heavily used by staff and students. It is 100 per cent timetabled together with after-school opportunities.' (Headteacher of a school using Global software.)

One English teacher had only a year to retirement and was not inclined to take on anything new. However, it seemed that he was being drawn in by SuccessMaker and it was helping his own self-esteem and confidence with IT.

At a site using the Jostens ILS one teacher discovered the benefits of using IT, where previously she had not been convinced. She admitted that she could never before see the advantage of using IT. It had taken her too long to familiarise herself with the operation of computer applications she had been introduced to before, and then she had had to think of ways that they might slot into the curriculum. It was obvious to her that the ILS software was immediately applicable in her classroom and that the information in the reports would inform the assessment and recording of her pupils' achievements.

The increased awareness of the learning process in teachers led to studying for further degrees in some cases and to promotion in others.

The headteacher of one of the project primary schools produced a thesis for a Master's degree on the management of ILS in a small school. In another school, a teacher conducted his own research on the impact of SuccessMaker on numeracy skills. An account of this research is included in Chapter 6.

Models of use employed

The various models of use employed in UK schools involved in the NCET study can be linked to their impact on teacher development. Where teachers are not directly involved in their pupils' use of the system they cannot move easily through the stages of development set out by Schnitz and Azbell.

In some schools the class teacher did not accompany his/her class to the ILS room. The pupils using ILS were supervised by a non-teaching assistant or the special needs co-ordinator. This model of use made it difficult for the teacher to be familiar with the work done on the system. Consequently, ILS was separate from classroom work. The teacher could not integrate it easily and sometimes resented the amount of time it took from classwork. The use of information in the reports was also very limited where this model of use was in place. The teacher remained at the novice stage of development, limited learning gains were achieved by the pupils and very little professional development took place as a result of the introduction of ILS.

However, some schools did not want to lose the advantage of having the ILS room supervised by a non-teaching assistant, so they set up a procedure which would enable each class teacher to observe his or her pupils on the system for half an hour per week. A further half an hour per week was allocated to each class teacher to analyse the reports. This meant that the teachers were better informed about the work done on ILS and the progress their pupils were making. It also enabled them to become more familiar with the management system so that they could adapt it to better meet the needs of their pupils.

In some schools, usually secondary schools, the teacher did accompany their class to the ILS room. Half the class would use the ILS whilst the other half were taught by the teacher. It appeared that this model allowed for more involvement on the part of the teacher. However, teachers found that they could not provide the support needed by children using ILS at the same time as teaching the other pupils. Neither did it allow them to observe their pupils using the system or to become familiar with the work done on ILS. Many schools using this model are now providing a support teacher for one of the ILS sessions to allow the teacher to become more involved. Teachers at these schools are moving onto the practitioner and integrator levels of the Schnitz and Azbell model.

In one or two schools pupils were removed from their lessons to use ILS in a largely unsupervised environment. Although the pupils completed the work and were generally well behaved they did not make significant gains in mathematics or reading. Teachers at these schools were not necessarily unfamiliar with the system, but they were unfamiliar with the work their pupils were doing on ILS and did not show the pupils that they valued it. The pupils began to see ILS as less valuable than their classwork because the teacher did not give them recognition for their achievements on the system. In these circumstances, teachers will remain at the practitioner level and learning gains will be small.

Management issues which influence teacher development

The introduction of an ILS into a school involves a great deal of planning and preparation. As shown above, the various models adopted by the schools each have a very different effect on teacher development. But this is only one of the management issues that need to be considered when a school plans to introduce ILS. It is essential for teacher development that teachers are as fully involved in their pupils' use of the system as possible. This need must be balanced against the financial necessities, perhaps to employ a non-teaching assistant to supervise the ILS room. In this case, it is essential that the costing of the introduction of ILS includes a training and development budget. Time for familiarisation is essential. A style of management that will encourage this level of familiarity with the system, promote a reflective attitude to the use of ILS and encourage professional development will ensure that ILS brings with it improved teacher development. Which comes first: a style of management that encourages reflection and teacher development, or the introduction of ILS which promotes this approach? To date, the research has not tackled this question.

Schools: Making ILS work – ILS: Making schools work

The evidence shows that there are some factors which are important preconditions if ILS is to work effectively. However, the evidence also shows that ILS can help make schools more effective according to the criteria set out in *Effective Schools* (Sammons *et al* 1995). This report established 10 factors identified as contributing to effective schools:

Professional leadership

Where strong leadership existed in ILS schools the use of the system was more effective. However, ILS has helped to develop more professional leadership in some schools.

Shared vision and goals

Schools which had a more successful experience had a clear vision of what could be achieved with ILS. This vision was shared by headteachers and staff.

Recognition of the potential of ILS to bring about school change has provided some schools with a vision and a framework for development.

Concentration on teaching and learning

The research has shown that SuccessMaker provides a calm, orderly environment in which students can learn. Students who usually find it difficult to learn appreciate the privacy and quiet created by ILS.

ILS are designed to make children achieve at a level to make them feel successful without developing complacency. The research has shown that this motivates them to repeat their success. This focus on achievement has had a positive effect on pupil cultures. These changes in pupil behaviour and performance have caused schools to re-examine teaching and learning styles.

Purposeful teaching

ILS provides effective management of learning. The production by the SuccessMaker Management System of objective and specific information has meant that class and subject teachers had to acquire knowledge of the curriculum content and to understand and interpret the reports produced by the management system.

The diagnostic nature of the reports from the SuccessMaker system provided teachers with objective feedback on pupil performance which enabled them to develop differentiated teaching strategies and to improve formative assessments. This resulted in more effective management of learning.

High expectations

It was noticeable that where teachers were enthusiastic about their involvement with the evaluation project pupils did better.

Messages about the importance or unimportance of the work on the systems came from teacher attitudes towards them. Most teachers had high expectations of their pupils and saw the project as an opportunity to help them achieve these expectations. Where students were sent to unsupervised environments and when the work completed on the ILS was not seen to be valued, projects were less successful.

Diagnostic feedback on individual students often surprised teachers and caused them to reassess their expectations of some students. The ability to provide greater differentiation through individual programmes of work helped teachers to support the realisation of their expectations for students.

Positive reinforcement

A major feature of ILS is positive reinforcement, and pupils have commented that they enjoy the instant feedback that they get on their work and the way in which the systems encourage them. Pupils frequently check their own results on the system to see further proof that they are doing well. In some schools our researchers noted a change in pedagogy in other classroom activities towards a greater use of praise.

Teachers using SuccessMaker software commented that the feedback on performance from the computer often supported their own judgements and this was regarded as positive reinforcement for the teacher.

Monitoring progress

An ILS will track pupils' responses and monitor their progress. The computer feedback on performance provided by ILS gives teachers an objective opinion on the progress of individual students and of whole groups.

Pupil rights and responsibilities

Schools have noted a rise in self-esteem in pupils using ILS, and students have enjoyed learning at their own pace and in private. Where schools have made sure that pupils know how to use the systems effectively by accessing help when they need it there has been a shift towards independent learning. Where teachers involve students in the interpretation of their reports from the system the students have been able to take a proactive part in the management of their own learning.

Home–school partnership

ILS project schools have provided information for parents. In some schools the systems have been used by parents and other groups after school hours.

Learning organisations

Where headteachers in both large and small schools have involved the whole school in the planning, implementation, monitoring and evaluation of the ILS project there have been useful opportunities for school based staff development.

In one special school the diagnostic nature of the reports from SuccessMaker has encouraged staff to discuss pupils and their progress in greater depth, to look closely at the learning styles of their pupils, and to explore alternative access devices for some of their children.

Teachers who had not previously used computers in the classroom have become confident users and have been encouraged by their use of ILS to explore other applications and computer based activities.

A small number of teachers within the project have undertaken accredited courses to gain further qualifications.

The future

Any further evaluation of ILS in UK schools should examine the issues raised in this chapter in more detail. In particular, a further evaluation should examine the claims made for the improvement of schools. Research evidence would need to focus on isolating the effects of the introduction of ILS and establishing which of the features of effective schools are prerequisites and which can be promoted by the introduction of ILS.

SECTION 4
Putting ILS into school

This section considers key management issues related to the introduction of ILS. Case studies of implementing ILS in a variety of learning environments provide evidence of the widespread applicability of the concept.

CHAPTER

Supporting learning in isolated environments

CHAPTER **15**

Don Passey

In Phase 2 of the NCET evaluation a third ILS system was introduced. This study reports on the use of software from Jostens Learning Corporation to support learning in isolated environments and within the learning resource area of a large urban comprehensive school.

Isolated environments for pupils

Children who become ill or who are hospitalised may be concerned about their state of well-being and this, coupled with the care offered to them by social and medical workers, often results in the emotional domain becoming a prominent element of their conscious working state. Children disturbed by trauma may exhibit attitudinal or behavioural characteristics which do not allow their intellectual domain to be readily approached.

In such cases, hospital schools, special schools, and pupil referral units may be a necessary means of supporting the pupil and providing more specific attention to the means of engaging the intellectual domain whilst accounting for emotional, social, attitudinal or behavioural needs. The DfEE (1994) has recognised the need to support these pupils, but has also indicated the need for these children to be challenged intellectually, and allowed opportunities to return to mainstream schooling as soon as possible.

For children experiencing such problems intellectual development may become temporarily halted. In such circumstances it is desirable for children to be given educational opportunities more specifically geared to their needs, but often this results in the children themselves being isolated from their peers in special units or special schools.

Teachers' needs in isolated learning situations

Teachers who work with children whose learning is disturbed in this way in special schools and units isolated from mainstream schools look for support both for their pupils and for the wider professional needs of their school or unit.

Teachers actively seek methods for pupils which can:

- engage children so that they concentrate on the tasks at hand;
- stimulate, so that children are interested by the material offered;
- challenge, by offering new material or familiar material in alternative ways;
- comfort, by providing known material with opportunities to succeed in undertaking activities to reassure and build self-esteem;

- offer analytical reports to identify children's needs and weaknesses more carefully;
- match pupils' needs when they may only be in school for short periods of time;
- record attainment and outcomes for transfer to other establishments;
- enable rapid assessment of a particular child's learning needs;
- provide educational material rather than mere games material.

For wider support and provision of the professional needs of the school or unit teachers in isolated situations value:

- technical support when things go wrong;
- training when they have problems or specific needs;
- communication to avoid social isolation;
- mechanisms to share ideas.

A range of studies and reviews already exist which support the notion that ILS could be a useful way to offer teachers a means to address some of these needs. For example, Hativa (1989) reported that the majority of students in a study indicated they enjoyed using ILS, and enjoyed the positive feedback the system gave them. Hoorvitch and Steimberg (1990) reported increased levels of self-confidence and self-esteem, and Clariana (1993) reported that positive feedback increased attendance rates.

Jostens ILS software

Jostens ILS used in the schools and pupil referral units in England contained material covering subject areas in reading, mathematics, science, writing, geography, history, skills for life and employment skills, and keyboarding.

Some authors might not regard the Jostens software as an ILS package (McFarlane 1995) as it does not have an automatic means to place pupils at a level of material to match their working abilities. However, the package provides material ordered progressively in levels of difficulty, with frequent feedback opportunities for pupils and teachers. The software also exists in both network and standalone versions, which makes it ideally suited for schools and units where resource opportunities are limited.

The NCET study

The purpose of this NCET commissioned study was to identify:

- the models of deployment and use in the sites;
- the effects of the software upon the perception of pupils, and teachers, and effects upon educational and attitudinal outcomes;
- the support required, available, and used;
- the effective management of isolated sites;
- teacher development arising from software use.

The study was conducted in five educational sites, and involved observation, interview and questionnaire data collection methods with vendor staff, NCET staff, Open School personnel, five project teachers, ten other teachers and 87 pupils. It should be recognised, however, that a short study of this nature always has limitations:

- initial responses and outcomes may not be continued as use progresses;
- initial studies may well be resourced and supported at higher levels than later use;

- involvement in pilot studies does not mean that use can be implemented in more routine ways.

Meeting the needs of teachers and pupils in isolated learning environments

Support and distant management

In studies of this nature the levels of support that sites receive should not be under-estimated. At the same time, the need for support during teething problems such as software not working well, certain facilities not being available, and breakdown of parts of the systems should also be recognised and balanced against the former. In this particular study the support available arose from a range of sources: the vendors; NCET; and the Open School based at Dartington Hall, Devon, which managed the Jostens ILS within the PRUs and hospital schools.

On balance it appears likely that larger schools may well be able to support themselves more effectively than small schools or PRUs in the use of this software. The hospital school, the school for children with specific medical problems and the two PRUs emphasised the value they had placed upon the support from the Open School in providing:

- technical support and liaising with software vendors and hardware suppliers;
- training support when staff were unsure about what to do;
- communication support in maintaining contact via the telephone, fax and e-mail, providing opportunities for the sharing of ideas through site visits, a newsletter, and local conferences.

Deployment and access

Some consideration of possible deployment patterns for ILS is provided within the latest NCET Phase 2 Evaluation Report (1996). Some authors report the critical importance of appropriate deployment to outcomes (Mageau 1990; and Shore and Johnson 1992).

In this report the models of use varied greatly. Within the secondary comprehensive school, a network of 15 machines was established in a resource area which could also house a class of 30 pupils. In the other sites single machines were deployed, one in a library resource area, one in a careers classroom, and the others in staff areas. In all cases the teachers had considered carefully what they felt were the most appropriate ways of using the equipment.

Time and frequency of use on the systems is also highlighted as an important factor of successful use and outcomes (NCET 1995; Becker 1994). In the NCET Jostens ILS study (reported in Passey 1995) access was provided in all sites at a minimum level, one session per pupil each week, to a maximum level of one session per pupil each day. The duration of sessions was usually of the order of 20 or 30 minutes, but in a few cases was less, and in a number of cases as long as two hours for a single session.

Engagement and concentration

If a software package engages attention and captures concentration then it is possible for other intellectual processes to follow. There is evidence that Jostens ILS captured and engaged attention over the time of the NCET study, particularly as teachers reported that pupil commitment to the use of Jostens ILS had not diminished significantly over the trial period.

In some cases increases of attention span were recorded which were considered by the teacher involved as being remarkable outcomes. In one instance a pupil, excluded from mainstream school for aggressive and violent behaviour, who had been reported as being extremely difficult to settle to work and had had difficulty in recognising letters and letter sounds, had managed to work on the Jostens ILS for between 15 minutes and two hours. Not only had the pupils concentration span been increased significantly, but he was also able to recognise for himself some of the learning outcomes he had achieved. In this case the use of the package was enabling the intellectual domain to be accessed. Furthermore, it was considered that the self-esteem of the pupil had been developed, so that the potential for further contact and learning was that much greater.

Stimulation and interest

The level of self-reported pupil enjoyment was similar to that found in Hativa (1989), with only seven from 87 pupils indicating that they did not enjoy using Jostens ILS. In some cases the lack of interest can be ascribed to a mismatch between learning style preferences. In one instance a pupil indicated a preference for using text as a form of internalisation. For this pupil, sounds and images were of secondary importance. In another instance a pupil indicated reliance upon sounds for learning. For this pupil images and text are of secondary importance and he would prefer that the program did not use them.

Stimulation and interest, therefore, appear to be related to the form of presentation used with the software package. It appears that some ten to 20 per cent of pupils may feel that the forms offered do not meet their own preferred learning styles.

Challenge and pursuit of learning

Whilst engagement and stimulation are prerequisites to learning, outcomes require application and persistence. These latter processes require a recognition of interaction between that which exists as knowledge and understanding already, and that which is recognised as being learned as an outcome.

Seventy-one pupils in this study were able to indicate specific learning outcomes which they believed had resulted from the use of the Jostens ILS package. In some instances pupils were able to indicate very clearly the ways in which the package had enabled them to achieve results. For example, one pupil was able to relate how osmosis had been understood as a process through the use of animated diagrams where teacher description and a practical demonstration had previously proved less successful.

Another factor which clearly emerged from the study was the need that some pupils had for social interaction to stimulate and challenge them. Some pupils need to verbalised their thoughts to develop cognitive understanding. They need a person to ask questions of when learning, and find this route a means of gaining greater understanding. Jostens ILS may not enable this route to be taken if the use of the packages is not adequately supported by teacher presence.

Comfort and reassurance

Many pupils require reassurance when learning. This often takes the form of the need for reviewing and revising, and the comfort of working through existing material and subsequently gaining high attainment scores.

In using the ILS both teachers and pupils indicated the value of being able to review existing material. Pupils indicated their increased confidence from doing this in a range of ways, such as:

'it explains things better';

'you can go back and listen again';

'(you) can go over it as many times as you want'!

Comfort and reassurance also result when pupils believe they are learning effectively. To reinforce this point, their own comments suggest that the use of the package encourages this:

'you can learn at your own pace';

'teachers cannot moan at you';

'you work on your own level';

'it tells you when you have done things right'!

Analytical approaches to identifying pupil needs and weaknesses

Jostens ILS is constructed in two major ways:

- as a set of learning instruments which offer auditory and visual routes for input, and tactile means for outputs of knowledge and understanding;
- as a set of progressively arranged exercises and activities which cover curriculum areas extensively and in small steps.

The software provides, therefore, the theoretical opportunity to consider in an analytical way a range of needs and the weaknesses of individual pupils. However, to access these data it is necessary to observe pupils using the system, to ask relevant questions of them, and to analyse the responses within a framework of possibilities. By asking pupils about their impressions of the software, it is possible to obtain some indicators about their needs in learning terms. For example, a pupil saying that the program 'speaks to you', suggests that the pupil is benefiting from what he hears and may be stimulated by them.

When a pupil says that the program helps 'because you are mainly on your own' he may well be indicating the need to learn in an environment which is free from distractions, or where building individual self-esteem without being viewed or judged by others externally is particularly important. A pupil saying that 'all that is learned could be done in class' might be indicating a need for more social interaction in learning. A pupil indicating that 'it can be hard to understand an American accent' may be indicating that what he hears is important, but that the sounds offered are not particularly helping the pupil.

Observation and questioning allow other areas of learning to be explored. For example, learning can be considered as a set of processes which can be considered to have associated direction. Forward learning can be defined as processes concerned with the desire or need by the pupil to tackle new or even unexpected knowledge and understanding. Backward learning can be defined as processes concerned with the desire or need by the pupil to review existing knowledge and understanding. Sideways learning can be defined as processes concerned with the desire or need to explore unexpected avenues which arise from cognitive stimulation, perhaps linked to lateral associations or ideas. Pupil responses to the program can offer some indications of these process and the importance or need that individual pupils place upon them. For example, a pupil saying that 'it is too easy if you are at a higher level of learning' might indicate that the pupil wishes to engage more in forward learning than in backward learning. A pupil saying that 'you can go over it as many times as you want' might well indicate the need that the pupil has for backward learning.

Whilst ILS offers possibilities for the exploration and analysis of pupil learning needs and weaknesses, it is also necessary to be aware of the demands that this range of possibilities offers. To utilise this level of detail teachers need time to observe and to question, and they need a framework against which to consider the outcomes of these observations and responses. This set of options is likely to place considerable demands upon the teacher, but without this application, and without being able to respond to pupil reactions and needs, it is quite possible that pupils may be given inappropriate material, which causes frustration and possible rejection of the opportunities which such software affords.

Matching ILS materials to pupil needs

The match of ILS material to pupil needs can be considered in two main ways:

- the ability of the ILS to offer material which is at a level appropriate to the learning needs of the pupil;
- the range of curriculum materials to offer pupils subject knowledge and understanding in appropriately structured forms.

Teachers in this study found that the ILS enabled them to find material appropriate to the learning needs and abilities of the range of pupils in the study. Those who saw the package could readily see opportunities for use by pupils after less than one day of exposure to the ILS. However, in some cases teachers did feel that the number of exercises offered was insufficient to allow pupils opportunities to reinforce their learning.

Teachers often felt that the range of material appropriate to pupils needs was good, and used their considerable experience to choose material for use in particular circumstances. To make a reasonable choice for their pupils they need to be aware of the range of materials within the Jostens ILS.

Teachers who did match materials to pupil needs found in about half the cases that the potential match produced a productive outcome. For example, one teacher saw the potential of using early reading material to support a 13 year old non-reader. The material was presented so that the pupil could relate spoken letters and words to visual images and symbols of letters and words. The pupil was content to be able to tackle this in isolation – the inability to read had given the child a low level of self-esteem. After some 20 sessions on the package the child could recognise a vocabulary of some 12 words; after a term the child began to recognise these words outside the context of the package. In this instance, the material had been presented through visual, symbolic and spoken language, associated in ways which enabled a match of pupil need. Strong spoken, visual and symbolic association offered within the package was enabling the pupils to learn from a combination of sound, images and symbols.

Recording attainment and outcomes

Teachers in the study used some of the wide range of records of attainment provided by the ILS. The options used were generally confined to printouts of lesson coverage (a list of activities undertaken), marks recorded (in percentages correct), and dates when exercises were undertaken. In general teachers were content with this form and level of data, but some teachers felt that access to the data was far from easy.

In no cases did teachers use the data to transfer results from the school or unit to another location, and in all cases the teachers kept additional notes or information (either formally or informally) which provided a more complete picture of individual pupil attainment. After about half a term of use some teachers began to consider how the records from the system would support their more general assessment needs for the pupil and for the school or unit.

Rapid assessment of pupil learning needs

Jostens ILS does not have a mechanism that automatically places pupils at an appropriate level. In the pilot study teachers placed pupils at levels which they considered appropriate. In some cases teachers felt that they had managed this well, while in others they felt the need to review the placing of the pupil after only one session. Teachers in the study indicated the importance of checking the appropriateness of level regularly after each day or each week. The management system of the ILS offered teachers printouts which they used as a part of their own assessment mechanism to judge how well pupils were scoring on the exercises and on the tests offered at the end of grouped exercises.

Where rapid assessment of pupil learning needs is required, Jostens ILS offers two practical advantages:

- the ILS is arranged in levels which can be roughly matched to UK year groups, and to UK National Curriculum levels;
- the range of curriculum material in the package offers teachers rapid access to exercises which may be able to assess ability.

However, the use of the package for rapid assessment of pupil learning needs still relies heavily upon the assessment and judgement capability of the teacher. Where teachers feel confident in their abilities to undertake such assessment Jostens ILS may well be able to support them.

Provision of educational material

There were no indications in the study that pupils or teachers considered the material offered by Jostens ILS to be anything other than educational material. The evidence indicated that many children were engaged and stimulated by the material, and that they believed they had learned specifically as a result of using it. Teachers considered that use of the material had enabled many pupils to gain in positive ways, particularly in terms of self-confidence and self-esteem where there were issues about pupil self-perceptions of their learning abilities and their own knowledge and understanding.

The educational material within the package is structured and offered in four main ways:

- as a set of exercises which demand pupil response;
- as a presentation of textual and visual material, followed by questions and opportunities to make notes;
- as a means of stimulating open-ended writing in essay, letters, and other forms;
- as exercises to support accurate use of the keyboard.

In the study the main forms of the material required pupils to respond by reacting to specific questions and ideas. Open-ended responses were used to a lesser extent. So within this study, Jostens ILS has largely offered opportunities for rapid response, and provided rapid feedback and praise for pupils using it. It is in this area that pupils and teachers feel there has been most gain.

Other studies (see Chapter 3) indicate that the use of Jostens ILS has produced quantifiable learning gains over particular periods of time. It has yet to be established whether this is also the case in the UK. There were no indicators within the study which could point towards sustained or quantifiable learning gains, but it did report the satisfaction of many pupils and teachers in its use.

Teachers managing the use of Jostens ILS

This study and others on ILS indicate a number of features and factors which teachers and schools should consider when contemplating the use of Jostens ILS:

- concerns about pragmatic problems such as the equipment functioning adequately should be preempted by having support available.
- provision of technical, training and communication support needs to be considered and established early.
- teachers need to see the package and be convinced of its potential before attempting to use it further.
- to get started teachers need approximately a single day of training, on-hand support in school, and timetabled opportunities to use the equipment.
- teachers need opportunities to share concerns and ideas when difficulties arise.
- on sites where it is only possible for one machine to be present, its siting and use need careful consideration.
- where networks are deployed their integration for subject use needs to be considered. Firm ideas about subject integration of ILS use may not emerge until the equipment has been used for half a term or more. This implies a need to retain initial flexibility when considering the siting, deployment and timetabled use of ILS.
- the frequency and duration of use needs to be considered in relation to pupil needs.

Teachers using Jostens ILS

The results from other studies indicate a range of features and factors which teachers and schools should consider when contemplating the use of Jostens ILS:

- the creativity of the teacher is a major factor for its successful use.
- where teachers are seeking solutions to address pupil needs, and analysing outcomes and possibilities for learning situations, Jostens ILS may provide opportuni-

ties for both the teacher and the pupil.

- pupils are likely to find the package easy to use.
- the teacher is still required to provide adequate and appropriate interaction and support for pupils, particularly for those who value a social means of learning.
- some pupils are likely to benefit from the use of the package more than others. Most pupils are likely to find the presentation of material stimulating, but some may not. Pupils may well find that the ways in which certain subject material is presented suits their learning processes more easily than it does in other subjects.
- pupils with low attention spans may well be supported through appropriate use of the package.
- the ILS may be able to provide alternative ways for pupils to consider concepts, but may also be able to offer ways to review existing knowledge. It does not allow pupils to explore easily ideas which arise in *ad hoc* ways.
- if exercises and activities demand responses as reactions from pupils, then they are likely to require further opportunities and alternative methods to reinforce and assimilate learning. The learning style used may well need specific activities in classrooms to be established for individuals or groups of pupils at specific times.
- the package can be used to support the analysis of pupil's learning and their learning needs, but this requires time for observation and questioning, and a framework in which to undertake subsequent analysis of the outcomes gained.
- the variety of material available from Jostens ILS is large but some areas may not provide the range of exercises required for pupils to fully assimilate some concepts and skills.
- the management system of the ILS provides printouts of certain attainment outcomes, but teachers are likely to require at least half a term using the ILS before being able to apply these data fully to school assessment needs.
- teachers wishing to undertake rapid assessment of pupils' abilities may be able to utilise the wide range of content in the ILS, but will still be required to apply their own assessment criteria and judgements.

Conclusion

In a limited study Jostens ILS has been shown to have the potential to support pupil learning, particularly in isolated learning situations where teachers need to explore ways to engage intellectual domains. Other studies (Columbus Public Schools 1994) would suggest that Jostens ILS has the potential of offering quantifiable learning gains within the UK. At present no studies have been conducted and completed in the UK to validate and support the findings of this small scale study. However, the evidence suggests that schools considering the use of ILS should not dismiss the opportunity to consider Jostens ILS.

Learning is a dynamic process, and teachers who can see potential have been able to apply their creativity in ways to support pupils in difficult situations. These circumstances often depend on the ability of the teacher to identify the means to stimulate and engage the intellectual domain in spite of the resistance caused by disturbances of the emotional, attitudinal or social domains. There is no suggestion in this or other studies that Jostens ILS will provide the entire answer. What it may do, however, is provide a link or key in a sequence or armoury of mechanisms which enable these other means to be tapped and used caused by disturbance of the the reluctant, the distracted, the distraught, the interested, the concerned, the unsure, or the low self-esteem child.

Ultimately education seeks to reward the isolated learner, and Jostens ILS is a resource which is likely to support a range of individuals. The focus of research attention should perhaps now be upon identifying for which individuals, in which circumstances, and over what periods of time this support might be most effectively gained.

Management issues

Maeve Stone and Jim Houghton

Evidence from the NCET pilot project has shown that the quality of management has a strong influence on the successful implementation of an ILS. An ILS will be a major investment for any school and the best returns will be ensured by good management at institution, department and classroom level. Decisions about the management of ILS taken at the pre-planning stage will be crucial to its successful implementation. As with any major innovation, careful consideration will need to be given to the following questions:

- Where are we now?
- Where do we want to be?
- When do we want to get there?
- What do we need to get there?
- When do we want to get there?
- How will we know when we are there?

Where are we now?

Having established the need for an ILS the senior management team will need to discuss where such a system would best support and extend work across the school. The school's training needs will need to be analysed and a curriculum audit carried out. It cannot be emphasised enough how important it will be to establish the school's present position before strategies for implementing an ILS are considered.

Where do we want to be?

To ensure effective implementation staff will need to be consulted and involved in the initial introduction of ILS and be aware of its potential impact on different curriculum areas. One outcome of this process would be to identify those areas likely to benefit most from involvement with ILS. Following on from this there will be a need to elicit what the school hopes to achieve by using an ILS, thus establishing clear goals by which the system can be evaluated.

When do we want to get there?

A carefully-phased timetable for implementation will smooth the process of implementation. In Florida, where ILS has been introduced state-wide, the implementation plan is spread over five years. It is unlikely that such a Utopian state of affairs will exist in many UK schools but time to embed the innovation will prove invaluable. Failure to allow an adequate period for this embedding process will lead sooner or later to significant frustration and disenchantment amongst both staff and pupils. For example students unfamiliar with a Windows environment could find their work wiped from the screen and have no idea how to get it back. Some ILS have a time-out algorithm. Any unanswered problem will be removed from the screen after a set period and treated as a wrong answer for the purpose of assessment. Unless teachers know how to alter the time allowance, students with slow response times could be timed out and marked down which could result in their being offered work below their capabilities. Sometimes systems will lock up; unless the student or the teacher knows how to circumvent the problem, the history of the student's work could be lost and whole sessions may have to be repeated.

What do we need to get there?

The first consideration will be the housing of the ILS. Planning for accommodation should include the selection of benching or other appropriate furniture, storage areas, rewiring and security measures. Where half the class is to be taught conventionally while the other half uses the ILS, an area must be set up which houses both groups. If ILS workstations are to be dispersed into individual classrooms, siting of the machines must be pre-planned taking into consideration both the class teacher's preferences and the requirements of the network.

At this stage the software will have to be selected. There are several ILS on the market and the school will need to consider which best fits their needs, ethos and budget. Once a particular ILS has been chosen the next decision will concern the hardware.

The ILS vendors will have given guidance on those computers which will run their programmes satisfactorily. Stand-alone machines will be able to run the programs from CD-ROMS but where several workstations are being installed a network would be more appropriate. Schools should take advice from the ILS vendors about file servers. On the whole a high capacity server will be a good investment for the future.

Schools will need to ensure they have clear contracts with suppliers which cover purchase, installation and the level of support which the school requires. Issues relating to system upgrades should also be clarified at the outset.

It would not be wise to skimp on staff training and development. An ILS is an expensive investment and its successful implementation relies crucially on the attitude and skills of the teachers using it. Teachers will need more than a superficial knowledge of the day-to-day running of the system. They will require time to become familiar with the units and, where appropriate, to integrate the contents of the ILS curriculum with normal class curriculum and practice, to ensure that the two complement each other. Once the system is in use they will need further training to become more sophisticated users of the ILS' management system.

After initial staff training, time will need to be set aside for ensuring appropriate student placement on the system or the setting up of work plans, depending on the ILS in use. Students will also require a structured introduction to the system. An initial period of experimental sessions with extra teacher support so that problems can be spotted and anxieties allayed should prove beneficial. For example, research has shown that to make progress students will need at least three sessions a week on SuccessMaker (Chapter 5). Efficient timetabling will be essential to ensure each student gets adequate time on the system.

How will we know when we are there?

As with all curriculum innovations it will be important to set up appropriate monitoring and evaluation procedures at the outset. These might include pre-testing and post-testing, questionnaires, observation and students' own assessments at planned intervals. Amongst schools involved in the NCET project, standardised tests such as Slaters and NFER have been used to establish scores in mathematics, reading and spelling prior to the implementation of ILS and again after a set period of use. A good ILS will also have its own built in system of recording progress but it must be borne in mind that this will only reflect work covered by the software.

The management of an ILS will need to include physical and curricular aspects and among the issues to be considered are:

Models of use

Once the decision to install an ILS has been taken, consideration has to given to its dispersal about the school. During the pilot project six different models for the location of ILS were used. The advantages and disadvantages of each of these models are shown in the following table:

Advantages and disadvantages of different locations for the ILS

Location	Advantages	Disadvantages
ILS room – set up for all to use ILS, with whole or part class groups attending	Supervision is easier and can improve pupil/teacher ratio Facilitates cross-curricular, flexible usage and whole school ownership Can facilitate involvement of cross-curricular specialists e.g. learning support	Might be perceived as separate, not integral to classwork Might cause timetable clashes, if using system flexibly as and when appropriate May require a large number of workstations
ILS Room/ classroom – set up for mixed work; typically half on and half off the system	Subject teacher can spend 'quality time' with smaller teaching group off system Subject teacher is available to deal with any problems ILS seen as integral to class work Subject teacher can become familiar with system Facilitates cross-curricular usage	Might cause timetable clashes, if using the system flexibly as and when appropriate Subject teacher may not become familiar with content due to focus on supervision of group working off-system
Specialist departmental room(s) – set up for ILS; typically half on and half off the system	No timetabling problems Subject specialist always available Individual support for small groups; increased "quality time' Flexibility of use – to support a range of teaching and learning styles May stimulate departmental teamwork	Limited cross-curricular access Problems may be caused by lack of whole school ownership

Advantages and disadvantages of different locations for the ILS (continued)

Location	Advantages	Disadvantages
Distributed network of ILS workstations throughout school	Facilitates cross-curricular use and whole school ownership Enables imaginative management Enhances possibilities for flexible learning and teaching Encourages pupils to take responsibility for their own learning	Costly if it is to be effective Timetabled use may be difficult Security more difficult Could promote ownership problems if not available throughout school Teachers may need training in classroom management of the resource.
Standalone ILS computer(s) installed for specific purposes using CD-ROM	Can be available to meet specific needs, even at short notice Can be particularly useful for emotional and behavioural difficulties or pupils with special educational needs. Can be used for cross-curricular work Can be used effectively with small groups, pairs etc.	CD-ROM limits amount of material Provides limited access
Library/open – ILS workstations as a central resource in open plan or library setting	Makes the resource available to all pupils Considerable learning asset to Learning Resources Centres Can promote autonomous learning	Lack of ownership by staff/pupils can lead to limited effect on learning gains Adequate supervision difficult Individual learning programmes needed to enable effective monitoring of progress

Advantages and disadvantages of different staffing models

Staffing	Advantages	Disadvantages
Teacher co-ordinator static in ILS lab – supervising most/all classes and groups	High level of individual support available Opportunity and records of achievement action planning with individual pupils relating to their work on ILS Continuity and coherence for staff and pupils Flexible whole school use possible Effective diagnosis can be fed back to class teacher	Subject/class teacher not directly involved, so reduced involvement and curriculum integration Uses one member of staff full time Can limit imaginative and creative use Reliant on one skilled member of staff
Teacher and class move to specialist ILS lab	Subject teachers very familiar with content so there are opportunities to integrate work on/off ILS Teacher uses subject expertise in support of individuals Can stimulate flexible usage as part of a range of learning and teaching styles Teachers begin to use reports information diagnostically	Timetabling can be a problem, unless used regularly in a predetermined way (which can be inappropriate) Some disruption to classes moving to and from the ILS lab
Teacher working in own subject room with her/his own pupils	No time tabling problems – subject specialist always available Quality time created with reduced number of pupils Teacher familiar with content and reports Flexibility of use to support variety of teaching and learning styles; can act as catalyst for other development Departmental ownership can increase teacher motivation May develop departmental team work	It can be difficult to involve all members of the department Limited access for cross-curricular use Problems caused by lack of whole school ownership – whole school strategy needed May constrain the development of other initiatives

Advantages and disadvantages of different staffing models

Staffing	Advantages	Disadvantages
Part or whole of class move to ILS lab with supervision by ancillary	Flexible, whole school usage possible Technical/operational support may be very good Subject teachers freed to have 'quality time' with smaller groups Can be economically staffed Provides opportunities for continuity and coherence	Subject/class teacher not directly involved, so reduced choice and integration Can limit imaginative and creative use
ILS self-standing with supervision either intermittent or indirect	Pupils who are self-sustaining may still gain from working on ILS in this way Very economical in staffing terms Can free class teachers to work with smaller groups whilst some are on ILS	lack of supervision can devalue the use of ILS in the eyes of pupils and result in limited learning gains Pupil access needs more flexible management

Setting up an ILS suite

The setting up of a dedicated ILS suite in a normal classroom is likely to involve a minor works contract to establish the appropriate infrastructure. An ILS suite requires benching, comfortable and adjustable seating, network and electrical distribution systems, security, adequate lighting, and probably window blinds. The requirements of children with special needs will need to be planned into the design, for example wheelchair access and different input devices. Where the model requires accommodation in which a whole class may be taught, some on ILS while the rest are working more conventionally with the teacher, thought will have to be given to whether the ILS stations are set around the outside of the classroom or at one end. ILS stations will need to be positioned so the student can work without distraction.

Classroom management

With all models of use there will be a need to look at classroom management and teaching styles. In common with other educational innovations the introduction of ILS will make significant demands on classroom organisation and management. Where group work is common practice ILS will be fitted into the normal classroom routine much more easily than where more formal teaching is the norm. Indeed, within the pilot project it was found that ILS was a stimulus for some teachers to expand their repertoire of teaching styles.

Software

Software will need to be chosen before hardware. Having chosen a particular ILS, a further decision will need to be made whether to purchase the whole package or some subset of it. Where a network is being used it will have a direct bearing on the specifications of the file-server. All ILS systems offer modules on literacy and numeracy but some have now expanded into other areas such as KS4 mathematics and English, science, modern languages and personal and social educatiom.The range is continuing to expand, particularly with the integration of third party software.

All the systems make some provision, to a greater or lesser extent, for the incorporation of third-party software. However, in the UK the Open Integrated Learning Systems (OILS) standard, now adopted by British Educational Suppliers Association, should provide the vehicle for the management system of an ILS to launch third-party software, and to extract performance data from that program for inclusion in management reports.This standard is embryonic at this stage but offers significant possibilities for expanding the content base on offer.

All software houses are actively improving their software in quality and range and the new versions often require more highly specified machines to run. Schools will need to consider whether the benefits of the upgrade are justified in terms of the increased machine specification and its associated cost.The involvement of staff in extra work in becoming familiar with and integrating the new content will also need be taken into account.

Hardware

Having selected the software the school will need to choose computers capable of running it reliably.The ILS in the project were all designed for use on PC or IBM compatible computers or Apple machines. Global software was adapted so it could also be run on Acorn Risc PCs. High specification machines are demanded by all the systems and care will need to be taken to ensure chosen computers match the specifications of the ILS vendors, particularly with regard to screen resolutions, system RAM and sound cards. Where a network is to be used, the server will need to be a very high specification machine with a hard disc capacity of several gigabytes.

With all equipment a degree of future-proofing will be advisable going well beyond the manufacturers' specification for the current version of the software. Once a network has been set up, care will need to be taken when adding extra machines. If the file server specification is not high enough delays in screen refreshing will occur which may affect students' concentration. In the pilot project, students with behavioural problems were particularly affected by such delays.

Peripherals

Headphones will need to be sturdy, comfortable and have individual volume controls for each ear. Provision for cleaning the earpieces will need to be considered. Baby wipes have proved a simple solution in some schools.

Input could be by keyboard, mouse or trackerball. Other input devices may need to be considered for students with special needs. Special arrangements such as induction loops and large screen monitors can be made for the hearing and visually impaired. Other useful devices to improve access are a touch screen, large key keyboard, or a glidepoint where finger movements and taps on a small pad replace the mouse and mouse buttons.

Security

As with all IT provision, there will be a need for security devices.These could include locks on doors, bars on windows, movement alarms and fluorescent post code markings on all machines.

Timetabling

Some of the skill development ILS modules are designed to be used for short but frequent periods whereas the more investigatory modules can be integrated more easily into the classroom teaching routine. The former case will necessitate additional detailed timetabling arrangements to incorporate ILS sessions into the teaching day. The latter will require more detailed planning by the teacher who will be required to put together individual or group programmes to support work within the existing structure.

Anecdotal evidence emerged during both phases of the evaluation project that students benefited from taking breaks away from regular use of the system. Many teachers felt the students returned to the ILS with renewed enthusiasm. If this is the case, a system of ILS use might involve students accessing the system for concentrated blocks of time at different periods in their school career or at different stages of individual development.

In primary schools, where a more informal timetable may be in place, it will be much easier to ensure a rotation of students giving easy access to ILS throughout the day and ensuring full use of the ILS stations.

In secondary schools this will not be so easy. Within the evaluation project some mathematics and English departments felt their share of the students' time for National Curriculum work was curtailed when students took time out to go on the ILS. Thought will need to be given to whether basic numeracy and literacy are entirely a matter for these departments or whether they could reasonably be considered a cross-curricular issue. If this is the case, time for ILS should not come only from the mathematics and English time allowance. The entire timetable should be top-sliced to allow students to access ILS without having to miss their normal mathematics and English allocation.

Staffing models

There were five different models of staffing in the project schools:

- **Teacher co-ordinator permanently placed** in ILS laboratory supervising most classes and groups
- **Teacher and class move** to specialist ILS laboratory
- **Teacher in own room** working with her/his own pupils
- **Ancillary** - Part or whole of class move to ILS laboratory with supervision by a non-teaching assistant
- **Indirect** - ILS self-standing with supervision either intermittent or indirect

The following tables identify the advantages and disadvantages of each of these models for different ILS:

Primary schools – SuccessMaker

Room model	Staffing model	School	Results	Comments
ILS room	**Teacher Co-ordinator**	A	Significant maths and very significant reading results	Pupils in class groups, half on computer, half with teacher
				Teachers using reports diagnostically
ILS room	**Teacher Co-ordinator**	C		Average results
				Special needs teacher supervises withdrawn groups, interprets reports and feeds back to colleagues
ILS room	**Ancillary**	D	Significant maths results	Half classes with ancillary; teacher has 'quality time' plus observation time
				Head modified model to allow class teachers time to observe their pupils and examine reports
ILS room	**Ancillary**	S		Good results
				Small school with family groupings i.e. children of mixed ages; pupils rotate to different activities, one of which is ILS
Library/ open access area	**Indirect**	R	No difference for early years	KS1 children have worked well and enthusiastically in a situation where supervision is spasmodic. Class teachers have not become involved and pupils feel ILS work is not valued by them.
Library/ open access area	**Indirect**	U	No difference	Pupils spasmodically supervised and observed not always to be on task.
Distributed in classrooms	**Teacher in own room**	B	Average results	Only two classrooms have workstations. School tried to re-schedule sessions to allow for more pupil access. Loss of regularity led to decline in learning gains.

Secondary schools – SuccessMaker

Room model	Staffing model	School	Results	Comments
ILS room	**Teacher and class move**	E	Very significant maths results	ILS group maintains advantage over control group once ILS usage stops
ILS Room	**Teacher and class move**	F	Significant maths results	Use of 'quality time' with half groups; curriculum integration has worked better in maths than in English.
		I	No difference	One 10–20 minute session per week only
		M	Significant maths results and very significant reading	Subject teachers in ILS session; model has worked well because of good whole school inset
ILS Room	**Teacher Co-ordinator**	G		Good use with E2L pupils Teacher using reports and selecting appropriate modules

Primary schools – Global

Room model	Staffing model	School	Results	Comments
Library / open plan	**Indirect**	O	No difference	Severe technical problems caused by the incompatibility of software and hardware delayed the start of the project
Library / open plan	**Indirect**	P	No difference	Severe technical problems delayed the start of the project

Secondary schools – Global

Room model	Staffing model	School	Results	Comments
Subject Department room	**Teacher in own room**	J		Good exam results Has worked well in maths, but so far less well in English. Part of an impressive school improvement. Teacher development in maths dept.
ILS Room	**Teacher and class move**	K	No difference	Time on system in phase 2 reduced to one half hour session per week
"		L	No difference	System relocated on a number of occasions
"		N	No difference	Severe technical problems delayed start of project
"		Q	No difference	Severe technical problems delayed start of project

Special school – SuccessMaker

Room model	Staffing model	School	Results	Comments
Distributed in classrooms	Teacher in own room	T		Good results. Model has worked well in this special school, where each classroom has a workstation, and this has led to improved management of learning, a more diagnostic approach to assessment and teacher development in both IT and curriculum.

Conclusion

Supervision and teacher intervention seem to be major factors in those schools with positive gains in numeracy. This may be related to ensuring pupils' time on ILS is spent on tasks. The attention may also improve their perception of the value of ILS. For early years and special needs there is evidence that a distributed model where pupils and teachers remain in their own classroom is more appropriate.

The involvement of class and subject teachers, either through being in the same room or by using the report information diagnostically in their teaching, aids curriculum integration and ensures that pupils recognise ILS as a positive part of learning. This is demonstrated in the two schools where learning gains were achieved in reading. In school A, a primary school, teachers saw from the SuccessMaker reports that children were avoiding work on comprehension. They were able to intervene to remedy this and children made significant gains in literacy. Clearly there is a significant correlation with the issues raised in the table on room use.

It will be crucial to give sufficient time for induction and familiarisation to all staff involved in the use of ILS. Without teacher commitment any innovation will be handicapped and may even prove fatally flawed.

Teachers will need time to understand the management system and become familiar with the software content of programs their students will be using. They will also need time to observe the students on the system, to print out reports and evaluate the information. This information will be critical to informed use of the system and for integrating ILS work into classroom practice.

After initial training, sessions will need to be arranged at regular intervals to continue the familiarisation process and to support the integration of skills acquired on the ILS into schemes of work. As teachers grow more at ease with ILS they will become ready to take on more of what the system offers. Responsibility within the management system can then be devolved, spreading the load.

Technical support

Although most systems have proved to be reliable there is an additional need to ensure technical support is available. This is particularly relevant during the bedding down stage but is also required to ensure smooth running of a network and individual stations. In secondary schools technical support may be supplied internally but primary schools are likely to be dependent upon external support.

The software and hardware houses involved in the pilot project are in the process of setting up a one stop technical support system. This has been found necessary because schools are not always sure whether a problem is caused by the ILS software or by the hardware/network. Those schools with an IT technician are ideally placed but all schools can make big savings on call out charges if at least one member of staff is able to deal with common problems. Again, special training may be necessary but savings in time as well as money will be made in the long run.

Schools should develop strategies for crisis management to cope with system crashes and the resultant loss of data and work plans. The regular backing-up of data should be incorporated into the job specification of a member of staff who need not necessarily be a teacher.

Community use

Outside school hours it would be possible to offer time on ILS systems to other groups within the community such as University of the Third Age classes, parents or former pupil groups and job seekers. Where appropriate, this could prove a useful income generator for the school.

US influences

In those systems originating in the US the sound track is spoken in an American accent. Moreover, the modules on money use US coinage and the spelling units contain some unfamiliar spellings. Some ILS vendors are in the process of customising units for the British market. However, it has been found that once students have become accustomed to the materials these issues are of decreasing importance. The pupils of today are the children of the television age and do not find the accents or the idiom at all strange.

Prerequisite student skills

The ILS used in the evaluation were not written for special needs students although the majority of such students encountered no difficulty in using ILS. Where problems occurred it was usually amongst those who had not yet become sufficiently mature or whose physical handicaps made computer use difficult. Access for the latter can often be facilitated by the use of specific input devices, but nevertheless individual students must meet essential baseline requirements in terms of sensory input, mechanical skills, visual and auditory perception, and ability to concentrate and follow instructions. They must have adequate keyboard skills and be able to follow the language of instruction and they must not be antagonistic to computer use.

The introduction of ILS into a school is only a starting point. To ensure full returns from the investment, a well thought out management model will need to be put in place at an early stage. It will need to be adequately funded in terms of money and time, and regularly revised to suit the school's changing needs and the advances being made in both hardware and software.

CHAPTER
17

Counting the cost of ILS

Malcolm R Hunt

The introduction and integration of ILS into an institution is not cheap. Nor is the cost purely a financial consideration; there are other prices to be paid in terms of time, planning and the general changes that such an undertaking involves.

This chapter is based on the key findings from interviews conducted with staff from three schools involved in the NCET ILS evaluation, who had identified a number of hidden costs associated with the use of ILS in their institutions. It is also informed by other desk-based research on the general cost issues associated with the use of information technology in education and training.

The findings are by no means comprehensive nor was the intention to arrive at a fully costed model applicable to every situation. Indeed it soon became clear as the project unfolded that it is difficult to cost such activities in detail as every institutional situation is unique. Rather an attempt was made to identify some of the key cost areas, especially the hidden costs that arise when working with a relatively new technology and to log them so that others can learn from the experience and hopefully overcome them or reduce their impact in the future.

A costing model for ILS

As the NCET ILS evaluation project developed it became clear that there are a number of expected and hidden costs involved in implementing and integrating a complex system such as ILS into a school. These have been based on a costing model adapted from two costing methodologies (Knapp and Orlansky 1983; Fletcher 1990) to meet the specific requirements of education and ILS in particular.

The stages in the model are as follows:

1) Research and planning
The costs associated with the planning and researching of which system/software to purchase and the implications for its introduction and use within a given institution.

2) Initial investment
The cost of the system consists of fixed and variable costs.

3) Operating and support costs
These relate to the managment, operation and maintenance of the system after implementation. It is possible to consider them annually or over a number of years, depending on how long it is considered that the system will be operative before it will need replacing, either because the hardware is out of date or because the software has become too sophisticated to run successfully on the equipment originally installed.

4) Disposal and salvage
The costs associated with the removal of a given intervention set against the salvage value of any equipment, assuming that it has a market value and is saleable. While this

Stage	Key items	Definitions/explanation
1. Research & development	• Staff time (internal) IT Co-ordinator ILS Co-ordinator Senior staff Subject staff Technician	Time spent by staff researching the various possibilities, planning meetings Report writing, feasibility studies, pilot trials, visits and consultations with suppliers
	• Staff time (external)	Cost of external consultant, LEA staff time or builders/architects needed to advise on changes to the buildings
	• Books & stationary	Purchase of research reports and support literature
	• Admin. time	Secretarial support to type reports and collate budget figures
	• Conferences	Fact finding at conferences/workshops
	• Travel and subs.	Travel costs for internal and external staff
	• Postage & telephone charges	
	• Displacement costs	Costs associated with the reciting of resources displaced as a result of ILS implementation
	• Public relations activities	Briefing meetings for parents, press and other interested parties
	• Telephone charges	Increased phone bills associated with ILS
2. Initial investment (a) Non-recurring costs	• Building costs	New building work and/or the refurbishment or alterations of existing buildings
	• Electrical work	Installation of new power cables, trunking and supply sockets
	• Network cabling	Installation of an Ethernet network system, including cables, sockets and infrastructure for 8 or 15 work stations
	• Furniture	Including chairs, tables, benching for each station, partitions and flooring materials
	• Security system	Provision of new alarm system, or extension of existing installation to protect network room and related measures such as window bars and locks
	• Fitments and fittings	e.g. blinds to prevent eye strain, carpeting
(b) Recurring costs	• Hardware: Client workstations File server	Machines capable of running a graphics-based interface at an acceptable speed, 4Mb RAM, a local hard disc & storage capacity 80Mb or greater e.g. 80486 DX with at least 16Mb RAM, large capacity in the order of 1 Gb
	• Peripherals	Printers, headphones, microphones and CD drives
	• Software: Network ILS management system ILS module software Licence agreements	Initial purchase costs e.g. Novell NetWare or AppleShare e.g. SuccessMaker or Global To use modules and management system
	• Initial installation costs	Initial installation of MIS and module software by the ILS developer
	• Support materials	Relating to the given software or locally produced materials required for induction, training or student support
	• Supplies	Printer paper, discs, ribbons, replacement leads
	• Insurance premiums	Increased insurance premiums to cover the new equipment and buildings as well as those relating to warranty cover
	• Staffing (internal) New staff	New appointments required to implement the new system, including a system manager if not an existing member of staff

(continued)		
	Existing staff	Costs of existing staff if not covered elsewhere and/or the time required to implement the system, where supply cover may be used
	Technician	Technical coordinator who can manage the network and hardware
	Non-teaching assistant	Teacher support for all groups using ILS, able to read and interpret reports and familiar with relevant curriculum software
	• Support staff (External) Installation Engineers	May need to consider those from a range of companies covering: hardware, software and network installation if not covered by warranty agreements
	Other consultants	
	• Training Internal	Time & resourcing for the training of staff within the institution who will be using the system and the development of curriculum support materials
	External	Time & resourcing for the training of individuals off site at the hardware or software provider premises
	• Travel expenses	To and from training sessions and meetings
	• Admin. support	To cover the cost of processing invoices, secretarial support and material production
	• Telephone call charges	Some ILS sites have incurred significant phone call charges associated with calls to suppliers over technical problems and system faults/failures
	• Energy costs	Institutions may wish to make provision for the increased electricity costs associated with the operation of large network systems
3. Operating & support costs (per year or for the estimated life time of the system	• Maintenance costs (a) Hardware Workstations Network	Including the file server and the Ethernet infrastructure
	(b) Software Network	The cost of maintaining the network software including call out charges
	ILS software	Covering the cost of maintaining the system, including call out charges caused by problems with the existing ILS module software
	(c) Peripherals (d) Security system	Printers, headphones, microphones and CD drives On going maintenance contracts, associated security costs, alarm systems and insurance premiums
	• Rental costs	If equipment has not been purchased outright
	• Support materials	Relating to the given software or locally produced materials required for induction, training or student support
	• Software upgrades Network ILS management software ILS module software Installation costs	Upgrades for both the network and ILS software New software to upgrade the management system Purchase of new software to upgrade the system New module software Costs associated with the installation of any new software which may have to be done by a hardware or software supplier
	• Hardware upgrades	Additional hardware upgrades caused by software upgrades and/or expansion of the system
	Workstations	Addition of new machines or improvements to existing workstations

(continued)	Network system	Expansion of the network to improve existing server Upgrade of the buildings, maintenance, repairs
	• Building repairs • Staffing (internal) New staff Existing staff Technician Non-teaching assistant • Technical support staff (external) Engineers	From a large range of companies covering: hardware, software and network installation, depending on the fault
	Other consultants	To advise on improvements to the system and software upgrades
	Maintenance/ warranty contracts • Other equipment upgrades	Cost of maintaining system after initial warranty agreements expire Additions to the system prompted by the upgrading of the software or as a result of experience gained from using the system
	• Staff training Internal	On going for system managers on software upgrades and in the use of advanced features. Also updating for staff and induction for new staff Off site at the hardware or software provider
	External • Travel expenses • Admin. support • Misc.	To cover such things as unforeseen breakages to peripherals
	• Evaluation	Evaluation of the system to date, the identification of problems, feedback to developers, planning for future use and integration with the curriculum
4. Disposal & salvage	• Equipment value • Disposal costs • Staff redundancies/ relocation/training • Other costs	Money gained from the sale of hardware Cost of equipment disposal if not saleable Cost of making staff redundant or re-training to a new role and job Cost of reorganising furniture and buildings to new activities. Reconditioning or changing hardware configurations to meet the requirements of a new role

Notes: The model seeks to be as comprehensive as possible and in doing so certain items may be inappropriate.
For example, an institution may wish to absorb building, staffing and training costs within existing budgets rather than assign them directly to ILS.

Aspects of the model have been adapted from the work of Knapp and Orlansky 1983, and Fletcher 1990.

Figure 1 NCET costing model for Integrated Learning Systems

terminology may be considered more appropriate to an industrial situation, it does highlight the need to see the introduction of ILS as an investment. If it is decided to discontinue using the system at any point in the future, or to upgrade the network with new machines, the equipment may still have a value to the institution, rather than being written off.

The more detailed version of the model in Figure 1 identifies specific costs in each stage. Traditionally costings are expressed in monetary terms, but it may be more helpful to consider costs in other ways, such as the numbers and types of work tasks required, and likely time considerations, as it may be difficult to put a monetary value on these costs.

The costing model includes sections for staffing and training; these may or may not be directly attributable to the introduction of ILS, as institutions may develop the job specification or description of staff to include work on ILS and cover the costs from existing staffing or training budgets.

Many schools have found that a proportion of the ongoing costs of ILS may be absorbed into general IT, departmental and training budgets, making it more difficult to assess the true costs of ILS. Indeed, once an institution or individual begins to consider how best to cost the introduction of ILS, the problems of which costs to include soon become apparent, along with the issue of how to measure them in a way that is most helpful to the institution. This raises qualitative issues about the planning and management of resources, and it may be helpful to see the model not so much as a comprehensive guide covering every possible cost likely to be incurred, but rather a checklist of key cost areas for consideration which will need adaptation to meet local need and specific situations.

The key costs of ILS

When costing this initial stage it may be more helpful to consider costs not just in monetary terms but also changes in the number and type of work tasks undertaken by staff, and time implications for those staff.

Time and planning

The introduction of any new educational intervention or technological approach to learning requires planning and preparation. In the case of ILS, given the size of initial investment many schools have taken the view that they want as many children as possible to use the system.

Recent evaluation reports (NCET 1996 and Underwood *et al* 1996) have stated that for those schools using SuccessMaker, the system will be most effective if students have three to five half-hour sessions a week. Any less exposure would appear to dilute the impact of the system on student learning. In many primary schools it may be possible for every child to use the system. Many have developed a rolling timetable programme for each school term: children are divided into small groups and allocated set time slots on the system, at varying times during the day for every week of the term.

There are as many approaches to the use of the system as there are schools, but the important issue is the thought, co-ordination and co-operation that this exercise involves: contingency planning for times when the network might be out of action or a given work station may be down; plans for dovetailing existing teaching staff, parent and teacher support staff in with the day to day operation of the system.

Where ILS responsibility were split between a member of the senior management team and the IT co-ordinator some schools found a pattern in the way staff time commitments developed. Senior staff were heavily involved during the initial planning, justifying the investment in ILS to other staff and governors. Educational benefits needed to be weighed against resourcing and other budget commitments. Once the system was installed and became operational the time commitment shifted towards IT and subject staff as technical and curriculum planning issues were worked through.

Schools have also identified the time spent on public relations issues and contacts with parents as a significant factor in initial planning. The introduction of ILS is a major undertaking and parents need to be briefed and introduced to the system. One primary head commented that:

> '... parents have to feel good about it (the ILS system) given that it is their children using the system...'

Some schools have run open evenings for parents and other people in the local community, including the local press. All these events require careful planning to ensure that they are a success and have to be fitted in alongside other school commitments.

There are also policy and planning issues surrounding how and why ILS is being introduced into school, with knock on effects for curriculum planning and whole school policies. Some schools see the network as being not just for the operation of ILS but as a vehicle for the delivery of other curriculum objectives. Depending on the software in operation these might include supporting the whole school IT policy, allowing greater differentiation within the curriculum, and enhancing the school assessment initiative. These matters need clarifying at the outset if the project is to be implemented successfully.

Many schools find that they need to renovate existing rooms or carry out extensive building work to accommodate the new technology. Such major activities need careful co-ordination and advance planning. As new space is created for ILS, other equipment and activities may be displaced and space will have to be found for them elsewhere in the school.

Hardware and software

All the schools in the evaluation received financial support from NCET/DfEE for the purchase of the hardware and software and many were able to increase the sum through initiatives by hardware manufacturers and grants from their LEA or TEC. Many schools have negotiated arrangements with their LEA or well-known hardware and software suppliers that have resulted in benefits for all parties over and above the initial commitment to work together on ILS. Having said this, the building of such relationships require time, effort and goodwill, all of which are 'costs' for all concerned. Many institutions, especially primary schools, felt that they would not have been able to fund such developments using their own resources and that grant aid was essential to fund the initial investment.

Hardware costs vary according to the size and type of network and the software employed. Several factors had a bearing on hardware and software selection, and ultimately on costs: specification of machine; level and type of technical support on offer inside the school and from suppliers; compatibility considerations relating to existing hardware, curriculum and IT policy. As a rough guide, the recent NCET report of Phase 2 of the ILS evaluation suggested the following costings for initial hardware investment:

Key item	8 station network	15 station network
Client workstations	£8,400	£15,525
File server	£5,000	£6,000
Peripherals	£1,200	£2,025

Equipment specification and compatibility

It is important when choosing what hardware to purchase to consider the technical spec-ification required very carefully. With such a complex system involving the interrelation of various pieces of software, the minimum hardware specification required to run the soft-ware, including the quality of sound cards fitted, needs to be determined. There is a strong case for ensuring that hardware is over specified to keep compatibility problems to a min-imum and allow for possible changes in specification that might be required to run the next software upgrade.

In cases where schools have used thoroughly tested and established hardware/software configurations, the level of technical problems and system down time appear to be mini-mal compared with institutions where untested combinations of hardware and software were adopted. In the latter, various technical problems arose which were not easily recti-fied without external technical support that in some cases resulted in the need to upgrade equipment.

Weighing competitive hardware prices against on-going technical support

Some schools found that when deciding on suppliers it was not just a question of consid-ering value for money in terms of the highest specification for lowest cost, although this was an important consideration. Technical support, especially where unusual combina-tions of hardware and software were involved, was also important, as was the time taken resolving technical issues or problems with late or incomplete deliveries of equipment, as this can quickly wipe out any of the savings made on hardware or software purchases.

Quality issues for hardware, peripherals, network infrastructure and furnishings

Many schools have found that to invest in cheaper equipment in a bid to cut initial costs did not in the long term save money. Schools reported that they had to replace cabling and network connectors with higher quality units after a year to 18 months of installation. Oth-ers felt that the same approach should also be applied when refurbishing rooms, purchas-ing window blinds and chairs and industrial standard carpeting, which would be more durable and help to provide a quality working environment. There was also a strong case for investing in a network infrastructure that was capable of future expansion and allowed for the upgrading of the file server at a future date.

Staffing time

A major consideration in the initial stages of the introduction of ILS was staff time costs. In many schools the ILS or IT co-ordinators recounted stories of hours spent trouble shoot-ing technical problems, and discussing them with the LEA, the software and hardware sup-pliers, often in their own time after school hours and in the holidays.

A factor in this issue is the level of technical knowledge that the school has in house. Where schools had staff able and willing to investigate the various faults and the time to liaise with manufacturers and suppliers, identify and rectify faults, this saved the school having to bring in an engineer. Schools needed to balance the time involved in such activities with the level of technical back up covered in any maintenance or warranty agreement. It is often difficult to identify the exact location of a given fault and where different suppliers are responsible for different components of the system expensive call out charges for engineers can be incurred if no comprehensive maintenance agreement is in place.

A number of schools have found that involvement in a national project has brought publicity and kudos to the school. This could be a double edged sword. On the one hand this required time and planning. There was a need to engage in awareness raising and public relations work with a number of groups including parents, staff, governors, colleagues in local schools, LEA officials and the local press. On the other hand, raising the profile of the institution and developing new links, partnerships and relationships, all takes time and the benefits can be difficult to quantify, although some schools have charged for the INSET work and thereby recovered some or all of their costs.

The time commitment of staff at all levels should not be underestimated. One ILS co-ordinator commented that:

'I could never have undertaken the implementation of ILS unless technology was both my hobby as well as my job...'

Similarly, a headteacher noted how important the contribution of all the staff had been to the successful operation of ILS:

'... Goodwill cannot be costed and a happy staff is essential to make ILS work...'

Training

In the build up to the introduction of ILS into one primary school £2,000 was invested in supply cover to support staff training and set-up activities in three key areas:

- concentrated in-service training in London and other off-site locations;
- attendance at conferences arranged by NCET;
- internal, on site training to discuss issues associated with the integration of ILS into the school curriculum and current learning strategies.

The latter was considered the most important by the headteacher and staff as it not only contributed to the smooth running and integration of ILS into the curriculum but also because such planning activities enhanced teamwork among staff, sharpened key aims and objectives and helped generate quality support materials.

Building and environmental work

Many schools have been able to fund environmental and building work through grants from their local authority or TEC. Costs of between £2,000 and £3,500 have been incurred by schools, but these figures vary according to the size of network and the extent of building alterations required.

Building work was often carried out in association with the local building inspector and many schools found it important to have staff on hand when installation work was taking place to advise on problems as they arose, especially during holidays or after school hours. In particular, staff were able to advise contractors on practical issues associated with the height of benching (especially important where young children or children of varying ages were using the system), and the location of trunking, cabling, connector boxes and electrical supply points.

Security of equipment and the building

For many schools the decision to invest in ILS represented a significant increase in IT equipment and a potential security risk. Many institutions have invested in new security alarm systems or extended existing provision, as well as providing protection for windows and new locks on doors and cupboards. Such developments also have long term implications: yearly maintenance contracts on alarm systems and increased insurance premiums for buildings and contents.

Security of data and back up facilities

The ILS system stores data about students which institutions back up on a daily or weekly basis. Some institutions have decided to buy extra back up tapes to ensure that information is backed up as regularly as possible. Some have fitted back up power supply units to their systems as they were concerned to ensure that no data was lost due to power cuts, electrical supply fluctuations or other accidental events such as floods, in between the time at which the system data are backed up.

Ongoing operating and support costs

The implementation of ILS involves ongoing commitments. While the level of effort, planning and capital investment may never be as high as that expended during the initial stages of implementation, it is important not to underestimate the level of support required to maintain the system once established in an institution. In its budget planning a school will have to consider the likely running costs of ILS in the current climate of static or declining funding and increasing pressures from other funding commitments as the responsibilities of LMS grow and LEA spending is squeezed.

Technical problems, fault finding and technical support

Feedback from ILS schools would suggest that initial technical support and maintenance costs can be rather high when working with Beta versions of software or when running new or unusual combinations of hardware and software. To some extent such costs can be planned for through warranty and maintenance agreements with suppliers and, in the case of certain equipment problems encountered by ILS schools, faulty or incorrectly specified units have been replaced free of charge by suppliers. Schools need to ensure that they budget for ongoing expenditure to allow warranty agreements to be extended beyond that which might come as standard with the hardware when first purchased.

However, this does not take account of the various hidden costs associated with technical problems such as the time associated with complex fault finding, increased telephone charges relating to calls to suppliers to discuss problems, knowing exactly where a given fault is located and which of a number of suppliers to call out, and other knock-on effects associated with the system being out of action for significant periods of time.

One possible approach to these problems where new technologies or combinations of hardware and software are being piloted for the first time, may be to consider a one stop shop for technical support, linked to yearly fixed-price support/maintenance contracts. The existence of one point of contact able to cover hardware, software and network problems would ensure that faults could be diagnosed and corrected quickly without the need to call out engineers from a range of companies.

In cases where software has been thoroughly tested and established hardware/software configurations are used, technical support costs would seem to be much lower in the first year of operation. Also in the second year of operation many ILS projects have indicated that technical support costs appear to drop considerably by virtue of the fact that the systems have all had time to bed in.

Maintenance costs

In the first year of the operation of ILS any equipment failure was generally covered by warranty agreements. Once these agreements run out a school will need to consider the extent and nature of the maintenance agreements they wish to put in place and ensure that, where possible, they have an all-embracing agreement that will cover them for all types of system failure. This is especially important given that the hardware and software may have been supplied by a range of companies and faults can be complex and difficult to diagnose. Also, where the system is in constant use, any 'down time' may result in serious disruption to the running of the school and timetable arrangements. In such situations the response time of an engineer is very important.

Staff development and training

Training is not a one-off expense. Many ILS schools are involved in a continuous and evolving programme of staff development. New staff are given induction training so they can start to use the system for the first time, while others need to familiarise themselves with other parts of the system and develop appropriate support materials and resources. Also, as pupils begin to use new modules of the software or upgrades are introduced further inset training will be required.

Hardware, peripheral, software and equipment costs

Leaving aside any costs associated with new versions of the software or upgrades to the file server and system software, schools will need to budget for the yearly renewal of licences and consider the likely increases which might result from upgrading the network and adding new stations to the existing system.

While replacement costs for all equipment may be kept to a minimum by ensuring that good quality equipment is ordered from the outset, provision still needs to be made for general wear and tear. Headphones are particularly prone to failure. One school, where ILS was used regularly throughout every school day, calculated that every set of headphones would be put on and taken off about 13 times a day. They estimated a replacement rate of three headphones per work station a year and investigated a higher specification replacement.

Other peripherals such as mouse and keyboards are also subject to wear and tear. Many schools have reported that it was considered to be most cost-effective in the long-term to invest in high quality equipment, be it headphones or network connectors, even though the initial costs might be appear to be high.

Upgrading costs

The developers of ILS software seek to improve their products and regularly bring out upgrades and improvements to their software. A school may wish to add new modules to existing systems or extend their network to include extra workstations. Such upgrades have a number of cost implications over and above the cost of purchasing new ILS software. Schools need to consider whether changes may have to be made to the network software, including the management system, or to the hardware specification of individual workstations or the central file server, to run new versions of the software successfully. Upgrades may also have implications for the costs of existing licensing agreements and require an engineer to undertake software installation or system reconfiguration, as well as any cabling and equipment improvements if the network is to be extended. Thereafter there may be training implications for staff and a need to make changes to existing curriculum support materials.

Building and furniture improvements

As a school develops the use of ILS it may wish to extend the number of machines on the network. One school estimated that it cost about £100 per workstation to extend the network. This approximate figure included workstation screening, chair, extra work surface on which to locate the equipment, wiring, and related electrical and joinery work, but did not include hardware or software expenditure.

Further integration and development of ILS across the institution

As a school develops the use of ILS there are implications for on going curriculum development for the whole school and for departments. A school may wish to devote time and resources to considering how best to exploit a given aspect of the system, such as the assessment facilities or diagnostic data on individual children, or extend the use of the software to support a new aspect of the curriculum. Other developmental issues, especially in primary schools, might include classroom management, and organising activities and small group work for children in vertically grouped classes, and relating this to the various Key Stages in the National Curriculum. Such work has implications for the use of training days. While it can result in some valuable resources and support materials being produced, ILS development work has to compete with all the other issues requiring attention by the staff.

Conclusion

The introduction and use of ILS is clearly a costly undertaking. However, before everyone reaches for the antidepressant tablets, it is important to see the costs identified in perspective. Costs vary over time, and, as the British experience of using ILS develops costs may be reduced and ways may be found to operate ILS more efficiently and effectively.

Costs are only one side of the cost-effectiveness coin in the ILS story. It is important, therefore, to weigh the not inconsiderable costs against the benefits. Other chapters, together with the various evaluation reports published by NCET, consider the benefits of ILS in detail.

From all my conversations with staff in the various ILS schools, few if any of them felt that on balance they regretted getting involved with ILS, although with hindsight they might all have done things differently had they had their time again.

CHAPTER
18

Conclusions

Jean Underwood and Jenny Brown

The current interest in ILS is a product of a number of factors that are impinging on our education system. The first is the rapidity of technological development. Increased computing power and storage, coupled with a very significant decline in costs, has made it possible to place larger, more stimulating and more interactive software into the classroom. The second factor is a political imperative: the national concern about standards in education. There is evidence that in areas of basic skills and knowledge the education of our children is less effective than that of our key economic competitors. That more than 15 per cent of the UK population should have too low a level of basic literacy or numeracy to equip them for many current occupations must be of continuing national concern. Linked to this political imperative is the need to promote the continuing professional development of the teaching profession in general and to up grade their information technology skills in particular.

In his introduction David Wood pointed out that the use of ILS in schools is relatively new but that the ideological and theoretical positions that divide opinion about their educational value are decidedly old. We know that many people are uncomfortable with the concept of ILS; it certainly does not produce the problem oriented curriculum advocated (Underwood and Underwood 1990). Wragg clearly articulates this discomfort:

'the majority of parents do not want their children to learn by sitting at a screen all day long. Most normal adult behaviour is interactive – and you get some strange people if they've been up in the attic staring at a computer screen from the age of five to 16.'

(in Picardie, 1995 p11)

This should not be an issue for ILS. The research presented in this text employs a multiplicity of methodologies, from the relatively large scale formal studies of learning outcomes, to surveys of pupil and teacher attitudes and ethnographic explorations of system use in a range of classroom settings. Collectively these studies taken from a range of perspectives provide a rich picture of likely costs and benefits associated with ILS usage in schools.

The need to monitor time-on-task is one such finding. More time with the system does not necessarily mean greater gains. Indeed, too much medicine in one large dose, as in those schools where a strategy of using SuccessMaker for an hour at a time was employed, can lead to pupil disaffection. Equally very limited exposure has no beneficial impact on learning. SuccessMaker appears to be slow-drip intervention; a little often appears to be the best way forward. The most important finding here is that we are not dealing with a 'quick-fix' intervention. There is evidence of the sustainability of learning gains for pupils a year after active intervention ceased. Such an intervention is necessarily resource hungry and has major financial implications both for individual schools and for local and national policy-makers.

Not all ILS packages are the same, however. The slow-drip approach so successful with SuccessMaker does not appear to be appropriate for our second package: Global mathematics. For this package learning gains were only recorded for pupils following a need-to-use revision strategy. Each ILS should be judged on its effectiveness in promoting children's learning but it should be noted that each package may have an optimal model of usage.

On reflection we should not be surprised that one of our systems proved effective in promoting basic skills learning. Howe (1992) has strongly argued that practice makes perfect – that we are too keen to attribute quality performance to innate talent compared to effort, and this works to the detriment of children. This assertion is supported by Ericsson, Krampe and Tesch-Romer (1993) whose study of ten violinists from the Music Academy of West Berlin shows that the exceptional performance of these talented performers is the result of intense practice extended over a minimum of ten years. They argue that many characteristics once believed to reflect innate talent are the end result of individuals' prolonged efforts to improve performance while negotiating motivational and external constraints. These conclusions are applicable to all domains that they reviewed including chess, physics, sports and music. Similarly Underwood, Deihim and Batt (1994) have found that expert performance in solving crossword puzzles is linked to a practice effect, that is good puzzlers have put in more time-on-task.

The results presented here show that ILS children are making learning gains through sustained effort, continually re-visiting and reviewing skills. The management system of SuccessMaker ensures this review process takes place by representing exercises covering previously learnt skills and knowledge. For the Global materials such skills review remains the responsibility of the teacher or the learner. One small teacher-led trial reported here does suggest that children achieving an automaticity of skill may benefit not only in an increased speed of performance but also from a release in cognitive processing capacity which they can then can bring to bear on higher order problems. This result does require full-scale replication, however.

One finding which may prove surprising is that where learning gains do occur it has not been possible to identify any one group that has gained differentially over another. We have recorded few if any gender effects and similarly few ability effects. All children appear to have gained from using the system, although there are still questions to be asked about the use of the system with very young learners. The most able children benefit from practice as do the least able.

One caveat to this general statement is that the software may need to be adapted to accommodate individual learning styles. Social, emotional or ability factors may result in some children requiring shorter sessions on the system, while more able children may need to speed up the system by turning off the visual rewards that can act as annoying distracters. The role of the teacher in tailoring the system to their pupils' needs is critical here. Software developers should consider facilitating this process by providing increasingly adaptive systems which support such teacher or indeed learner intervention.

The credibility of ILS is also being strongly questioned in the US not just by theorists such as Roy Pea (1993), arguing that this is a poor model of learning, but also by school boards who have not seen the promised eradication of poor numeracy and literacy skills. In the latter case the schools' administrators have often operated a 'teacher deficit model of education' based on the assumption that the children's failure to learn is caused by lack of teacher expertise.

The negative feedback from the US contrasts sharply with our study. We believe that there are a number of key differences between ILS usage in the UK and in parts, but not all of the US. One such difference is the UK perception that ILS delivers a significant but limited part of the curriculum. It is not the total solution. A second is that many of our teachers, as in some US schools, have made a conscious effort to come to a fuller understanding of the system, and through that understanding have started to integrate the ILS into their practice. They do not see the introduction of ILS as teacher replacement, rather they are looking at a new and effective tool in the teacher's armoury. Throughout our study it has become apparent that an ILS in the classroom is not a substitute for teachers. A representative comment from the teachers in this project is:

> ' I would be very reluctant to allow the system to be taken away. BUT it does matter how you use it. It's not a delivery system but a partner with children and teacher in the learning process. You must think of a partnership to get the full benefits out of the system.'

However, interacting with the system has proved to be a stimulus to teachers' professional development. At one level teachers have seen the ILS as a support tool helping them to identify weaknesses in their children's understanding. This has allowed them to be more effective managers of the learning environment. In addition, for a few teachers it has led to a rethinking of what it is to teach.

Our understanding of 'what is an ILS' has grown during this evaluation but there are still unanswered questions. Although we have shown that basic numeracy can be acquired through the use of an ILS we have still to establish whether other mathematical skills are being acquired from the system or, perhaps as importantly, at what level the development of well-practised basic skills is underpinning traditional mathematics teaching. The value of ILS in the development of basic literacy remains open. Also, we have not reached a collective agreement on what makes any one ILS effective. Further models of use may prove critical for the different software packages. For example several schools argue that they are achieving positive outcomes using the Global software. Such outcomes were not apparent in the formal evaluation although the results of the YELLIS comparisons are more promising. What is clear is that those schools where there is some indication of positive results all have a working system, and this was not true for the formal evaluation. They are also using the software either as part of a carousel of interventions, for example one of the schools is combining Global English with Reading Recovery reinforcement, or as a revision tool.

Answers to many of the outstanding questions may be achieved through an analysis of evidence from international projects to inform schools, support agencies and providers. Such an analysis could help to identify any outstanding questions and help inform those setting future research agendas. For example, we have still to develop a full understanding of why such systems work, nor do we know if they are more effective than other intervention strategies including non-technology based approaches. The link between Global English and Reading Recovery reinforcement suggests that we should look at combinations of strategies. To return to the medical analogy of Chapter 4, it may well be that a cocktail of interventions will prove most effective both in terms of learning outcomes and cost. Judging the combination and dosage of interventions may prove tricky but we might start by considering how the so-called superhighway can facilitate the delivery of materials to schools.

This call for further research should not be viewed as a lack of confidence in the research findings presented here, rather it is an awareness of the importance and sensitivity of the issues surrounding ILS. As David Wood stated in the introduction, there appears little doubt that some form of large-scale, computer-based, networked, adaptive technology will soon find its way into most or all of our classrooms. Such technologies will be found at all levels of education, even at degree level. It is imperative that the use of such technologies is based firmly on research evidence and not on the entrenched beliefs of either the technophiles or the Luddites. The evidence presented here shows that there is a role for ILS in supporting basic skills development. Whether it can or should do more is a key question we have yet to ask.

References

References

Amarel, M. (1984) Classrooms and Computers as Instructional Settings. *Theory into Practice,* **22,** 220-226.

APU (1991) *APU Mathematics Monitoring: (Phase 2).* London: HMSO.

APU (1991) *The Assessment of Performance in Design and Technology* London: HMSO.

Azevedo, Roger and Bernard, Robert M. (1995) The Effects of Computer-Presented Feedback on Learning from Computer-Based Instruction: A Meta-Analysis. Paper presented at the Annual Meeting of the American Educational Research Association, San Francisco USA.

Backman, C. W. and Secord, P. F. (1968) *A Social Psychological View of Education.* NY: Harcourt, Brace and World.

Bailey, G. D. (1992) Wanted: A Road Map for Understanding Integrated Learning Systems. *Educational Technology,* **32** (9), 3-5.

Bailey, G. D. and Lumley, D. (1991) Supervising Teachers who Use Integrated Learning Systems: New Roles for School Administrators. *Educational Technology,* **31** (7) 21-24.

Baker, Eva *et al* (1990) *The Apple Classroom of Tomorrow: 1989 Evaluation Study.* University of California: Los Angeles Centre for Technology Assessment.

Balajthy, E. (1987) What Does Research on Computer-Based Instruction Have to Say to the Reading Teacher? *Reading Research and Instruction,* **27** (1) 55-65.

Balajthy, E. (1988) Recent Trends in Minicomputer-Based Integrated Learning Systems for Reading and Language Arts Instruction. Paper presented at the Rutgers University Spring Reading Conference, New Brunswick, New Jersey USA.

Ball, S. (1977) *Motivation in Education,* London: Academic Press.

Becker, H. J. (1983) School Uses of Microcomputers: Reports from a National Survey. (Issue No 1) Baltimore MD USA: Center for Social Organization of Schools, Johns Hopkins University.

Becker, H. J. (1990) Effects of Computer Use on Mathematics Achievement: Findings from a Nationwide Field Experiment in Grade Five to Eight Classes. Paper presented at the Annual Meeting of the American Educational Research Association.

Becker, H. J. (1992) Computer-Based ILSs in the Elementary and Middle Grades: A Critical Review and Synthesis of Evaluation Reports. *Journal of Educational Computing Research,* **8** (1), 1-42.

Becker, H. J. (1992b) A Model for Improving the Performance of Integrated Learning Systems. *Educational Technology,* **32** (9).

Becker, H. J. (1994) Mindless or Mindful Use of Integrated Learning Systems. *International Journal of Educational Research,* **21** (1).

Becker, H. J. and Hativa, N. (1994) History, Theory and Research Concerning Integrated Learning Systems. *International Journal of Educational Research,* **21** (1) 5-12.

Ben Dror, Y. (1991) Differences in Effects of TOAM-based Practice in Arithmetic among Disadvantaged Students with Intensified and Regular Practice and Advantaged

Students, during the Academic Year and the Full Calendar Year. Unpublished Masters thesis, Tel Aviv University, School of Education (Hebrew).

Bentley, E. (1991) Integrated Learning Systems: The Problems with the Solution. *Contemporary Education, 63* (1) 24-27.

Biott, C. (1987) Co-operative Group Work: Pupils' and Teachers' Membership and Participation. *Curriculum, 8* (2), 5-14.

Blickhan, D. S. (1992) The Teacher's Role in Integrated Learning Systems. *Educational Technology, 32* (9) 46-48.

Blum, W., Burghes, D. N., Green, N. and Kaiser-Messmer, G. (1993) British/German comparative project: Some preliminary results. *Teaching Mathematics and its Applications, 12,* 16-19.

Bracey, G. W. (1992) The Bright Future of Integrated Learning Systems. *Educational Technology. 32,* 60-62.

Braun, L. (1990) Vision: TEST (Technologically Enriched Schools of Tomorrow) Final Report: Recommendations for American Educational Decision Makers. Eugene, O. R.: The International Society for Technology in Education.

Brooks, G., Foxman, D. and Gorman, T. (1995) Standards in Literacy and Numeracy: 1948-1994. *National Commission on Education Briefing,* **New Series 7,** 1-4.

Brown, J. S. (1990) Towards a New Epistemology for Learning. In Frasson, C and Gauthier, G (eds), *Intelligent Tutoring Systems: At the Crossroads of AI and Education.* Norwood, NJ USA: Ablex.

Brown, R. (1988) *Group Processes: Dynamics Within and Between Groups.* Oxford: Basil Blackwell.

Burns, R. (1982) *Self Concept Development and Education.* London: Holt, Rinehart and Winston.

Buzan, T. (1989) *Use your Head.* London, BBC Books.

Campione, J. C. (1989) Assisted Assessment: A Taxonomy of Approaches and an Outline of Strengths and Weaknesses. *Journal of Learning Disabilities, 22* (3), 151-165.

Carey, S. (1986) Cognitive Science and Science Education. *American Psychologist, 41* (10), 1123-30.

Cavendish, S. (1988) Sex Differences Relating to Achievement in Mathematics. Unpublished PhD thesis, Leicester: University of Leicester.

Clare, J. (199) 'Hey! Just look what I can do' *The Daily Telegraph.*

Clariana, R. B. (1990) The Teacher is a Variable in Computer-Based Instruction. ERIC Document Reproduction Service: ED 317 966.

Clariana, R. B. (1992) Prescriptions in Reading Computer-Assisted Instruction: Reading versus Writing. *Journal of Computer-Based Instruction, 19* (2) 58-63.

Clariana, R. B. (1992b) Integrated Learning Systems and Standardized Test Improvement. Invited presentation, WICAT Users Conference; Sandy, Utah USA; ERIC Document Reproduction Service: ED 349 943.

Clariana, R. B. (1992c) The Effects of Public Reports of Progress on Rate of Lesson Completion in Computer-Based Instruction. *Journal of Computing in Childhood Education, 3* (2) 127-136.

Clariana, R. B. (1993) The Motivational Effect of Advisement on Attendance and Achievement in Computer-Based Instruction. *Journal of Computer-Based Instruction Spring, 20* (2) 47-51.

Clariana, R. B. and Schultz, C. W. (1993) Gender by Content Achievement Differences in

Computer-Based Instruction. *Journal of Computers in Mathematics and Science Teaching,* **12** (3/4) 277–288.

Clark, R. (1983) Reconsidering Research on Learning from Media. *Review of Educational Research,* **4** 445–459.

Clark, R. E. (1984) Learning from Computers: Theoretical problems. Paper presented at AERA, April, New Orleans USA.

Cockcroft Report (1982) *Mathematics Counts.* London: HMSO.

Cockcroft, W. H. (1983) Mathematics Counts: Report of the Committee of Inquiry into the Teaching of Mathematics in Schools. London: HMSO.

Columbus Public Schools (1994) Vocational Programs Pilot Study on Integrated Learning System Computer Software: Columbus Public Schools 1993–1994. Columbus Public Schools Day (1995).

Collins, J. (1994) Computers in Classroom and College. *Computer Education,* **77** 30–33.

Dalton, D. W. and Hannafin, M. J. (1988) The Effects of Computer-Assisted and Traditional Mastery Methods on Computation Accuracy and Attitudes. *Journal of Educational Research,* **82** 27–33.

Dehaan, R. F. and Havinghurst, R. J. (1961) *Educating Gifted Children.* Chicago: University of Chicago Press.

Denton, C. and Postlethwaite, K. (1985) *Able Children: Identifying them in the Classroom.* Windsor: NFER-Nelson.

DFE (1994) *Code of Practice on the Identification and Assessment of Special Educational Needs.* London: HMSO.

DFE (1994) *Pupils with Problems.* London: HMSO.

DFE (1995) Survey of Information Technology in Schools. *Statistical Bulletin Issue No 3/95.* HMSO.

Driver, R. and Bell, B. (1985) Students Thinking and Learning of Science, *New Zealand Science Teacher,* **46** 4–12.

Dwyer, D. C., Ringstaff, C. and Sandholtz, J. H. (1990) *Teacher Beliefs and Practices Part 1: Patterns of Change* (Apple Computer, Inc: ACOT).

Edwards, D. and Mercer, N. M. (1987) *Common Knowledge.* London: Methuen.

EPIE Institute (1990) *The Integrated Instructional Systems Report.* New York, USA: Water Mill.

Ericsson, K. A., Krampe, R. T. and Tesch-Romer, C. (1993). The Role of Deliberate Practice in the Acquisition of Expert Performance. *Psychological Review,* **100** 362–406.

Erlwanger, S. H. (1973) Benny's Conception of Rules and Answers in IPI Mathematics. *Journal of Children's Mathematical Behavior,* **1** (2) 93–98.

Fitz-Gibbon, C. T. (1996) *Issues to be Considered in the Design of a National Value Added System.* CEM Centre report for SCAA. London: School Curriculum and Assessment Authority.

Fletcher, J. D. (1990) Computer-Based Instruction: Costs and Effectiveness. In Sage, A. P. (ed): *Concise Encyclopaedia of Information Processing in Systems and Organisations.* Oxford: Pergamon Press.

Foxman, D., Hagues, N. and Ruddock, G. (1990) *Practical Maths Assessments.* Windsor, UK: NFER-Nelson.

France, N. (1979) *Profile of Mathematical Skills.* Middlesex: Nelson.

Fraser B. J. and Teh, G. (1994) Effect Sizes Associated with Micro-PROLOG-based Computer Assisted Learning. *Computers and Education,* **23** 187-196.

Freeman, J. (1991) Recent Developments for the Highly Able in Britain. In: Monks, F. J., Katsko, M. W. and Van Boxell, H. W. (Eds) *Education of the Gifted in Europe: Theoretical and Research Issues.* Amsterdam: Swets and Zeitlinger.

Galton, M., Simon, B. and Croll, P. (1980) *Inside the Primary Classroom.* London: Routledge & Kegan Paul.

Galton, M. and Willcocks, J. (1983) *Moving from the Primary Classroom.* London: Routledge & Kegan Paul.

Galton, M. and Williamson, J. (1992) *Group Work in the Primary Classroom.* London: Routledge.

Gross, M. U. M. (1993) *Exceptionally Gifted Children.* London: Routledge.

Hativa, N. (1986) Computer-Based Practice in Arithmetic (TOAM): Dreams and Realities, an Ethnographic Study. The Pinchas Sapir Center for Development, Discussion Paper No. 7-86.

Hativa, N. (1988a). Computer-Based Drill and Practice in Arithmetic – Widening the Gap between High and Low Achieving Students. *American Educational Research Journal,* **25** (3) 366-397.

Hativa, N. (1988b). CAI vs Paper and Pencil – Discrepancies in Students' Performance. *Instructional Science,* **17** (1) 77-76.

Hativa, N. (1989) Students' Conceptions of and Attitudes Towards Specific Features of a CAI System. *Journal of Computer-Based Instruction,* **16** (3) 81-89.

Hativa, N. (1990) Students' Attitudes towards Arithmetic Practice with the WICAT System in Glen Cove School District. An unpublished report.

Hativa, N. (1994) What You Design is Not What You Get (WYDINWYG): Cognitive, Affective, and Social Impacts of Learning with ILS – an Integration of Findings from Six Years of Qualitative and Quantitative Studies. *International Journal of Educational Research,* **21** (1) 81-111.

Hativa, N. and Becker, H. J. (1994) Instructional Learning Systems: Problems and Potential Benefits. *International Journal of Educational Research,* **21** (1) 113-119.

Hativa, N., Lesgold, A. and Swissa, S. (1993) Competition in Individualized CAI. *Instructional Science,* **21** 393-428.

Hawkins, J., and Collins, A. (1992) Design Experiments for Infusing Technology into Learning. *Educational Technology,* **32** (9).

Hermon, B. (1994) Computer-Assisted Instruction Projects. Unpublished paper.

Holt, J. (1984) *How Children Fail.* Revised edition. Harmondsworth: Penguin.

Hoorvitch-Steimberg, Y. (1990) *The Low-Achieving Student in TOAM System.* Unpublished Master's thesis, Tel Aviv University, School of Education (Hebrew).

Hopkins, M. (1991) The Value of Information Technology for Children with Emotional and Behavioural Difficulties. *Maladjusted and Therapeutic Education,* **9** (3) 143-151.

Howe, M. (1992) *The Origin of Exceptional Abilities.* Oxford: Blackwell.

Hoyle, E. (1976) Strategies for Curriculum Change; Unit 23 in *Innovation: Problems and Possibilities.* Milton Keynes: Open University Press.

Johnson, D. W. and Johnson, R. T. (1975) *Learning Together and Alone*. Englewood Cliffs, N. J., USA: Prentice Hall.

Kay, R. H. (1992) The Computer Literacy Potpourri: A Review of the Literature or McCluhan Revisited. *Journal of Research on Computers in Education,* 24 446–456.

Kelly, A. (1976). A study of the comparability of external examinations in different subjects. *Research in Education,* 16 50–63.

Kerry, T. and Sands, M. (1982) *Handling Classroom Groups.* Nottingham: Nottingham University, School of Education (mimeo).

Klahr, D. and Carver, S. M. (1988). Cognitive Objectives in a LOGO Debugging Curriculum: Instruction, Learning and Transfer. *Cognitive Psychology,* 20, 362–404.

Knapp, M. I. and Orlansky, J. A.: (1983) *A Cost Element Structure for Defence Training.* IDA paper P- 1709, Alexandria, Virginia USA, Institute for Defence Analyses.

Kulik and Kulik (1987) Review of Recent Computer-based Instruction. *Contemporary Educational Psychology,* 12, 222–230.

Lange, P. C. (Ed) (1967) *National Society for the Study of Education Yearbook,* 66 (Part II). Chicago: University of Chicago Press.

Lave, J. and Wenger, E. (1991) *Situated Learning: Legitimate Peripheral Participation.* Cambridge: Cambridge University Press.

Lewis, A. (1995) *Primary Special Needs and the National Curriculum.* London: Routledge. 2nd edn.

Light, P. (1992) Collaborative Learning with Computers. In P. Scrimshaw (ed) *Language, Classrooms and Computers.* London: Routledge.

Macdonald, G. (1994) 'Computers Lead to 20-Month Gain' *Times Educational Supplement* November 18, 1994.

Maddux, C. D. and Willis, J. W. (1992) Integrated Learning Systems and their Alternatives: Problems and Cautions. *Educational Technology,* 32 (9).

Mageau, T. (1990) ILS: its New Role in Schools. *Electronic Learning,* 10 (1) 22–24, 31–32.

Mager, J. (1989) Using Computer-Assisted Instruction to Improve Basic Skills in Second and Fourth Grades. A Practicum Report Submitted to the Faculty of the Center for the Advancement of Education at Nova Scotia University.

Maines, B. and Robinson, G. (1993) *B/G Stemm: A Self-Esteem Scale with Locus of Control Items.* Avon: Lame Duck Publishing.

Marland, S. P. (1972) Education of the Gifted and Talented. Report to Congress by the US Commissioner for Education. Vol 1. Washington, DC: US Office of Education.

McFarlane, A. E. (1994) 'Progress on Prescription'. *TES 25* March p26.

McFarlane, A. (1994) 'More homework, please' *TES Update* 17 June.

McFarlane, A. (1995) *Integrated Learning Systems: A Review of the Literature.* Coventry: NCET (unpublished paper).

McGill, P. (1994) 'Screen Stars' *The Times* Monday 21 November.

Mellar, H., Bliss, J., Boohan, R., Ogburn, J. and Tompsett, C. (1994) *Learning with Artificial Worlds: Computer Based Modelling in the Curriculum.* London: Falmer Press

Mevarech, Z. R. (1994) The Effectiveness of Individualized Versus Cooperative Computer-Based Integrated Learning Systems. *International Journal of Educational Research,* 21 (1).

Mortimore, P., Sammons, P. *et al.*(1988) *School Matters: the Junior Years.* London: Open Books.

NCET (1994) *Integrated Learning Systems – A Report of the Pilot Evaluation of ILS in the UK.* Coventry: National Council for Educational Technology.

NCET (1996) *Integrated Learning Systems – A Report of the Phase II of the Pilot Evaluation of ILS in the UK.* Coventry: NCET.

Neuman, D. (1991) Learning Disabled Students' Interactions with Commercial Courseware: A Naturalistic Study. *Educational Technology Research and Development,* **39** 1, 31–49.

Nisbet, J. F. (1891) *The Insanity of Genius.* London: Paul.

OFSTED (Office of Standards in Education) (1995) *Key Characteristics of Effective Schools,* Salmons, P. *et al.* London: Institute of Education.

Office of Technology Assessment (1988) *Power on! New Tools for Teaching and Learning.* US Government Printing Office: Washington D C.

Ogilvie, E. (1973) *Gifted Children in Primary Schools.* London: Macmillan.

Osin, L. and Nesher, P. (1988) Comparison of Student Performance in Arithmetic Exercises: TOAM vs Paper-and-Pencil Testing. *International Journal of Man-Machine Studies,* **31** 293–313.

Olson, J. (1988) *Schoolworlds – Microworlds.* Oxford: Pergamon.

OTA (1988) *Power on! New Tools for Teaching and Learning.* Congress of the United States, Office of Technology Assessment.

Parr, J. M. (1944) Report of the Evaluation of the Computer Assisted Learning Project at Rutherford High School. Auckland: University of Auckland.

Passey, D. (1995) *Use of Jostens ILS Products in UK School: An Evaluation Report for NCET.* Lancaster: STAC.

Pea, R. (1985) Beyond Amplification: Using the Computer to Reorganise Mental Functioning. *Educational Psychologist,* **20** 167–182.

Pea, R. (1993) Practices of Distributed Intelligence and Designs for Education. In Salomon, G. (ed) *Distributed Cognitions.* New York: Cambridge University Press.

Percival, F., Craig D. and Buglass D. (1987) *Flexible Learning Systems.* London: Kogan Page.

Perkins, D. (1992) Technology Meets Constructivism: Do they Make a Marriage? In Duffy, T. and Jonassen, D. (eds) *Constructivism and the Technology of Instruction: A Conversation.* New Jersey: Lawrence Erlbaum Associates.

Perry, N. (1990) The Relationship Between Students' Advancement in Practice Problems in Arithmetic by Computerized Management of Instruction, and Students' Command of Arithmetic Material (the TOAM system). Unpublished Masters' thesis, Tel Aviv University, School of Education (Hebrew).

Piaget, J. and Inhelder, B. (1947) Diagnosis of Mental Operations and the Theory of Diagnosis. *American Journal of Mental Deficiency,* **51** 401–406.

Picardie, J. (1995) 'Have Traditional Schools had their Day?' *The Independent on Sunday Review,* 2 April.

Posner, G. J., Strike, K. A., Hewson, P. W. and Gertzog, W. A. (1982). Accommodation of a Scientific Conception; Towards a Theory of Conceptual Change, *Science Education,* **66**, (2), 211–29.

Ragosta, M., Holland, P. and Jamison, D. (1982) *Computer-Assisted Instruction and Compensatory Education: The ETS/LAUSD Study.* Princeton, NJ: Educational Testing Service.

Ragsdale, R. (1991) Effective Computing in Education: Teachers, Tools and Training. *Education and Computing,* **7** 157-166.

Ramey, M. (1991) Compensatory Education Sustained Gains from Spring 1988 to Spring 1990. Report No 91-1. Seattle, WA: Seattle Public Schools.

Renzulli, J. S. (1978). 'What Makes Giftedness? Re-examining Definition', *Phi Delta Kappa,* **60,** (3), 180-184.

Roberts, V. A. and Madhere, S. (1990) Chapter 1: Resource Laboratory Program for Computer Assisted Instruction (CAI) 1989-90. Evaluation Report. Washington, DC: District of Columbia Public Schools (ED334299).

Robinson, S. (1992) Integrated Learning Systems: Staff Development as the Key to Implementation. *Educational Technology,* **32** (9).

Robitatille, D. F. and Garden, R. A. (1989) *The IEA Study of Mathematics II: Contexts and Outcomes of School Mathematics.* London: Pergamon Press.

Ross, S. M., Smith, L. S. and Morrison, G. R. (1991) The Longitudinal Influences of Computer-Intensive Learning Experiences on At-Risk Elementary Students. *Educational Technology Research and Development,* **39** (4) 33-46.

Ross, T. W. (1992) A Principal's Guide to ILS Facilities Installation. *Educational Technology,* **32** (9) 33-35.

Ryan, D. (1987) 'Innovation in Teaching; Educational Technology as Opportunity vs Educational Technology as Constraint' in Percival, F., Craig, D. and Buglass, D. *Flexible Learning Systems.* London: Kogan Page.

Saettler, P. (1990) *The Evolution of American Educational Technology.* Englewood, CO: Libraries Unlimited.

Salomon, G. (1990) The Changing Role of the Teacher: from Knowledge Transmitter to Exploration Orchestrator. Paper presented at *International Symposium on Research on Effective Teaching,* Fribourg, Switzerland.

Salomon, G., Perkins, D. N. and Globerson, T. (1991) Partners in Cognition: Extending Human Intelligence with Intelligent Technologies. *Educational Research,* **20,** 2-9.

Schnitz, J. E. and Azbell, J. W. (1990) Training for Third-Generation Management Systems Effecting Integrator Implementation Models. Proceedings of the Eighth Annual Conference on Interactive Instructional Technology, 1990.

Schunk, D. (1990) 'Self-Concept and School Achievement' in Rogers, C. and Kutnick, P. (eds) *The Social Psychology of the Primary School.* London: Routledge.

Sherry, M. (1992) Integrated Learning Systems: What May We Expect in the Future? *Educational Technology,* **32** (9) 58-59.

Shore, A. and Johnson, M. F. (1992) Integrated Learning Systems: A Vision for the Future. *Educational Technology,* **32** (9) 36-39.

Slavin, R. L. (1986). Best-Evidence Synthesis: An Alternative to Meta-Analytic and Traditional Reviews. *Educational Researcher,* **15** 5-16.

Slavin, R. E. (1987) A Theory of School and Classroom Organization. *Educational Psychologist,* **22** (2) 89-108.

Slavin, R. E. (1987) Mastery Learning Reconsidered. *Review of Educational Research,* **57** 175-213.

Stoddart, T. (1992) Commentary: Fostering Coherence Between Constructivism on Campus and Conventional Practice in Schools. The Holmes Group Forum; **6** (2) 26-28.

Stradling, B., Sims, D. and Jamison, J. (1994) *Portable Computers Pilot Evaluation Report.* Coventry: NCET.

Suppes, P. and Morningstar, M. (1972) *Computer-Assisted Instruction at Stanford, 1966-68, Models and Evaluations of the Arithmetic Program*. New York: Academic Press.

Taylor, D. M. (1990). *Computer Based Integrated Learning Systems in Rural Alaska: An Evaluation of the Jostens Learning System*. Anchorage: Alaska Association for Computers in Education.

Terman, L. M. (1925) *Genetic Studies of Genius. Vol 1 Mental and Physical Traits of a Thousand Gifted Children*. Stanford, CA: Stanford University Press.

Thorndike, R. L. and Hagen E. P. (1977) *Measurement and Evaluation in Psychology and Education*. New York: Prentice-Hall.

Turner, J. (1982) 'Towards a Cognitive Redefinition of the Social Group' in Tajfel, M (ed) *Social Identity and Intergroup Relations*. Cambridge: Cambridge University Press.

Underwood, J. (1986) The Role of the Computer in Developing Children's Classificatory Abilities. *Computers and Education,* **10** 175-180.

Underwood, G. and Batt, V. (1996). *Reading and Understanding*. Oxford: Blackwell.

Underwood, G., Deihim, C. and Batt, V. (1994). Expert Performance in Solving Word Puzzles: from Retrieval Cues to Crossword Clues. *Applied Cognitive Psychology,* **8** 531-548.

Underwood G. and Everatt J., (1995) Automatic and Controlled Information Processing: the Role of Attention in the Processing of Novelty. In O Neumann and A F Sanders (eds), *Encyclopaedia of Psychology: Attention*. London: Academic Press.

Underwood, J., Cavendish, S., Dowling, S., Fogelman, K. and Lawson, T. (1994) *Integrated Learning Systems in UK Schools*. Coventry: NCET.

Underwood, J., Cavendish, S., Dowling, S. and Lawson, T. (1996) *Integrated Learning Systems: A Study of Sustainable Learning Gains in UK Schools*. Coventry: NCET.

Underwood, J., Cavendish, S. and Lawson, T. (1995) Integrated Learning Systems in FE Institutions (unpublished report prepared for NCET).

Underwood, J. and Underwood, G. (1990) *Computers and Learning: Helping Children Acquire Thinking Skills*. Oxford: Blackwell.

Underwood, G., Underwood, J. and Turner, M. (1993) Children's Thinking during Collaborative Computer-Based Problem Solving. *Educational Psychology,* **13** 345-357.

Van Drusen, L. M., and Worthen, B. R. (1992) Factors that Facilitate or Impede Implementation of Integrated Learning Systems. *Educational Technology,* **32** (9) 16-21.

Van Drusen, L. M. and Worthen, B. R. (1994) The Impact of Integrated Learning System Implementation on Student Outcomes: Implications for Research and Evaluation. *International Journal of Educational Research,* **21** (1) 13-24.

Venezky, R. L. (1983) Evaluating Computer-Assisted Instruction in its Own Terms. In A. C. Wilkinson (ed) *Classroom Computers and Cognitive Science*. New York: Academic Press.

von Wright, G. H. (1971) *Explanation and Understanding*. London: Routledge and Kegan Paul.

Watson, D. M. (1993). The ImpacT Report, An Evaluation of the Impact of Information Technology on Children's Achievements in Primary and Secondary Schools. King's College, London.

West, R. C. and Marcotte, D. R. (1994) The Effects of an Integrated Learning System (ILS) Using Incremental Time Allotments on Ninth Grade Algebra Achievement. *Journal of Educational Technology Systems,* **22** (3) 283-94.

White, M. A. (1992) Are ILSs Good Education? *Educational Technology,* **32** (9) 49–50.

White, R. T. (1973) 'Research into Learning Hierarchies', *Review of Educational Research,* **43** (3) 361–75.

White, R. T. and Gunstone, R. F. (1989) 'Meta-learning and conceptual change', *International Journal of Science Education,* **11,** Special Issue, 577–86.

Wilson, J. (1990) *Integrated Learning Systems: A Primer. Classroom Computer Learning,* **10** (5) 22–23, 27–30, 34, 360.

Wishart, J. and Canter, D. (1988) *Variations in User Involvement with Educational Software.* Computers and Education, **12** 365–379.

Worthen, B. R., Van Drusen, L. M. and Sailor, P. J. (1994) A Comparative Study of the Impact of Integrated Learning Systems on Students' Time-on-Task. *International Journal of Educational Research,* **21** (1).

ILS reader glossary and explanatory notes

Adaptive feedback   feedback which adjusts to individual learning needs which are assessed from student performance.

Attainment targets   see: National Curriculum

AVG levels   SuccessMaker provides placement information and ongoing assessment in terms of "AVG' levels. These represent US grade equivalents and although preliminary work to cross reference them to UK measures seems to indicate that they are reasonably accurate, they have been treated with caution by evaluators in this study.

Behaviourism   A theory and method of psychological investigation based on the study and analysis of behaviour. The emphasis in this approach on observable and measurable behaviour, and the systematic reinforcement of desired responses is reflected in the use of computers in education through drill and practice programs.

Comprehensive school   (UK) non-selective school providing all types of education for all or most of the children in a neighbourhood or area.

Constructivist theory   A theory of teaching and learning implying an active view of learning, in which the learner reviews experiences and interprets them in terms of general ideas or categories, that is the learner constructs 'knowledge' of the world in his or her head.

In Piagetian terms the student is to be helped to develop meta-cognitive self-regulation over the processes of learning. The most sophisticated form of self-regulation occurs when students exhibit conscious, reflective surveillance of thought and the ability to critique their own problem solving behaviour.

also see Vygotskian

Dyspraxia   an impairment or immaturity of the organisation of movement resulting in poor understanding of the messages that senses convey and difficulty in relating those messages to actions. Dyspraxic children of normal intelligence may have great difficulty in planning and organising thoughts.

Ecological validity   grounded in the real 'world' as opposed to the artificial or man-made 'world' of the laboratory

Effect size	(in this research) the difference in performance between the ILS and control groups, expressed as a proportion of one standard deviation of pre-trial scores for the combined ILS and control groups.
Elementary school	(US) school catering for grades 1 to 6
Grade levels	A class at school (US) in relation to advancement.
Hermeneutic	belonging to or concerned with interpretation; especially as distinguished from exegesis or practical exposition.
Junior High School	(US) school catering for grades 7 to 9
Locus of control scale	standardised measure of independence in learning
Logical positivism	the name given to the theories and doctrines of philosophers active in Vienna in the early 1930s (the Vienna Circle), which were aimed at evolving in the language of philosophy formal methods for the verification of empirical questions similar to those of the mathematical sciences, and which therefore eliminated metaphysical and other more speculative questions as being logically ill-founded. Every basic statement must, in order to be meaningful, be verifiable in isolation.
Management system	in ILS the management system links and controls the flow of data and may perform some or all of the following functions: interpretation of pupil responses to tasks; updating of student records; choice of pathways through curriculum content; delivery of appropriate sequence of modules; provision of feedback to students and teachers.
Meta-cognitive skills	higher order thinking skills, an awareness of one's own thinking. From cognition, the faculty of knowing as distinguished from feeling and volition.
National Curriculum	(UK) applies to all pupils of compulsory school age in maintained schools. Organised on the basis of 4 Key Stages:

Key Stage 1: ages 6-7 years – subjects included: English, mathematics, science, technology, history, geography, art, music and physical education.

Key Stage 2: ages 7-11 years – subjects included: as at Key Stage 1

Key Stage 3: ages 11-14 years – subjects included: as at Key Stages 1 & 2 plus a modern foreign language.

Key Stage 4: ages 14-16 years – subjects included: English, mathematics, science, physical education , technology, and a modern foreign language.

For each subject and for each Key Stage *programmes of study* set out what pupils should be taught and *attainment targets* set out the expected standards of pupils' performance.

Nomothetic	that which pertains to or is concerned with the study or discovery of general (scientific) laws. Nomothetic theories are concerned with the similarities between people and seek to understand each person in terms of laws which apply to all people, as contrasted with idiographic theories which attempt to understand each person as a unique entity.
Operant-conditioning	also instrumental conditioning. The method of 'operant conditioning' in a Skinner box can be used to investigate physiological changes that accompany habit formation. In operant conditioning reinforcement is provided when a desired action or behaviour is forthcoming, thus encouraging the learner to repeat that response. This is termed shaping the behaviour.
	The contemporary view of conditioning is more complex and subtle than that expounded by the early behaviourists. Conditioning is a universal mechanism by which we and other animals intuitively detect and store information about the causal structure of our environment.
	see Behaviourism
Position paper	summary paper outlining the current state of research within a given area.
Primary school	(UK) catering for children at Key Stages 1 & 2 aged 5-11 years
Programmes of study	see: National Curriculum
Ravens Progressive Matrices	a standardised test of non-verbal ability.
Secondary school	(UK) school catering for children at Key Stages 3 & 4 aged 11-18
Semi- structured interview schedule	Structured interviewing is the systematic recording of responses to pre-set largely closed questions. In semi-structured interviews a framework for the interview is established but questions are more open and responses, while more varied and elaborate, often achieving higher ecological validity, are also more difficult to code and therefore to analyse.
Senior High School	(US) school catering for grades 10 to 12
Semi- structured observation schedule	Structured observation is the systematic recording on grids or checklists of specific behaviours. In semi-structured observation a framework for observation is established but, as for semi-structured interviews, greater ecological validity may be gained by recording notable events as they occur rather than rigidly applying the pre-set observation criteria. The difficulty with informal observation is the tendency to observe what the researcher is aware of as

these observations are necessarily selective. Ecological validity might be achieved but there may be a subsequent loss in the reliability of the observations and important detail may well go unnoticed.

Special needs co-ordinator	(UK) The 1993 Education Act requires all schools to appoint an individual to co-ordinate the provision for pupils with special educational needs. A Code of Practice issued by the Department for Education and Employment in 1994 offers guidelines for this co-ordinator.
Spooncer	a group literacy assessment test for children aged 10.5 to 12.5 developed by Frank A Spooncer and published by Hodder & Stoughton.
Standardised test	a test for which norms of performance for a given population have been made available.
Year groups	(UK) within schools children are grouped according to their age and these groups are called Years 1 - 11. These year groups relate to National Curriculum Key Stages as follows:

Key Stage 1   Years 1-3
Key Stage 2   Years 4-6
Key Stage 3   Years 7-9
Key Stage 4   Years 10-11

YELLIS	Year Eleven Information System, this is a broadly based monitoring system which collects data on some 44,000 Year 11 (aged 16) students before they sit the General Certificate of Secondary Education. These data can be compared with the students results to measure the value added benefits of specific changes.
Vygotskian theory	following the ideas of L.S. Vygotsky a Soviet psychologist who defined intelligence as the ability to learn through instruction. Vygotskian theory suggests that co-operatively achieved success in both formal and informal contexts and with more knowledgeable others (peers, siblings, parents, friends etc.) lies at the foundations of learning.

Index